Financing Local Government in the
People's Republic of China

Financing Local Government in the People's Republic of China

Edited by
CHRISTINE P. W. WONG

Published for the Asian Development Bank
by Oxford University Press

HONG KONG
OXFORD UNIVERSITY PRESS
OXFORD   NEW YORK
1997

Oxford University Press

Oxford New York
Athens Auckland Bangkok Bogota Bombay
Buenos Aires Calcutta Cape Town Dar es Salaam
Delhi Florence Hong Kong Istanbul Karachi
Kuala Lumpur Madras Madrid Melbourne
Mexico City Nairobi Paris Singapore
Taipei Tokyo Toronto

and associated companies in
Berlin Ibadan

Oxford is a trade mark of Oxford University Press

First published 1997
This impression (lowest digit)
1 3 5 7 9 10 8 6 4 2

Published in the United States
by Oxford University Press, New York

Published for the Asian Development Bank by
Oxford University Press

British Library Cataloguing in Publication Data
available

Library of Congress Cataloging-in-Publication Data

Financing local government in the People's Republic of China/
edited by Christine P.W. Wong.
p.   cm.
Includes bibliographical references and index.
ISBN 0-19-590027-8
I. Local finance—China. I. Wong, Christine, date.
HJ9590.F56   1996
336' .01451—dc20   96-31869
                                          CIP

Printed in Hong Kong
Published by Oxford University Press (China) Ltd.
18/F Warwick House, Taikoo Place, 979 King's Road,
Quarry Bay, Hong Kong

CONTENTS

TABLES

FIGURES

TEXT BOXES

PREFACE

Financing Local Government in the People's Republic of China is the logical sequel to *Fiscal Management and Economic Reform in the People's Republic of China*, published for the Asian Development Bank by Oxford University Press. It is the second in a series of studies on fiscal policy reform in the PRC. Two other ongoing studies, "Fiscal Policy and Regulatory Framework for Social Security System Reform" and "Strengthening Budget and Revenue Systems," cofinanced by the Ministry of Finance of the PRC and the Asian Development Bank, further support the PRC's fiscal reform process.

This publication is very timely because the success of the sweeping fiscal reforms of 1994 depends critically on the rationalization of revenue and expenditure responsibilities at the subprovincial levels. A key objective of the Ninth Five-Year Plan (1996–2000), launched in March 1996, is to reduce the gap between the rich and poor regions in terms of income as well as access to social services. This study identifies some inequalities and recommends corrective measures.

While the reforms of 1994 have moved the fiscal system significantly toward greater transparency and a sounder basis for revenue sharing, they are incomplete. These measures have addressed the intergovernmental division of revenues but have left subprovincial expenditure assignments largely intact. The tax-sharing reform has had two opposing effects on local budgets. The reform shifted revenues toward the central government, reassigning to it most of the revenues from the largest taxes—the value-added tax and the consumption tax. At the same time, the reform assigned to local governments some taxes with significant potential for revenue generation—the personal income tax and the property tax. Local governments also gained the right to retain revenues from the sale of land; land-lease rights are becoming a major revenue source in some cities in the PRC.

This study focuses on the level and composition of revenues and expenditures at the city (prefectural), county, and township levels. It assesses the adequacy of revenues at these levels to finance expenditure assignments, and the likely effects of the new tax-sharing system on the status of the local governments. In view of the dearth of information about local public finance in the PRC, this study devotes considerable attention to describing the current system and placing it in international perspective.

The major finding of the study is that fiscal reforms over the past decade have not kept pace with the rapid changes in demand for government services at the lower levels. Cities have generally lagged in supplying infrastructure to support their rapidly growing economies and populations. Moreover, they have not developed coordinated plans for revenue generation. They have relied instead on ad hoc sources of revenue and used a variety of user charges and asset sales (land and housing) to finance new infrastructure while neglecting the maintenance and use of existing facilities. In the rural sector, the disbanding of agricultural collectives left many services unfunded, and local governments (including villages) have levied various fees and charges to raise revenues. In both the urban and rural sectors, there are large disparities in expenditure and service provision between regions. Revenue adequacy is a serious concern for poor regions, and basic services such as primary education and public health are well below levels prescribed by national policy.

The study is based on the work of a team of consultants who visited the PRC in September 1994. The team comprised Christine Wong (team leader), Christopher Heady, Loraine West, and Kam Wing Chan, and was assisted by Alice Chien and Zhang Tao. Some information for the book was also drawn from a pilot study done by Christine Wong in Hebei Province in September 1993. The opinions expressed here are entirely those of the authors.

The study owed much to the strong support of the Ministry of Finance, particularly the Statistics Division of the Comprehensive Planning and Reform Department (CPR) and the Local Budget Department (LB), which collaborated with the team in the fieldwork. Vice Minister of Finance Xie Xuren gave overall guidance and support to the study. Logistical support was provided jointly by the CPR Department under Deputy Director General Kang Xuejun and by the LB Department under Division Chief Wang Lifeng.

During the month-long visit to the PRC, the team studied local-government finance in Shandong and Guizhou provinces. The team was accompanied during all or part of the fieldwork by officials of the Ministry of Finance including Kang Xuejun, Deputy Division Chief Chen Weiqun, and Guo Zhiwei, all from the CPR Department, and by Wang Lifeng, Zhang Jian, Zhang Zhihua, and Zhou Jizhou of the LB Department.

The Asian Development Bank thanks the Ministry of Finance and its counterparts in Guizhou and Shandong provinces for their unstinting guidance, help, and support to the study team throughout the fieldwork. The study benefited as well from the comments and suggestions made at the international conference in Changchun, Jilin, in September 1995, at which a preliminary draft of the study findings was presented to many senior government officials including Vice Minister of Finance Xie Xuren, officials of local finance departments, and senior scholars from research institutes. Professors Roy Bahl and Susan Whiting also gave helpful comments. At the Asian Development Bank, the project was supervised by Senior Economist V. N. Gnanathurai under the guidance of Bruce Murray, Manager, Division I, Programs Department (East).

EIICHI WATANABE
Director, Programs Department (East)
Asian Development Bank

ACRONYMS

ADB	Asian Development Bank
CEH	culture, education, and health
EBF	extrabudgetary funds
FYP	five-year plan
GDP	gross domestic product
GNP	gross national product
GVIO	gross value of industrial output
ICT	industrial-commercial tax
MCH	maternal and child health
MOF	Ministry of Finance
NTS	national tax system
PRC	People's Republic of China
SCMP	South China Morning Post
SESRC	State Economic System Reforms Commission
SEZ	special economic zone
SOE	state-owned enterprise
SRF	self-raised funds
SSB	State Statistical Bureau
TSS	tax-sharing system
TVE	township and village enterprise
UMCF	urban maintenance and construction funds
UMCT	urban maintenance and construction tax
VAT	value-added tax

SUMMARY

CHAPTER 1
OVERVIEW OF ISSUES IN LOCAL PUBLIC
FINANCE IN THE PRC

Over the past one-and-a-half decades, reforming the fiscal system has been an increasingly urgent concern in the PRC, as the revenue capacity of the old Soviet-type fiscal system was inexorably eroded by emerging market forces, and the budget fell from 35 percent of GNP in the late 1970s to 12.7 percent in 1994. In 1994, a comprehensive fiscal reform package was implemented to arrest the decline in revenues, clarify fiscal responsibilities, and separate central and local systems and thus strengthen macroeconomic control at the center. The reform simplified and unified taxes to rationalize the tax structure and separating central and local tax administration, and produced a shift from tax contracting to a combination of revenue sharing, tax sharing, and tax assignments. A revamp of intergovernmental revenue-sharing arrangements was considered central to the reform package as it was widely believed that the fiscal decline had been caused partly by the poor incentives for local revenue collection.

This book examines the status of local government finance at the subprovincial levels. Past studies of central-local fiscal relations focused largely only on the provincial level and its interaction with the central budget. The sharing of revenues among the lower tiers of government significantly affects the incentives for resource allocation and revenue mobilization at the local levels. Moreover, as public goods and services are provided by all tiers of government, expenditure assignments and the existence of appropriate financing mechanisms jointly determine the efficiency and equity of their provision.

A study of subprovincial finance is long overdue. Through the 1980s and 1990s, while the Ministry of Finance was reforming its revenue-sharing relations with the provinces, little attention was paid to how these changes were transmitted to the subprovincial levels, leaving the provinces with virtually complete autonomy in the subprovincial sphere. Gaining a better understanding of how fiscal responsibilities and resources have evolved at the lower levels of government through 15 years of transition to the market is an essential first step to designing policies in support of the 1994 reform.

The effect of the 1994 reforms on local finance is uncertain, especially since the Ministry has once again juggled the intergovernmental division of revenues but left expenditure assignments intact. Even on the revenue side, opposing tendencies were introduced. On the one hand, the tax-sharing reform was designed specifically to shift revenues toward the central government, and should lead to a squeeze on local budgets unless offset by increased transfers from the central government, or unless new local revenues can be found. On the other hand, for the first time, local governments have been assigned some taxes with significant revenue-generating capacity as local taxes. These taxes include the personal income tax, the business tax, and the real estate tax. The expected growth in the taxes should provide local governments with a substantial independent tax base. In addition, the tax-sharing system (TSS) formally assigned revenues from land sales to local governments. In some coastal cities, they have already become a major source of local revenues.

One clear effect is the unequal impact of the reform across regions. For one, the reassignment of taxes on liquor and tobacco as central taxes will exact a heavy toll on localities like Guizhou Province, which derived some 45 percent of its revenues from the two products in 1993. More importantly, since the TSS has shifted revenue sharing to the derivation principle, whereby retained revenues are proportional to locally raised revenues, regional disparities will be magnified unless corrective action is taken. This disequalizing effect is amplified by the fact that rich regions will have far more opportunity than poor regions to offset the loss of value-added tax (VAT) and consumption tax revenues with revenues from local taxes and asset sales.

Government administration is divided into five levels: central, provincial, prefectural, county, and township. More than a division of responsibilities, as in many countries, the different levels of government in the PRC also form a monohierarchical system, with lower levels entirely subordinate to governments of higher rank.

Revenue-sharing arrangements in the PRC are bilateral, involving only two tiers of government at a time. Given the five tiers of government, there are four layers of revenue-sharing relationships: between the central government and the provinces, between provinces and prefectures or cities, between cities and counties, and between counties and townships. At each layer, the superior level has virtually absolute authority over the setting of contracts.

Subprovincial sharing arrangements generally imitate central-provincial arrangements. Through the 1980s, as central-provincial revenue sharing changed from sharing specific revenue to sharing total revenues, subprovincial arrangements followed suit. Since the late 1980s, with the introduction of fiscal contracting at the central-provincial level, subprovincial arrangements have most often been some variation of fixed-term contracts.

The revenue-sharing process will be simplified under the TSS, which provides a clearer delineation of revenues by tax types. However, the reform itself specified only the division between the central and provincial governments, and left the provinces to decide how to divide up the "local" share between the province and the lower levels. Through September 1994, neither Shandong nor Guizhou Province had yet announced the new formulas for revenue sharing with prefectures and cities. Moreover, some taxes, such as the farmland occupation tax and the agricultural special products tax, continue to be shared separately, outside the "regular" pool.

Before revenue sharing, the central government accounted for the largest proportion of own revenues among the five levels of government in 1993 (34 percent), followed by prefectures/cities (29 percent), counties (16 percent), and provinces and townships (11 percent each). The dominance of cities in revenue shares is actually understated because the provincial share includes the shares of Beijing, Tianjin, and Shanghai, cities with provincial status. During the 1980s, the provincial share of own revenues generally fell while the shares of cities/prefectures and counties rose slightly.

The province and county levels spend a greater share of revenues than they collect, while the inverse is true for prefectures/cities and townships. This vertical imbalance reflects the tax system's reliance on industry and commerce to generate the bulk of revenues. It also highlights the dependence of these levels on transfers.

Intergovernmental expenditure assignments roughly follow international practice. The central government spends for national defense and external relations while local governments are responsible for day-to-day administration and for social services. For some major expenditures, however, there is a high degree of overlap among levels of government, resulting in some ambiguity in the division of responsibility. Most notable are responsibilities for basic education and capital expenditures.

A decentralizing trend for budgetary expenditures is observed at the subprovincial levels. In Shandong, the provincial share of total expenditures fell from 34 percent in 1980 to 17 percent in 1993. The share of prefectures/cities rose from 16 percent to 26 percent during the same period, while the combined share of counties and townships rose from 50 percent to 57 percent. The shift to lower levels is driven by the same factors contributing to the declining share of central expenditures relative to the local: the transfer of investment finance to enterprises and the banking sector, which reduced capital investment outlays at the center, and the rise in wages borne primarily by city, county, and township budgets, which raised the costs, primarily to the lower levels, of day-to-day administration and service provision.

A notable aspect of subprovincial finance has been the growing importance of off-budget funds in financing government, especially at the lower levels. Off-budget finance consists of extrabudgetary funds under the control of local governments and administrative agencies, as well as "self-raised funds" at the county and township levels. The exact size and distribution of these funds are difficult to ascertain as local governments are reluctant to disclose fully all the resources available to them.

CHAPTER 2
THE ROLE OF SUBNATIONAL GOVERNMENTS:
THEORY AND INTERNATIONAL PRACTICE

The allocation of public expenditure and tax powers between levels of government lies at the heart of any system of public finance. The theory that has been developed to analyze this allocation is the "Theory of Fiscal Federalism," which applies to unitary states just as much as to countries with federal constitutions.

In relation to expenditure responsibilities, the theory recommends that local services be provided by local governments because they have better information about the needs and wants of the local population. On the other hand, central government should be responsible for the provision of public services that spread beyond a particular area, because it can take into account the needs and wants of people in all the affected areas.

Application of these simple principles can lead to an efficient allocation of expenditure responsibilities. However, two complications must be considered. First, different local services cover localities of different sizes. This can lead to a system with more than one level of local government, each with particular responsibilities. Second, some services have both local and national characteristics. In such cases, different levels of government must be allowed to participate together in financing projects.

In relation to tax powers, the theory is mainly concerned with the distortions that might arise from different local governments setting different tax rates. The case for allowing local governments to set at least one rate of tax arises from their need to respond to the needs and wants of the local population. If one local government is to decide to increase expenditure in its area, it must be able to increase tax revenue. However, the setting of different tax rates in different localities can distort the allocation of resources in the economy, and the theory is concerned with identifying which taxes would have the smallest distortionary effect.

Theoretically, the only nondistortionary tax is a land tax, and many countries give their local governments control over some tax of this sort (such as a property tax). However, land taxes are often thought to be inequitable and are usually not sufficient to cover local-government expenditure needs.

These theoretical arguments lead to a position in which a large part of public expenditure should be the responsibility of local governments but only a small part of tax revenue (the property tax) should be under their control. This leads to a mismatch between the revenues and expenditures of different levels of government. There are three ways of dealing with this. First, subnational governments can be given control over major taxes, but at the cost of causing economic distortions. Second, the central government can give grants to lower levels of government, but this reduces the autonomy of local government. Third, as is the case in the

PRC, local governments can directly receive some or all of the tax revenues collected from their area, even if the tax rate is chosen by the central government. The disadvantage of this system is that it encourages fiscal competition, whereby local governments try to induce enterprises to move from other areas into their own to increase their tax base.

In practice, funds for financing local governments come from various sources. Local taxes, particularly property taxes, are the most natural source of finance. However, they are frequently unpopular, for reasons of unfairness and inefficiency. For this reason, there is a growing move toward the use of service charges, although these are not suitable for financing all types of services. Government grants are another major source of local-government finance. The use of grants prevents great inequalities in basic service provision and encourages local governments to provide services that have a national, as well as a local, characteristic. Loans and asset sales can be attractive sources of finance because they allow increases in expenditure without immediate increases in taxes. However, they have to be used with caution. It is important to note that, from a purely financial point of view, asset sales are just like loans. If a profitable state-owned enterprise is sold, the government receives a lump sum but then ceases to receive the profits of the enterprise. Therefore, asset sales can lead to future financial deficits unless the funds from asset sales are invested in the same careful way as the funds from loans.

The final aspect of the division of fiscal responsibility between levels of government is the responsibility for tax administration. Generally, when central and local governments have separate tax sources, each level administers its own tax. However, when two levels of government share the same tax base, there is an argument for one level to collect the tax for both levels. Such arrangements need to be considered with caution to avoid a situation where one level of government grants concessions that reduce the revenue of another level of government.

CHAPTER 3
URBANIZATION AND URBAN INFRASTRUCTURE SERVICES IN THE PRC

Cities in the PRC have been the primary producers of state revenues. However, in the pre-reform era, they generally suffered from underinvestment in urban infrastructure.

Administrative changes since reform have aimed at reviving cities as centers of exchange. This is done by lowering vertical bureaucratic barriers and promoting market exchanges and horizontal linkages between nearby administrative entities and between the rural and urban sectors. Changes include the reestablishment of "line-item" cities and the creation of "coastal open cities," the policy of putting counties under city administration, and programs wherein counties are turned into cities and townships into towns. All these involve granting more power to cities and elevating their administrative status. The gravitation of power to major urban centers, especially coastal cities, has also been favored by the market-oriented reform and open-door policy, which have placed a premium on technology and savings generated by urban agglomeration economies and their historical and commercial linkages with the outside world. The rationale for these administrative changes was economic: improved coordination of governments and economic activity at the regional level. Since these administrative changes inevitably redistribute power over resource allocation, the issues are the subject of contention between levels of government.

Unlike the restricted urbanization and tightly controlled migration of the post-1961 Maoist era, urban population has grown at a steadily high rate since the economic reforms of the late 1970s. Urban population rose by 126 million, or by 61 percent, between 1982 and 1993, from 208 million to 334 million. The urban share of the population grew from 21.1 percent to 28.1 percent in the same period. In addition, there has been a significant expansion in the size of the unregistered, "floating," population in many cities.

This rapid expansion of urban growth has been attributed to high levels of migration and extensive urban aggrandizement. More than 300 cities and about 13,000 towns have been newly designated since 1983. Agricultural reform and decollectivization have also turned previously disguised rural unemployment into tens of millions of footloose rural laborers, many of whom have been absorbed by the rapidly expanding urban-industrial economy, especially in the nonstate sector. The shift was also made easier by relaxed controls on migration and employment as the government came to realize the value of cheap labor to the economic boom. Hard-labor jobs and factory positions in many coastal cities, which offer low pay, are mostly filled by rural migrants. With the introduction of new policies allowing self-initiated migration, and a rapid erosion of mechanisms of social control based on urban residence permits, foodgrain rationing, employment controls, and neighborhood watch systems, the population of the country has been increasingly mobile since the mid-1980s.

There has also been a general recognition of the importance of municipal planning. City mayors are empowered to oversee the development of urban infrastructure. A rudimentary legislative and administrative framework for coordinating urban construction was set up in the 1980s. This includes the establishment of city planning departments at various levels, the enactment of the Law of Urban Planning in 1989, and the drawing up of master plans for almost all cities.

Increased budgetary allocations and new sources of revenues have produced more funds for the construction of urban infrastructure. The new revenue sources were taxes on enterprises and fees on new users (including a new levy on urban construction introduced in 1979), as well as foreign private-sector investment. In recent years, many local governments have also raised revenues by selling urban residency rights and land. Land sales are especially popular in coastal cities and are increasingly being carried out by other local governments as well.

Urban housing construction has moved rapidly in the last 15 years. However, there has been only limited success in commercializing the sale of public housing. Until recently, public housing was sold in many cities at greatly discounted prices. Although housing rentals have been raised in the last few years, they remain far below costs.

Figures for per capita availability of several types of urban infrastructure services place the PRC broadly in the category of lower middle-income countries. Compared with cities in most other Third World countries, cities in the PRC probably provide a higher percentage of their populations with access to piped water, housing, paved roads, and green areas. On the other hand, cities in the PRC are probably behind other Third World cities in the provision of public transportation, waste treatment, telecommunication facilities, and electricity for domestic use.

Differences in provincial averages in the level of provision of many types of basic infrastructure between the cities of Shandong Province and those of the less-developed Guizhou are strikingly small. Nevertheless, Shandong still has higher levels of provision per capita (nonagricultural population) when it comes to paved roads, garbage and night-soil treatment, and gas supply. Generally, larger cities in the two provinces tend to provide more infrastructure per capita in most sectors than do smaller cities, with the exception of housing and possibly paved roads.

CHAPTER 4
MUNICIPAL PUBLIC FINANCE

The financing of urban infrastructure is an important responsibility of municipal governments. The best methods of financing this infrastructure depend on whether the infrastructure services are "private goods" or "public goods." The use of a private good can be clearly attributed to particular people or households, and levying some form of user charge on such groups would therefore be both efficient and equitable. On the other hand, the use of public goods is fundamentally collective and cannot be attributed to individuals. These should therefore be funded from tax revenue. In both cases, the cost of providing the good can be so large that it is more practicable to finance the cost with a loan and make repayments from user charges or tax revenue, whichever is appropriate.

The experience of other countries shows that the provision of urban infrastructure is expensive, and financing comes from a variety of sources, with user charges generally financing private goods, and tax revenues of central and local governments, as well as loans, financing public goods. In the PRC, funding sources are also varied. However, the country has not been as successful as other countries in applying user charges. The financing of roads, water supply, and housing shows that user charges could raise much greater revenue, although some user charges currently in use are not appropriate.

There has been a large recent increase in the use of revenue from asset sales for urban construction in the PRC. This can be seen as part of the move to a market economy, but it does raise some concerns. As explained above, asset sales are similar to loans in their financial effects, and so the revenue raised must be used carefully. Also, opportunities for asset sales will eventually diminish and an alternative source of revenue is therefore needed. Increased user charges will have an important role in filling the gap.

An examination of the budgets of the four main cities in the study shows how variations in revenue capacity, revenue growth, and contracting arrangements have led to very large differences in per capita expenditure on local services. The level of expenditure on peripheral areas of cities is also shown to be substantially lower than at the center. To some extent, poorer local governments respond to the lack of money by allocating a higher proportion to basic needs, such as education and health. However, this still does not permit them to spend as much on these services as the richer cities, and has the disadvantage of diverting money from much-needed infrastructure investment. The system of allocating funds between local governments needs to be fundamentally revised to provide adequate services to all citizens.

In health and education, richer cities, in general, provide higher-quality services, as the four cities show. This is particularly true for health, where there are very large differences in provision between the richer and the poorer cities. The pattern is less clear for education: the richer cities do not necessarily provide better service, despite higher expenditure. Although the data are not fully comparable, there could be substantial differences in the efficiency of service provision.

The citywide social insurance schemes that have developed since 1984 are an important area of municipal provision. Such schemes play an important role in the development of the market economy, by providing pensions and other labor-market insurance independently of individual enterprises. However, there is considerable evidence that their financial base is not sufficiently strong. The current benefit rates are made affordable only by enrolling new groups of workers which include few pensioners. The rapid growth in the proportion of the population above retirement age requires a fundamental reform of the pension schemes, or else they will soon start to place a heavy financial burden on the cities that are responsible for them. These reforms will probably include raising the retirement age, finding additional ways for workers to save for their old age, reducing administrative expense, and finding investments with higher rates of return.

CHAPTER 5
RURAL PUBLIC FINANCE

Despite concerns expressed by the government of the PRC that county and township budgets are hard-pressed and are often in deficit, the study of rural public finance has received little attention. Chapter 5 provides a systematic examination of rural public finance by giving a brief overview of the role of rural governments and their expenditure assignments, assessing the status of rural finance at the county, township, and village levels, and evaluating the role of off-budget finance.

The rural sector is primarily responsible for expenditures in agricultural investment, rural education and health care, administration, welfare assistance, and aid to poor regions. On the average, capital expenditures account for 10-15 percent of county budgets, while social expenditures absorb 40-45 percent of expenditures (with 20-30 percent for education) and administrative expenditures take up another 25-30 percent. Concerns of urban governments, such as provision of infrastructure and housing, have become part of the county's responsibilities as many counties have acquired city status and manufacturing has come to dominate the rural economy in many counties.

However, as one important legacy of the self-reliant rural finance inherited from Cultural Revolution policies, expenditure assignments are necessarily murky, with a high degree of overlap in services between county, township, and even village levels. This is because the principle called on each administrative unit to minimize "dependence" on aid from higher levels by providing as much as possible for itself. As what each unit (or level) could do depended on its resource endowment, the result was differing expenditure responsibilities across regions. In education, for example, even though primary schools were provided mainly by production brigades, middle schools by communes, and senior middle schools by counties, a good deal of variation emerged. In richer areas, some production teams had their own primary schools, while brigades ran middle schools, and some communes operated senior middle schools. The same applied to the provision of medical clinics and hospitals.

The township, which was restored as a level of rural government when people's communes were abolished in 1983, provides social services and administers disaster relief and law and order. Because of its short life span to date, the township is far less autonomous in fiscal matters than other levels of government. This is evidenced not only by the high share of revenues remitted and subsidies received, but also by the extensive overlap in responsibilities with the county in the provision of education, health, and welfare services.

With the disbanding of agricultural collectives, the production brigades and teams reverted to their traditional name of "village." Even though a village is not a formal level of government, it has expenditure responsibilities inherited from the collective economy including payment of salary or subsidies to village cadres and provision of social welfare. These expenditures, which were financed from the proceeds of the collectives in the old system, are now usually financed through nontax levies on rural income and production.

Unlike cities, rural administrative units are revenue-poor. Per capita revenues are low and county budgets are, on the average, in deficit in both Shandong and Guizhou. However, data for four counties, Qufu, Penglai, Zunyi, and Puding, reveal a remarkable growth in revenue collection from the late 1980s to the early 1990s. This was accounted for by growth in industrial and commercial taxes (ICT), particularly turnover taxes. As a percentage of total revenues, ICT and turnover taxes were on the rise in all four counties, agricultural taxes had a flat or declining share, and direct taxes from state-owned enterprises declined.

Transfers in the form of remittances and subsidies have declined as a proportion of revenues in three of the four counties. In Puding, the portion of the budget financed by subsidies fell from 80 percent in the mid-1980s to 40 percent in 1993. While the decline in transfers reflects greater self-sufficiency in revenues and should be taken as a positive development, the situation in Puding is cause for concern because fiscal expenditures remain very low. Pushing the county toward self-financing means prolonging the government's inability to meet its basic service responsibilities.

The shares of remittances of Zunyi, Penglai, and Qufu are inversely related to their per capita income ranking. The situation in Zunyi County is noteworthy because its remittance rate seems too high for its income and budgetary status and it has been rising through the late 1980s and early 1990s, contrary to the national trend. These observations suggest that provincial location may be the most important determinant of fiscal status. In a poor province, rich counties have to bear a greater burden for financing intraprovincial redistribution than similar counties in a richer province. The rising remittance rates for Zunyi were likely to have been the result of the declining transfers from the central government to Guizhou Province and the cost of self-financing at the provincial level.

Since the late 1980s, all provinces except Tibet have set up fiscal departments at the township level, but the process of separating township finance from counties has proceeded at different rates across provinces. Resources available to townships vary widely. At the aggregate level, the township budget registered a surplus. Given the limited buoyancy of agricultural taxation, townships are also dependent on industries for revenue growth.

Subsidies are an important source of finance at the township level. These are dominated by funds for welfare and disaster relief, which are mostly passed through from the central and provincial governments.

Villages do not have independent budgetary status. However, depending on whether production continues to be collective in nature and whether the village owns a significant amount of collective assets that are revenue-producing, additional resources could be generated to supplement transfers from higher levels of government. Village expenditures are not included in budgetary statistics, and this causes an underestimation of the amount of total government expenditures as well as the extent of regional disparities in service provision in the PRC.

While all levels of government depend to a varying extent on off-budget resources, there is explicit official recognition of these to finance government expenditure at the township level. Since 1986, townships have been required to report budgetary as well as off-budget revenues and expenditures.

The uses of extrabudgetary and self-raised funds are virtually identical to those of budgetary revenues. They are spent on education, health, road maintenance and construction, family planning, and other things to supplement the budget. While extrabudgetary and self-raised funds alleviate fiscal pressures for many local governments, their growth has hastened the decline of the formal fiscal system. It has created incentives for local governments to shift funds from the sector where they are taxed to the off-budget sector. It has also created a quasi-tax system that is increasingly beyond the central government's control and whose structure of fees and charges is extremely chaotic, nontransparent, and often inequitable.

The most important problems identified in this chapter are the large regional disparities and revenue inadequacy in poor localities. Evidence suggests that counties in richer provinces face lower remittance requirements which leave more for local allocation. In poor provinces, however, surplus counties face high remittance rates, while poor counties receive dwindling subsidies as central subsidies to the province have diminished during the reform period. In Guizhou, since 1988, the entire rural sector has acquired net remitter status, so that the rural sector may be supporting the urban sector.

The horizontal inequalities are partly due to the substantial variation in revenue capacity across regions. These are likely to have grown in recent years because of the fall in the relative size of vertical and horizontal transfers that characterize all administrative levels. The growing importance of off-budget finance heightens these regional inequalities because this type of finance is not subject to revenue sharing, so that a shift from budgetary finance to a mix of sources reduces the overall proportion of funds that are redistributed. With the growing importance of off-budget finance, tax reform must be extended to rationing the structure of levies and quasi-taxes. In effect, the present system cedes a large share of rural taxation to the off-budget sector. The prevalence of rural levies on farm households belies the government's claim that new taxes cannot be imposed on the farm sector because of low incomes.

The loss of indirect tax revenues in the rural sector will have a severe impact on the fiscal status of rural governments and may reverse the recent trend of a rising share of total revenues accruing to the township level. It will also worsen the problem of poor incentives for tax collection from township and village enterprises. While shifting consumption tax revenues on liquor and tobacco entirely to the central government will help to eliminate the scramble to build local wineries and cigarette plants, its effect is likely to be even more severe and regionally unbalanced. If fully implemented, its impact on localities like Qufu will be devastating since the city had grown so dependent on liquor taxes.

CHAPTER 6
PROVISION OF PUBLIC SERVICES IN RURAL PRC

Revenue adequacy at the county and township levels can be assessed only by comparing their expenditure needs with their actual provision of key services, such as education, public health care, and social welfare. For each of these services, goals and targets have been enunciated in state policy which may be interpreted as guidelines for expenditure needs. In assessing local public finance in the PRC, it is important to know whether the methods and sources of financing allow counties and townships to provide the desirable level and quality of services to rural residents.

In the case of education, the Chinese government passed the nine-year Compulsory Education Law in 1986, calling for six years of primary school and three years of junior high school for every child, tuition-free. The overall goal of the Compulsory Education Law is not only to increase the number of children completing nine years of education but also to improve the quality of the education they receive. A second education goal articulated by the government is the elimination of illiteracy among the young and middle-aged population. In addition to these two major goals, the central and provincial governments have established a number of education standards for teacher qualifications, classroom equipment, and school facilities.

On close scrutiny, education attainment levels and indicators of the quality of education reveal that most rural areas fall short of the targets and standards set by the government, with the gap being wider for poor counties and townships. For example, rural areas in Shandong Province expect to be able to meet the target of nine years of universal education in 1997. On the other hand, most counties in Guizhou will be unable to meet this target even by the end of the century. In fact, one-third of Guizhou's counties still have not attained universal primary education. Throughout rural PRC, many primary and secondary teachers lack the required academic credentials to meet present standards. The proportion of teachers lacking adequate training is higher in poorer townships and counties. While most rural communities have solved the problem of dilapidated and dangerous schools, in the poorest rural areas the problem remains serious. Only schools in the economically developed rural areas of the coastal provinces are able to meet first-class standards in terms of libraries, laboratories, music and art equipment, computers, and other facilities.

Government budgetary appropriations account for the majority of funds spent on education. In general, the lowest levels of government, the county and the township, are responsible for allocating funds to support rural basic education. Budgetary expenditures for education by the central and provincial governments are concentrated on tertiary educational institutions and their support for rural education is limited. Education grants by the central government to lower levels are only about Y2 per rural primary and lower secondary student. The specific assignment of expenditure responsibility to the county and township depends on the fiscal strength of the township. The village, a nongovernmental unit, also plays a major role in supporting primary education.

The budgetary appropriations of counties and townships are typically sufficient to cover only personnel costs in rural primary and secondary schools; therefore, schools must rely on other sources for additional recurrent expenditures, capital outlays, and teachers' training. One source local governments have turned to is extrabudgetary revenue in the form of ad hoc fees and tax surcharges levied on rural residents and enterprises, which are then earmarked for education. As education costs rise and government funding does not keep pace, students are also being forced to help meet the shortfall. During compulsory education, students are to pay only a miscellaneous fee; however, many schools charge other fees as well. Among the four counties studied, an inverse relationship was found between wealth and the reliance on tuition and fees to fund education. Self-raised funds are another important source of supplementary funds for education. With the exception of village *tongchou* funds raised to supplement community teachers' salaries, self-raised funds are primarily used to invest in fixed assets of schools, filling the gap left by government appropriations. Even though upper levels of government provide more generous matching funds to poorer areas under programs expanding the education infrastructure, the burden of raising funds is still very heavy on the local government and the community in these areas.

With respect to public health care, the government has set targets for establishing health stations in all villages, reducing infant and maternal mortality rates, and increasing immunization coverage for children. Specific programs are also under way to renovate township and county-level health facilities and to upgrade medical equipment in these facilities.

The size and condition of township health centers and county hospitals vary tremendously within and across regions. Township health centers visited ranged from a single rented room in Guizhou, classified as dangerous and equipped with a pressure cuff, thermometer, and stethoscope, to a new, multistoried building in Shandong with specialized rooms for minor surgery, orthodontic care, obstetrical deliveries, examinations, and a medical dispensary and equipped with ultrasound and x-ray machines. Villages without a health-care facility are concentrated in provinces such as Guizhou. Hospital beds and medical personnel have a higher per capita availability in richer areas. Health outcomes mirror the range in quality of facilities and service. Poorer regions have infant and maternal mortality rates matching those of low-income developing countries, while developed rural areas in coastal provinces have rates comparable to those of upper middle-income countries. The outbreak of childhood diseases is also more prevalent in poorer areas.

As hospitals and other health institutions were instructed to become more self-financing by increasing their earnings from services in the 1980s, a large share of the financing burden was shifted to patients in the form of higher fees, and government budget appropriations covered a smaller share of total health-care expenditures. Because budget appropriations only partially fund their salaries, rural medical personnel are dependent on service fees and profits from sales of medicine for the remainder. In poorer areas, these supplementary revenues are limited and medical salaries are consequently much lower. Lower salaries, in turn, make it difficult to attract and retain highly qualified medical personnel.

Government budgets at all levels include appropriations for capital investment in public health facilities and equipment. However, with few exceptions, access to higher-level funds is contingent upon the ability of the lower level to raise matching funds, such that central government funds represent only a fraction of total investment in rural medical facilities while self-raised funds and local budgets account for the overwhelming majority. This funding arrangement allows areas that can raise these funds to provide better service while, at the same time, placing poorer areas at a disadvantage.

Less than 20 percent of the rural population is currently estimated to be insured under government, labor, or cooperative health insurance programs. Those insured under rural cooperative medical insurance programs have limited benefits which depend on the size of the village public welfare fund and township fiscal resources. With the shrinking role of government appropriations and the high cost of medical goods and services, the financing burden on rural patients, most of whom are uninsured, has risen dramatically since the onset of reforms.

The delivery of social welfare services is also very dependent on local-government and community resources. With the exception of disaster relief, other social welfare programs require substantial local financial support. In fact, villages provide the majority of support to participants in *wubaohu,* one of the principal income maintenance programs. If the village and local governments lack the financial resources, eligible individuals receive less or no support.

CHAPTER 7
EQUALIZATION ISSUES

Fiscal systems play an important distributional function and can be used to address a number of social equity concerns. The distribution of fiscal resources has direct consequences for disparities in the provision of public services across administrative levels and regions in the PRC.

Sizeable horizontal variation in fiscal revenues is found at all administrative levels—province, city, county, and township—making it all the more important to ensure that effective mechanisms are in place in the fiscal system for equalizing expenditures. Mechanisms for the vertical and horizontal redistribution of revenues across administrative units include remittances under revenue-sharing contracts, quota subsidies, earmarked subsidies, and budgetary grants. At each administrative level—province, city, county, and township—per capita expenditures are less widely dispersed than per capita revenues, providing some evidence that leveling is effected through these transfer mechanisms. These mechanisms differ, however, in their effectiveness in achieving equalization.

Revenue-sharing contracts are, on the whole, equalizing: at the provincial level, richer provinces remit part of their surplus to the central government, and these surpluses go to financing quota subsidies to poorer regions. However, remittance rates have fallen through the transition period, thus weakening the central government's ability to finance transfers to poor provinces. It is hoped that the new tax-sharing system will reverse this decline. Below the province level, a sizeable gap in revenue resources exists between cities and counties, largely owing to the industry-centered tax base. Redistribution serves to moderate city expenditures and to enhance slightly the fiscal resources of counties.

Earmarked subsidies, on the other hand, are found to be distributed in a way that favors rich provinces and negates the equalizing effect of other transfer mechanisms. Through the 1980s, earmarked subsidies grew rapidly and were dominated by grain subsidies. These were obviously disequalizing since the more urbanized provinces received higher subsidies even though they also had higher incomes.

Budgetary grants for equalization are extremely small, the principal ones being welfare assistance and aid to poor regions, which accounted for only 4-5 percent of consolidated expenditures in the 1990s—not enough to make a significant difference in equalizing expenditures across localities.

Data limitations preclude a separate examination of transfer mechanisms at the subprovincial levels; however, the gap between revenues and expenditures represents the consolidated transfer and is assessed to determine the net redistributive effect. A weak positive correlation is found between per capita consolidated remittance and revenue for townships, counties, and cities, indicating that transfers are mildly equalizing. However, numerous exceptions are found within subsamples for each administrative level. In fact, among the four counties surveyed, both Zunyi and Penglai have lower per capita revenues than Qufu; however, their remittance rates are more than double Qufu's.

These disequalizing outcomes of intergovernmental transfers occur when revenue-sharing transfers are dominated by earmarked subsidies. Even though some earmarked subsidies can be targeted to poorer localities, such as capital construction subsidies for the education and health sectors, the requirement to provide matching funds often excludes poor localities from participation, reinforcing the disequalizing effect of these subsidies.

Off-budget revenue is more unequally distributed than budgetary revenue because extrabudgetary fees are frequently levied on the same tax base as budgetary taxes and extrabudgetary revenue is not subject to sharing with higher levels of government. Thus, areas with high per capita revenues also tend to have high per capita extrabudgetary revenues, which are not subject to redistribution either vertically or horizontally. The growing reliance on off-budget finance for local governments means increasing regional disparities and erosion of the equalization achieved through the redistribution of budgetary revenues.

The inequality in fiscal resources and the limited effectiveness of the redistribution mechanisms result in great disparities in the provision of services by governments. Substantial variation exists across provinces, between urban and rural areas, and within urban and rural areas in the provision of basic services. For example, urban areas are able to offer the basic services of education and health care in far superior quantities and quality than most rural areas.

Disparities in the provision of public services can be noted across cities in the PRC. The advancement of compulsory education, the number of hospital beds and doctors, and infrastructure vary from high levels in provincial capitals and major coastal cities to lower levels in other cities. The fiscal resources of these cities differ because of varying levels of industrial concentration and because of varying opportunities for generating off-budget revenue.

Variation in the provision of social services is seen across rural areas as well. Every education and health indicator reflects the higher quantity and quality of social services provided in Penglai and Qufu, as compared with Zunyi and Puding. In poor rural areas such as Puding, per capita expenditures are inadequate to sustain education and public health services at levels set in government programs and targets. If these government targets are taken as defined service needs of the community, these shortfalls in provision indicate fiscal gaps.

The findings in this chapter reveal the ineffectiveness of current redistribution mechanisms in the fiscal system. First, at the subprovincial levels, vertical redistribution mechanisms, through which substantial resources at each level are transferred upward and downward, are extremely active; however, these transfers are, in net terms, not significantly equalizing. Second, the government's passive strategy of permitting a growing reliance on off-budget funds has failed to meet fiscal gaps in the poor areas, while exacerbating regional disparities. More transfers that are better targeted are urgently needed to provide minimum social services in poor regions.

CHAPTER 8
POLICY RECOMMENDATIONS

This report has identified local public finance as an area requiring urgent policy action. Economic reforms and emerging market forces have affected the roles, revenues, and expenditures of local governments. However, despite the recent reforms in central-provincial fiscal relations, subprovincial public finance has not been reformed to take new realities into account. This has meant that many rural local governments have insufficient funds to meet the basic needs of their communities, while urban local governments have difficulties in financing the urban infrastructure required for further economic growth. These difficulties have led to undesirable financial practices: the unplanned sale of state assets (at low prices), the growing role of off-budget funds (which are outside normal rules of accountability), and the development of payment arrears.

The study-tour reports on Australia, New Zealand, France, Norway, Canada, and the US provide useful insights into how a reformed system of subprovincial finance might be set up in the PRC. Despite substantial differences in their systems of local government finance, the six study countries share certain important features. First, the tax powers and expenditure responsibilities of each level of government are clearly specified, normally by law or in the constitution. Second, in most cases local governments have control over the rate of at least one substantial tax, so that the community can decide on the level of local service provision that it wishes to pay for. Third, a high proportion of local-government expenditure is financed by grants from higher levels of government. These grants are based on transparent and objective formulas to ensure that all local governments are able to meet nationwide minimum standards of service provision, and have the effect of reducing the inequality in financial resources between local governments.

None of these three features are present in the current system of local-government finance in the PRC. First, the new tax-sharing system between the center and the provinces has not been reflected in changes at the subprovincial level, where local governments are unsure about future arrangements. Also, the allocation of expenditure responsibilities requires clarification. Second, local governments do not have the formal power to choose local tax rates (apart from taxes with insignificant revenues), and many have responded to local expenditure needs by imposing a variety of fees and levies with no clear legal status. Third, despite very large vertical transfers between levels of government, the allocation of these funds is not transparent and does not provide all local governments with the finance required to meet even very basic levels of service provision in health and education.

Many of the current inadequacies in PRC local-government finance arise from the economic transition. The major change is in the role of government from direct management of production to indirect management. However, there are also other important changes in the economy. The decollectivization of agriculture and the increase in rural-urban migration means that the rural population cannot be excluded from the public services that urban residents receive. These changes have also produced a local-government responsibility for pensions that many will not be able to afford. Reform of local government finance must address these issues, but also recognize that financial resources are limited.

At the same time, the rapid growth of cities and the changes in urban economic activities have resulted in an enormous demand for infrastructure improvements. The need to finance these infrastructure requirements has led to the unplanned sale of assets, at below their true values. These developments must be funded more rationally, through the greater use of user fees (although these are already too high in some cases) and through reduced expenditure on unnecessary items such as food subsidies.

Rural public finance needs thorough reform. It needs sufficient resources to provide adequate local services and develop rural infrastructure without imposing large, arbitrary levies on the rural population. This will require greater transfers from higher levels of government, but also consolidation of local government at a single level.

Poverty assistance in rural areas should move away from revenue-generation schemes that run against the principles of a market economy and should concentrate on investment in infrastructure and education, which can produce greater revenue growth in the long run. Food for Work should be used as a method of alleviating extreme poverty.

In summary, the main policy recommendations are as follows. The PRC should:

- set up a formal program of intergovernmental transfers;
- reform off-budget finance;
- rationalize the system of earmarked funds;
- give local governments (especially municipal governments) greater autonomy to set local taxes and user charges and to borrow for infrastructure;
- consolidate county and township finance;
- clarify the expenditure responsibilities of different levels of government;
- clearly define revenue division and tax assignments for different levels of government;
- refocus poverty alleviation programs;
- set up procedures for arbitrating taxpayer complaints; and
- combine the local pension schemes into a national scheme.

Table S.1: Recommended Sequence of Implementation of Reforms

Immediate (within 1 year)	Short-Term (1 to 3 years)	Medium-Term (4 to 6 years)	Supplementary Notes
Revisions in revenue and expenditure assignments			
Ensure that tax-sharing system reforms are passed down to subprovincial levels along with rebates to provide sufficient revenues at lower levels.			
Clarify expenditure responsibilities of different levels of government.	Clearly define revenue division and tax assignments of different levels of government and provide legal/constitutional guarantees.		
	Consolidate rural finance at the county or township level.		Administration should, however, be left at the village and township levels.
	Inject funds to clear up payment arrears in the fiscal system.		Distortions would be corrected and the proper incentives restored in the system.

(cont'd)

Table S.1: Recommended Sequence of Implementation of Reforms (cont'd)

Immediate (within 1 year)	*Short-Term* (1 to 3 years)	*Medium-Term* (4 to 6 years)	*Supplementary Notes*
Intergovernmental transfers			
	Set up a formal program of intergovernmental transfers to achieve a few well-defined policy goals.	Increase the size of interprovincial transfers by raising the central government's share of revenues and using the additional revenues to finance transfers.	These measures will achieve equalization and ensure that every locality can provide at least minimum standards for basic services.
Social safety nets			
Refocus programs for poverty alleviation and assistance to deficit counties. Adopt instead a mix of consumption relief and long-term development assistance aimed at improving resource conditions.		Combine local pension schemes into a national scheme under centralized management.	

(cont'd)

Table S.1: Recommended Sequence of Implementation of Reforms (cont'd)

Immediate (within 1 year)	Short-Term (1 to 3 years)	Medium-Term (4 to 6 years)	Supplementary Notes
Autonomy to local governments			
Encourage local governments to set user charges at cost-recovery levels.	Empower local governments to set the base and rates for a few local taxes.		These measures should provide local governments with a significant and stable base of revenues to finance local needs.
	Permit local governments to borrow for infrastructure investment through a national financial intermediary.		
Earmarked funds			
Improve the efficiency of earmarking and set up funding programs to ensure financing for all announced national goals; end unfunded mandates.			The multitude of earmarked funds should be greatly reduced to give greater discretion to local governments in the use of funds.
	End urban subsidies for food, housing, urban transport, and public utilities and redirect the resources to funding equalization grants.		

(cont'd)

Table S.1: Recommended Sequence of Implementation of Reforms (cont'd)

Immediate (within 1 year)	Short-Term (1 to 3 years)	Medium-Term (4 to 6 years)	Supplementary Notes
Off-budget finance			
	Reform off-budget finance.		Legitimate fees and levies are to be included as taxes or user charges in the formal system of budgetary accounting.
	Set up procedures for arbitrating taxpayer complaints about nonbenefit-based fees and levies imposed by local governments or agencies.	.	For grievance procedure to be effective, progress must be made in reducing local-government leverage over enterprises and other tax-payers, to ensure access to resources outside local-government control and to reduce the value of official patronage.
Others			
	Strengthen supervision and regulation over sales of state assets to ensure rational pacing and prudent use of funds generated.		

Chapter 1

OVERVIEW OF ISSUES IN LOCAL PUBLIC FINANCE IN THE PRC

by Christine P. W. Wong

O ver the past one-and-a-half decades, reforming the fiscal system has been an increasingly urgent concern in the People's Republic of China, as the revenue capacity of the old Soviet-type fiscal system has been inexorably eroded by emerging market forces. In the pre-reform system, government revenues were drawn heavily from profit remittances from state-owned enterprises (SOEs).[1] The revenue capacity of the system depended on three features of the planned economy: fixed prices rigged to favor industry, which transferred surpluses from other sectors to create bloated profits in many industries; state ownership of industry and restricted entry; and compulsory procurement of agricultural products and mandated trade among producers at plan prices. After the reform that began in 1979, these features were gradually eliminated, weakening revenue capacity, and the budget fell from 35 percent of gross national product (GNP) in the late 1970s to 12.7 percent in 1994. While "downsizing" the government should be considered a desirable outcome of the reform and decentralization process, there is nonetheless a level below which inadequate budgetary revenues begin to hinder the government's ability to provide basic services or to respond to the new demands of the

---

[1] At their peak, in 1965-1966 and in the early 1970s, profit remittances from SOEs accounted for about 60 percent of all government revenues. Despite growing losses through the 1970s, enterprises still accounted for about half of all revenues on the eve of reform (Ministry of Finance 1992, pp. 20-21).

emerging market economy. Since the late 1980s the government has concentrated on attempting to reverse the downward trend in revenue collection.

Revamping intergovernmental revenue-sharing arrangements has been a major focus of these efforts since it is widely believed that the fiscal decline is partly caused by the poor incentives for local revenue collection. Under the pre-reform Soviet-type fiscal system, revenues were collected by local governments and shared upward with the central government. The system was highly redistributive, requiring rich provinces to hand over large portions of their revenues to the central government to finance transfers to poor provinces (Lardy 1978). The adverse effects of the very poor incentives thus created were held in check by fairly straightforward monitoring, where revenue capacity was relatively easy to determine given the fixed prices and the tight central control over entry into industry. In any case, local government could not easily hide unauthorized expenditures when budgets were centrally controlled. In the reform period, in contrast, monitoring of the tax effort has become virtually impossible, as large shifts in prices and unrestricted entry into industry have caused large shifts in tax capacity in every region. At the same time, decentralization of budgetary control has also given local governments both the motive and the opportunity to shield local revenues from sharing with higher levels. The history of this evolutionary process was discussed in *Fiscal Management and Economic Reform in the People's Republic of China* (Wong, Heady, and Woo 1995).

The present book extends the exploration of intergovernmental fiscal relations downward by assessing the problems of financing local government, including the subprovincial levels, in light of public finance theory and the practice in other countries. Past studies of local finance were limited to the provincial level and its interaction with the central budget. Under decentralized tax administration, however, taxes are in fact collected primarily at the subprovincial levels, by agents in cities, counties, and townships. Revenue-sharing arrangements are bilateral—involving only two levels at a time—so that there are four layers of sharing: between the central and provincial governments, between the provincial governments and prefectures/cities, between the prefectures/cities and counties, and between counties and townships. Revenue sharing among the lower tiers of government shapes local incentives to allocate resources and mobilize revenues. At the same time, expenditure assignments and the availability of financing jointly determine the efficiency and equity of public goods and services provided by all tiers of government.

A study of subprovincial finance is therefore timely. Throughout the 1980s and 1990s, as the Ministry of Finance was reforming its revenue-sharing relations with the provinces, it paid little attention to how the changes were to be transmitted to the subprovincial levels. The latter, in effect, were left under the near-complete control of the provinces. (The only exception was the central government's attempt to draw selected prefectural-level cities into its own orbit and away from provincial control through the "line-item cities" program, a topic discussed in Chapter 3.) Knowing how fiscal responsibilities and resources at the lower levels of government evolved through more than a dozen years of market transition is an essential first step to designing policies in support of the fiscal reform of 1994. Local finance will be especially affected by the new tax-sharing system (TSS), which has revamped revenue-sharing formulas in a way that is intended to shift revenues toward the central government. Being able to anticipate the direction and magnitude of these changes will greatly strengthen the Ministry of Finance's ability to guide the successful implementation of the reform package.

This book on local finance will focus separately on the urban and rural sectors, with their equally important but different concerns. Municipal finance is an increasingly urgent issue in the PRC's transition to a market economy. As will be explained in greater detail in Chapter 3, cities were generally undervalued and underdeveloped in centrally planned economies, where the plan displaced cities from their coordinating role as centers of information and exchange. In the rush to industrialize, resources were drained from cities for investment in the material sectors (considered the only productive sectors), starving investment in urban infrastructure. This was especially true during the 1950-1980 period, when coastal cities like Shanghai, Tianjin, and Guangzhou were allowed to decay as their weight in GDP, industrial output, and exports generally declined (Davis et al. 1995).

In the transition period, as market exchanges gradually replace plan directives, and as horizontal interaction among economic agents replaces vertical interaction dictated by the plan, the agglomeration economies offered by cities reassert their importance, and cities regain their economic role. Urbanization accelerates, and municipal governments are faced with huge appetites for investment in infrastructure, as well as increased demand for services to support the rapidly growing population. In this process of transition, new tensions are created in the fiscal system, which was designed to produce revenues in urban centers but transfer them for centralized allocation. Unless revenue-sharing rules are changed, cities often do not have sufficient resources to meet their expanded role in the market economy. These issues of urbanization and municipal finance are examined in Chapters 3 and 4.

Rural public finance also faces new pressures in the transition process, since reforms have brought a squeeze on both the revenue and expenditure sides. On the revenue side, rural budgets are generally revenue-poor under the industry-centered tax structure. At the county level, which is responsible for rural governance, government budgets are on the average in deficit, and depend on transfers from higher-level governments. In 1993 an average county had revenues of Y57 million but spent Y74 million; the shortfall of Y17 million was financed by transfers.

Amid the overall fiscal decline, intergovernmental transfers have fallen in absolute and relative size. Data on Guizhou Province show how the poorer counties have been affected. In the early 1980s subsidies from the central government financed nearly 60 percent of the budgetary expenditures of the province. By 1993 they financed less than 20 percent. As its budget was squeezed, the province not only ended subsidies to the lower levels but by the early 1990s was extracting a surplus from the counties to finance provincial government.

On the expenditure side, the share of counties and townships has generally risen in the transition period, mainly because wages and salaries have risen rapidly, and these form the bulk of local-government outlays (accounting for as much as 80 percent of county-level expenditures). Moreover, the shift to household farming and the disbanding of agricultural collectives in the early 1980s meant that rural governments have had to find new ways of financing public services, including education, health care, old-age support, and welfare for poor families, which had been financed from the collective public accumulation funds. In other words, while the Chinese countryside, as usual, had to provide for itself, this time the financing mechanisms of collective agriculture were gone. With higher-level governments themselves under severe fiscal strain, rural governments have had to find their own solutions. Armed with no formal taxing authority, they have resorted to imposing a variety of user fees and charges that are the bane of rural livelihood in many regions. The problems of financing rural government are treated in Chapters 5 and 6.

This chapter provides the background to the discussion of local-government financing in the PRC by describing the present status of local finance at the subprovincial levels, the administrative setup, revenue-sharing arrangements, trends in the vertical distribution of revenues and expenditures, and off-budget finance. We begin by reviewing the 1994 fiscal reforms and their likely impact on local finance. A brief discussion of public finance theory and practice in relation to the role of subnational governments is presented in Chapter 2 to provide the analytical and comparative framework for examining local public finance in the PRC in later chapters.

THE FISCAL REFORM OF 1994

PROVISIONS

A comprehensive reform of macroeconomic management was announced by the government at the Third Plenum of the 14th Party Congress in November 1993. Among the provisions of the "Decision on Issues Concerning the Establishment of a Socialist Market Economy" was a package of measures aimed at reforming the fiscal system. The program addresses three areas of concern: providing adequate revenues for government, especially central government; making the tax structure nondistortionary and more transparent; and revamping central-local revenue-sharing arrangements.

A key provision of the package is a major reform in indirect taxes which extends the value-added tax (VAT) to all turnover, eliminates the product tax, and replaces the business tax on many services. The previous 21 product tax rates (ranging from 3 to 60 percent), 13 VAT rates (8-45 percent), and 4 business tax rates (3-15 percent) have essentially been combined into a single rate of 17 percent, thus greatly simplifying the tax structure. Through a "transitional" period, however, "preferential rates" of 13 percent and 6 percent are applied to some basic necessities for which the government wants to limit price increases (such as urban water supply), and a few low-profit industries (e.g., coal mining).[2] The reform also includes uniform treatment of the turnover tax on domestic and foreign enterprises by eliminating the consolidated industrial and commercial tax (with 40 rates ranging from 1.5 percent to 69 percent) on foreign enterprises and applying the VAT to them as well.

The reform in direct taxes has unified the tax rate on profits for state-owned, collective, and private enterprises, thus eliminating the distortionary unequal treatment of enterprises under different ownership. The top nominal rate of taxation has been reduced from 55 percent to 33 percent. The income adjustment tax has been abolished, along with contributions to the Energy and Key Transport Fund and the Budget Adjustment Fund, which used to absorb 25 percent of enterprise after-tax profits. Offsetting these reductions is the elimination of a number of exemptions, most notably the pretax repayment of loans from enterprise profits.

A new personal income tax has replaced three former taxes: the personal income tax, the personal income adjustment tax, and the individual enterprise income tax. Chinese citizens and foreigners are now on the same tax schedule, although the unequal treatment of different incomes by source still persists.

Reform has reduced the types of taxes to 18, from the previous 32. Among the taxes abolished were the bonus tax, the wage adjustment tax for SOEs, the special fuel oil tax, the market transaction tax, and the livestock trading tax. New taxes include the consumption tax, an excise tax levied in addition to the VAT on luxury goods such as alcohol and tobacco products; the land appreciation tax; the inheritance tax; and the securities trading tax. Some taxes, like the salt and resource taxes and the turnover and income taxes mentioned above, were combined. In preparation for membership in the World Trade Organization, the reform also cut import duties on 1,898 products in November 1993, and on another 234 products in 1994.[3]

---

[2] The 6 percent rate is applied to small river ports and urban water supply companies. It is also applied as a flat rate to gross receipts of small enterprises. The 13 percent rate is applied to iron ore mining operations (but not if they are part of an integrated iron and steel company), coal mining, farm machinery, and chemical fertilizers.

[3] Zhou and Yang (1994).

The centerpiece of the reform package is the new tax-sharing system (*fenshuizhi*), which has fundamentally changed the way revenues are shared between the central and provincial governments. The TSS has reassigned taxes between the central and local governments. Central taxes (or "central fixed incomes") comprise customs duties; the consumption tax; VAT revenues collected by customs; income taxes from central enterprises and from banks and nonbank financial intermediaries; the remitted profits, income taxes, business taxes, and urban construction and maintenance taxes of the railroad, bank headquarters, and insurance companies; and resource taxes on offshore oil extraction.

Local taxes (or "local fixed incomes") consist of business taxes (excluding those named above as central fixed incomes), income taxes and profit remittances of local enterprises, urban land use taxes, personal income taxes, the fixed asset investment orientation tax, the urban construction and maintenance tax, real estate taxes, the vehicle utilization tax, the stamp tax, the animal slaughter tax, agricultural taxes, the title tax, inheritance and gift taxes, the capital gains tax on land, state land sales revenues, and resource taxes on land-based resources.

Shared taxes are the VAT and the new securities trading tax. The central government gets 75 percent of VAT revenues and the local government, 25 percent. Revenues from the security trading tax, on the other hand, are shared equally between the central and local governments.

To phase in the new revenue divisions, the central government modified the TSS in two ways. First, to guarantee each province base revenues in 1994 that at least equaled 1993 base revenues, the central government committed to making a transfer to each province of:

$$PBR - LT - 0.25 \times VAT$$

where:
PBR is the province's base retained revenue
LT is the province's local tax revenue in the base year (1993)
VAT is the VAT revenue from that province

In other words, the base revenue of each province for 1994 was taken to be its retained revenue in 1993 (total revenue of the province minus the amount remitted to the central government). The transfer was meant to allow the province to maintain the same level of expenditure in 1994, after accounting for its local tax revenue and its share in the VAT.

The sharing of increases in revenue was also modified. Thirty percent of any increase in the central government's revenue from VAT and consumption tax in a particular province over the previous year's level goes back to that province. In other words, the province receives from the center an extra transfer of:

0.3 x [0.75 x (VAT increase) + (CT increase)]

where:
CT is the consumption tax revenue from that province

This means that for any increase in provincial revenue that results from increases in consumption tax and VAT, the province receives 30 percent of the gain to the central government, and the results of the system are as follows:

- For an increase in consumption tax, the province receives 30 percent of the increase, and the central government receives 70 percent.
- For an increase in VAT, the province receives 47.5 percent (0.75 x 30 percent + 25 percent), and the center receives 52.5 percent.

These formulas for sharing additional revenues are particularly significant in that the base revenue figures are stated in nominal terms. As inflation through the 1990s gradually erodes the role of the 1993 base revenue figures, the revenue shares going to the provinces will increasingly be determined by the formula for the division of revenue increases.

One additional measure to smooth the transition was the permission given to some SOEs under profit and tax contracts to continue those contracts through 1994 and 1995.[4] These SOEs must accord-

---

[4] These contracts were approved by provincial authorities. One such contract was signed in 1990 by the Confucius Family Winery in Qufu City, Shandong, and the city. It set the lumpsum remittance at Y11.5 million, including shared profits and income and turnover taxes. The lower tax rate under this lumpsum contract permitted the winery to keep more funds for investment in expansion. The winery was allowed to stay under this contract through 1995. (Fieldwork data)

ingly pay taxes as assessed, and the provincial government shares these payments with the central government as stipulated under the TSS, but the province receives a special rebate from the central government equal to the difference between the taxes paid and the contracted amount of taxes. This arrangement should end in 1996 with the expiration of the contracts.

To deal with the problem of poor local collection of central-government taxes, the 1994 reform program established a national tax system (NTS) to collect central-government revenues, and a local tax system to collect local taxes. For this purpose, existing tax bureaus were split into national and local tax offices. The national tax office was supposed to collect the VAT and the consumption tax and then to transfer 25 percent of the VAT revenue to the local government. In most localities the split was achieved by reassigning staff according to their functions: those in charge of turnover taxes were assigned to the NTS, and those assigned to local taxes went to the local tax bureaus.

In the administration of the VAT, tax payments due were calculated through the "invoice method" instead of the previous chaotic system which allowed taxpayers to choose from among different methods.[5]

With these new measures, Chinese tax administration has moved significantly closer to international standards.

IMPLEMENTATION OF THE REFORM PACKAGE

Timing Problems. One major concern in implementing this reform was that the tax administration did not have enough time to prepare for the change. The experience of other countries suggests that substantial periods of time are required. For example, a two-year period of planning and taxpayer education is generally advised before the introduction of the VAT. In the case of the PRC, the reforms were implemented only a few months after they were approved, although many of the proposals had been discussed for several years. Hence, the tax bureaus

---

[5] Wong, Heady, and Woo (1995).

could not be split before the new rules came into effect. Moreover, neither the taxpayers nor many of the local tax officials were fully prepared for the implementation of the VAT and the first-time use of the invoice method.

The speed of implementation also left the provinces little time to establish tax-sharing schemes with the levels of government under them. Through 1994, cities and counties were in doubt as to whether the rules of the contract system would still govern the tax sharing with their provincial government or a formula similar to that between provinces and the central government would instead apply. Such uncertainty hampers proper planning of local expenditures.

Also as a result of the 1994 reform, many local governments reported severe cash-flow problems through 1994 and 1995 in the transition to the new tax-sharing system. The NTS collects revenues from the VAT and the consumption tax directly and channels these to the central treasury. The central government is expected to return 25 percent of the VAT and a portion of total revenues to the provinces each month. But delay in the return of these funds has reportedly caused many local governments to defer all capital expenditures and even wage payments to civil servants and teachers. These problems are more serious at the lower levels, which have to wait for disbursements from the province, and where wages are a major part of total expenditures.

Renewed Bargaining. The new revenue-sharing system is intended to eliminate the bargaining that used to take place between the center and provinces under the contract system. This change will be very welcome, but the new system is very much affected (at least until inflation erodes them) by the base revenue figures used to calculate the central-government transfers to the provinces. The announcement in August 1993 that transfers under the TSS would henceforth be based on the 1993 retained revenues prompted many provinces to make a special effort to increase their revenues by the end of the year. Improved enforcement as well as the collection of owed back taxes caused a reported surge in tax revenues (turnover tax revenue increased by 49.6 percent over the 1992 figure). The Ministry of Finance, however, believes that some of the increase may not be genuine, and that some enterprises may have been persuaded to pay taxes in advance to boost the figures.

To prevent provinces from gaining from artificially inflated revenues in 1993 and to ensure revenue growth in 1994, the Ministry of

Finance set targets for revenue growth for each province, with the threat of reductions in base revenues for those provinces that failed to meet their target. The Ministry set higher targets for those provinces suspected of submitting misleading 1993 figures. This was a fairly clever way of dealing with the problem of inflated base figures, but it also reintroduced the harmful individual negotiation between province and center that characterized the contract system.

There is also some doubt as to whether other aspects of the 1994 reform have been successful in eliminating harmful individual negotiation. The tax preferences granted in 1994, under State Council supervision, gave concessions, such as a new 6 percent VAT rate, to specific industries such as water and brick making. Enterprises in financial difficulty were also allowed concessionary income tax rates of 18 percent and 27 percent. This case-by-case examination was worrisome, since it threatened to erode the objectivity of the new tax system and undermine the whole spirit of reform. Fortunately, the concessions appear to have been limited, and were applied to entire industries, rather than to individual firms.

IMPLICATIONS FOR LOCAL FINANCE

The 1994 fiscal reform package was remarkable for its comprehensiveness. Since the start of reform in 1979, numerous attempts had been made to alter the tax structure and improve incentives for local tax collection (Oskenberg and Tong 1991; Wong 1992). However, these attempts were aimed at marginal changes and left intact two central features of the Soviet system that have proved problematic in a decentralized economy: the differential rates of indirect taxes across products and sectors which allowed taxes to play an unintended resource-allocation function, and the joint "ownership" of revenues which required negotiated sharing between the central and local governments and eroded incentives for local tax collection. The 1994 package, in contrast, marked the first attempt by the government to fundamentally change the fiscal system by rooting out these troublesome features and overhauling tax administration. The greatly simplified tax structure and improved transparency should, in turn, aid monitoring and improve revenue collection over time.

While the 1994 reforms have moved the fiscal system significantly toward greater transparency and a sounder basis for revenue
sharing, they are very much incomplete. The Ministry of Finance has
once again juggled the intergovernmental division of revenues but left
expenditure assignments intact. Since the tax-sharing reform was designed specifically to shift revenues toward the central government, it
will squeeze local budgets unless there is an offsetting increase in transfers from the central government, or new local revenues can be found.
The reforms did not authorize local governments to impose new types
of taxes or set tax rates, but they did, for the first time, assign some
taxes with significant revenue-generating capacity to local governments.
Unlike the local taxes of the past, the personal income tax, the business
tax, and the real estate tax can be expected to grow to provide local
governments with a substantial tax base; indeed, these taxes are the
mainstay of local revenues in many countries. The TSS also formally
assigned revenues from land sales to local governments (formalizing a
practice for some years). Some coastal cities already derive a major
part of their revenues from this source.

The effects are likely to have unequal impact across regions. For
example, the reassignment of taxes on liquor and tobacco as central
taxes will exact a heavy toll on Guizhou Province, which derived some
45 percent of its revenues in 1993 from the taxes on the two products.
More importantly, the very large differences in income between regions in the PRC have produced large disparities in tax capacity and
service provision between provinces. Among the provinces, the ratio
of highest to lowest per capita income is about 6 to 1. Even bigger
ratios are common at the subprovincial levels: among the dozen villages in one township in Guizhou, for example, the ratio was 10 to 1.
Since localities differ greatly in their revenue-raising capacity, and since
the TSS has made retained revenues proportional to locally raised revenues, according to the derivation principle of revenue sharing, regional disparities will intensify unless corrective action is applied.

THE LOCAL ADMINISTRATIVE SETUP

Government administration in the PRC is divided into five levels: the
central level; the provincial level, consisting of 22 provinces, 5 au-

tonomous regions, and 3 cities (*shi*, or municipalities) directly under central administration (Beijing, Shanghai, and Tianjin);[6] the prefectural level, with 101 prefectures and 196 prefectural-level cities at the end of 1993; the county level, with 1,617 counties, 371 county-level cities, and 178 other types of county-level administrative units; and the township level, with more than 50,000 towns and townships. Figure 1.1 shows a generalized scheme of the spatial administrative structure in the reform era. One feature worthy of note is that the prefecture has no constitutional status (i.e., no corresponding People's Congress) and in theory is only an agency of the provincial authorities, but prefectures at present function as another level of government with an organizational setup similar and largely parallel to that of other levels of local government. More than a division of responsibilities, as in many other countries, the different levels of government in the PRC also form a monohierarchical system, with lower-level governments wholly subordinate to governments of higher rank.

While provinces and prefectures are area-based administrative units, encompassing both urban and rural units, cities and counties (and their subordinates) were originally conceived as urban and rural administrative units, respectively. In the PRC, cities are where industries, especially those owned by the state, are concentrated and where most of the government revenues are produced. Cities are thus the core of the "state sector," even if their population is only a small part of the nation's total. Besides producing a large portion of government revenues, they also receive most of the funds from the central government, whether directly or indirectly, for such items as infrastructure development, food subsidies for urban residents, and industrial investment. Until very recently, only urban governments (cities and towns) could raise certain taxes such as the urban maintenance and construction tax and, in some cases, approve foreign investment projects (Koshizawa 1988; Yeh and Xu 1989). Counties, on the other hand, are mainly concerned with agriculture, and have neither the tax obligations of cities nor the financial support they get from the central and provincial governments.

---

[6]   This count excludes Taipei,China. *Shi* is also translated as "municipality" in the literature, but, for consistency, the term "city" is used here throughout.

Figure 1.1: China's Spatial Administrative Hierarchy in the Post-1983 Era: A Generalized Schema

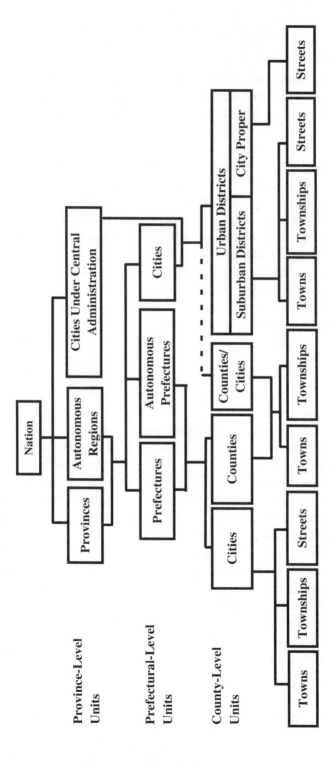

Note: The dotted line represents an optional relation—not all cities have counties under them.

Source: Chan (1994a).

The administrative setup in the countryside is relatively straight-forward. Below the prefectures are the counties and below these are the township-level units, townships, and towns. Villagers' committees at the subtownship level are not government bodies but also perform some local-government functions such as providing social services and ensuring public security.

The system of urban government is more complicated. The definition of cities (*shi*) is a very complex issue by itself (discussed in Chapter 3). Cities are moreover differentiated with reference to their levels in the administrative hierarchy (Figure 1.1). Three cities directly under central administration (*zhixiashi*)—Beijing, Shanghai, and Tianjin—are provincial-level units and occupy the highest positions in the urban hierarchy. Next are prefectural-level cities (*dijishi*), which are directly under provincial administration. A special feature of provincial-level and prefectural-level cities is the subdivision of their urban areas into city or urban "districts" (*shiqu or shixiaqu*). Many of them also administer counties within their jurisdictions. County-level cities (*xianjishi*), at the lowest rung of the city hierarchy, have no urban districts and do not administer any counties.

The present study examines six cities and two counties (and their townships) in two provinces, Shandong and Guizhou (see Annex) and draws additional information from Hebei Province. Three of the six cities (Qingdao, Taian, and Guiyang) are at the prefectural level, and the three others (Qufu, Penglai, and Anshun) are county-level cities. The evolution and reorganization of the PRC administrative structure during the transition have given rise to changes that are not totally consistent with the formal setup. Qingdao, for one, is formally a prefectural-level city and also a "line-item" and "open coastal" city enjoying many economic management and fiscal powers equal to those of a province. These new urban forms will be discussed in greater detail in Chapter 3.

The overall structure of the provincial, prefectural, and county government units (including cities and nonurban units) has remained relatively stable throughout the 1980s and the early 1990s (Table 1.1). In the country as a whole, only one additional provincial unit, Hainan, has been created. Between 1982 and 1993, a total of 16 new prefectural-level units were created, and 100 county-level units were abolished, largely as a result of the amalgamation of counties into new

Table 1.1: Administrative Units in the PRC, 1982-1994
(Number at year-end)

| | Provincial Level | | Prefectural Level | | County Level | | Cities at | City |
	All	Cities	All	Cities	All	Cities	All Levels	District
Nation								
1982	29	3	319	109	2,266	133	245	527
1988	30	3	334	183	2,186	248	434	647
1994	30	3	333	206	2,148	413	622	697
Change, 1982-1994	1	0	14	97	-437	211	377	170
Shandong								
1982	-	-	14	5	112	8	13	24
1988	-	-	15	10	100	20	30	34
1994	-	-	17	14	95	32	46	44
Change, 1982-1994	-	-	3	9	-17	24	33	20
Guizhou								
1982	-	-	9	2	82	3	5	5
1988	-	-	9	2	81	6	8	6
1994	-	-	9	2	80	9	11	6
Change, 1982-1994	-	-	0	0	-2	6	6	1

"-" Not applicable.

Source: SSB (1983, 1989, 1994a, 1995).

county-level cities. The number of prefectural-level units accordingly increased by 5 percent and the number of county-level units dropped by 4 percent.

In contrast to the stability at the three broad levels of government, many nonurban units have been reclassified into urban units within the categories of prefectural and county-level units. This explains the fact that, while the number of prefectural and county-level units has changed only slightly, the number of cities has more than doubled since 1982, from 245 in 1982 to 570 in 1993. All the newly designated cities are reclassified counties which retained their administrative rank and boundaries, and for this reason are known as county-level cities. The prefectural rank, on the other hand, admitted 87 more cities. Most of these prefectural-level cities were formed by combining county-level cities with some of their neighboring counties. In many cases, they simply occupied the areas of the former prefectures.

Similar patterns of change can be seen in the provinces of Shandong and Guizhou, but the changes are more pronounced in the more developed Shandong than in Guizhou. To illustrate, the total number of cities increased by 30, to 43, in Shandong in 1993 but by only 6, to 11, in Guizhou. The differences are more significant in individual categories of cities. In the same period, the number of county-level cities multiplied by about four times, from 8 to 31, in Shandong, but only by three times, from 3 to 9, in Guizhou. Of Shandong's prefectural units in 1993, about 70 percent, or double the 1982 figure, had been prefectural-level cities. The prefectural administrative structure in Guizhou, on the other hand, has remained unchanged since the early 1980s, and only 2 of the 9 prefectural-level units are cities. In our case studies, the county-level cities Taian, Qufu, and Penglai were all once counties; Taian became a county-level city in 1982, Qufu in 1986, and Penglai in 1991. In 1985 Taian was upgraded once more into a prefectural city.

Generally, these changes in the administrative system in the 1980s and the early 1990s reflect the growing urbanization (and the application of broader criteria for designating urban areas) and the recognition by the PRC leadership of the importance of local government, especially medium and small-sized cities, in the regional economies. The administrative changes were also attempts to remedy problems in economic development coordination at the local regional levels which the vertical, bureaucratically organized system (examined in Chapter 3) had left behind. To a great extent, these efforts parallel the post-Mao administrative decentralization and growing local financial autonomy. The creation of prefectural-level cities to replace prefectures also indicates the gradual phaseout of prefectures, which, as pointed out earlier, do not have a constitutional basis for their administration.

REVENUE SHARING AT THE SUBPROVINCIAL LEVELS

As noted in *Economic Reform and Fiscal Management in the People's Republic of China*, revenue-sharing arrangements are bilateral, involving only two levels of government at a time. Given the five tiers of government in China, there are four layers of revenue-sharing relationships: between the central government and the provinces, between provinces and prefectures or cities,[7] between cities and counties, and between counties and townships. At each layer, the superior level has virtually absolute authority over the setting of contracts, subject to resource constraints but with little interference from the next higher level.[8]

Subprovincial sharing arrangements generally mimic central-provincial arrangements. Through the 1980s, as central-provincial revenue sharing changed from "sharing specific revenues" to sharing all revenues, subprovincial arrangements generally followed suit, albeit with a lag. Since the late 1980s, with the introduction of fiscal contracting at the central-provincial level, subprovincial arrangements have most often been some variant of fixed-term contracts stipulating a lumpsum remittance or subsidy, with the lumpsum sometimes pegged to grow with total revenue. For example, from 1987 to 1993, Shandong Province had a contract that set remittance to the central government at a flat Y289 million per year. In turn, the province had contracts with prefectural cities that called for lumpsum remittances increasing by 0-

---

[7] Consistent with the replacement of the prefectures with the city as the administrative unit between the province and the county, the term "city" is used in this book to denote a prefecture or a prefectural-level city. A city at any other level will be so specified, e.g., a "county-level" city.

[8] In extreme cases, the lower-level unit can appeal to the next higher level for intervention, as Shijiazhuang City did in the mid-1980s, when it pleaded with the Ministry of Finance to grant a special allowance to offset the adverse effects of price changes on the city's textile industry.

10.1 percent per year (Table 1.2; Box 1.1 presents an illustrative set of four tiers of revenue sharing in Hebei Province).

Within this framework of uniformity, however, significant differences across regions reflected substantial local autonomy. Several local governments in the fieldwork sample experimented with forms of revenue sharing, such as the introduction of lumpsum contracts at the subprovincial levels in Shandong Province as early as 1985 (in Taian City), which were later implemented nationwide.

More interestingly, an early version of the tax-sharing system was introduced in Hebei in 1987 when, to stop the province's share of revenues from slipping after most enterprises were transferred to city control, provincial officials put in a special claim on the most buoyant tax type, turnover taxes. The turnover taxes (product, value-added, and business taxes) of six prefectural-level cities placed under the program

Table 1.2: Revenue Sharing
in Shandong Province, 1988-1993

Prefecture/City	Remittance Base[a] (Y million)	Provision for Annual Incremental Remittance (%)
Zibo	233.93	8-10.1
Taian	22.17	8
Jinan	557.40	8-10.1
Jining	25.95	8-8.35
Weifang	300.13	8-10.1
Yantai	312.27	...
Dezhou	-65.42	0
Huimin	-55.03	0
Heze	-139.43	0
Liaocheng	-66.12	0
Zaozhuang	-16.31	0
Linyi	-49.78	0
Dongying	-24.53	0

... Not available.
[a] 1988 was the base year.
Sources: Huang Kehua (1993); Shandong Provincial Budget Department.

Box 1.1: Four Levels of Fiscal Contracts in Hebei, 1988-1991

I. Contracting with the central government. Hebei was assigned a base remittance quota of Y1.52 billion in 1988, with an annual increment of 4.5 percent. In 1991 the province remitted Y2.02 billion.

IIa. Provincial contract with Shijiazhuang. Shijiazhuang's base remittance quota in 1988 was Y384 million, with an annual increment of 5.5 percent. In 1992 Shijiazhuang remitted about Y500 million under the contract. In addition, 50 percent of the city's turnover tax revenues were set aside as provincial fixed revenues, under the tax-sharing arrangement introduced in 1987.

IIb. Provincial contract with Xinji. Counties normally have revenue-sharing arrangements with prefectures/cities. As one of the nine "line-item county cities," however, Xinji has a direct budgetary link with the province, bypassing the prefectural level. Placed under fiscal contracting in 1986, Xinji was assigned a remittance quota of Y27.41 million, with an annual increment of 5.5 percent. Its remittance in 1992 was Y35.91 million.

IIIa. Shijiazhuang's contracts with its six city districts. Each district has a base remittance quota with an annual increment of 6.5 percent.

IIIb. Shijiazhuang's contracts with its four suburban counties. Each county has a contract with a base remittance quota and an annual increment of 7.5 percent. The higher incremental growth in the counties' remittance quotas is justified by the fact that the counties are excluded from the provincial tax-sharing arrangement, and will therefore have higher buoyancy in their revenue base.

IV. Xinji's contract with Nanzhiqiu Township. Townships gained increasing budgetary autonomy through the late 1980s. They have fixed expenditure assignments (to cover agricultural expenses and water conservation, basic education, health, and welfare). In 1986-1988, Nanzhiqiu had a fixed-rate revenue-sharing contract with Xinji which allowed it to retain 11 percent of total revenues up to the revenue base, and 80 percent of revenues beyond that. The revenue base was set at Y656, and the remittance base was set at Y584,000.

In 1989-1991, the township was on a contract that fixed quotas for revenues and expenditures, with a 90 percent retention rate on excess revenues. The "base numbers" were fixed at Y925,000 for revenues and Y267,000 for expenditures. In 1992 the township was placed on a three-year contract, with a fixed remittance quota of Y1.275 million. The remittance quota was to increase by 8 percent in 1993 and by 9 percent in 1994. In addition, the new "special agricultural products tax" introduced in 1989 is treated separately outside the revenue-sharing base. Eighty percent of the revenues from this tax go to the city, and the township retains only 20 percent.

Source: Wong, Heady, and Woo (1995).

were set apart from other tax revenues and shared separately. The province claimed 30-60 percent of these turnover tax revenues *prior* to revenue-sharing contracts, with a different ratio for each city; only the remainder entered the pool of revenues to which fiscal contracts were applied. Shijiazhuang, for example, was allowed to retain 50 percent. In a treatment that foreshadowed the nationwide implementation of the tax-sharing system in 1994, the provincial portion of turnover tax revenues was channeled directly into provincial accounts at the Treasury.

Until the TSS reform, revenues were shared between the central and provincial governments from a general pool. This pool included about 50 percent of revenues after excluding central taxes (about 30 percent of the total), local taxes (less than 10 percent), and special shared taxes (mainly for liquor and tobacco, which composed another 10 percent of revenues) (Wong 1991a; Wong, Heady, and Woo 1995).

This pattern of sharing was replicated at the local levels, where revenues were similarly divided in two stages. First, revenues were divided into three categories: fixed revenues for each of the two levels of government, and shared revenues. Then, revenue-sharing contracts were applied to shared revenues and the fixed revenues of the lower level. The fixed revenues of the province generally included the leftover portion (after the central government took 70 percent) of the turnover tax revenues from the four centralized industries (power, petroleum, petrochemicals, and nonferrous metals), business tax revenues from banks and insurance companies, direct tax revenues and profit remittances from provincial-owned enterprises, and a portion of resource tax revenues. For the city, fixed revenues comprised the 13 minor taxes that were turned over to local ownership in 1988, including the real estate tax, vehicle utilization tax, urban land use tax, stamp tax, animal slaughter tax, animal trading tax, banquet tax, market trading tax, urban maintenance tax, pollution fees, and water resource tax. In Shandong Province, these taxes accounted for less than 9 percent of total tax revenues in 1992 (Huang Kehua 1993, p. 290). Revenues shared between the provinces and the cities came from the direct taxes and profit remittances of city-owned enterprises, turnover taxes, income taxes on collective enterprises, the construction tax, and agricultural taxes.

The TSS, which divides revenues more clearly by tax types, will simplify the revenue sharing. However, the reform itself specified only the division between the central and provincial governments, and left the provinces to decide how to divide up the "local" share between the province and the lower levels. Through September 1994, neither Shandong nor Guizhou Province had yet announced the new formulas for revenue sharing with prefectures and cities. Moreover, some taxes, such as the farmland occupation tax and the agricultural special products tax, continue to be shared separately, outside the "regular" pool.

Aside from own and shared values, local governments also receive transfers from higher levels. Before TSS, there were four channels of such transfers (Figure 1.2). Aside from the quota subsidies under revenue contracts (S_1), there were also earmarked and other subsidies, some of which came from the central government and were passed through the lower levels (represented by S_2). At the provincial level, earmarked subsidies primarily consisted of funds for social and disaster relief; price subsidies for grain, cotton, and oil; grants for large-scale flood and drought prevention projects; and special subsidies for health and education in poor and border areas. County subsidies were disbursed primarily for social and disaster relief. Table 1.3 gives the remittance and quota subsidy figures for each province, and Table 1.4, the earmarked and quota subsidies provided by the central government in selected years. Tables 1.5 and 1.6 classify earmarked subsidies by use and by province. Table 1.7 shows the levels and composition of subsidies and remittances for the four county-level administrative units in our sample to illustrate the multistranded fiscal flows.

TRENDS IN THE VERTICAL DISTRIBUTION OF REVENUES AND EXPENDITURES

The division of expenditure responsibilities among administrative levels is discussed in detail in later chapters. This section presents the vertical distribution of revenues and expenditures in the aggregate, to provide a context for situating the fieldwork sites and their experiences.

Before revenue sharing, the five levels of government in 1993 had own revenues as follows:

Figure 1.2: Intergovernmental Transfers

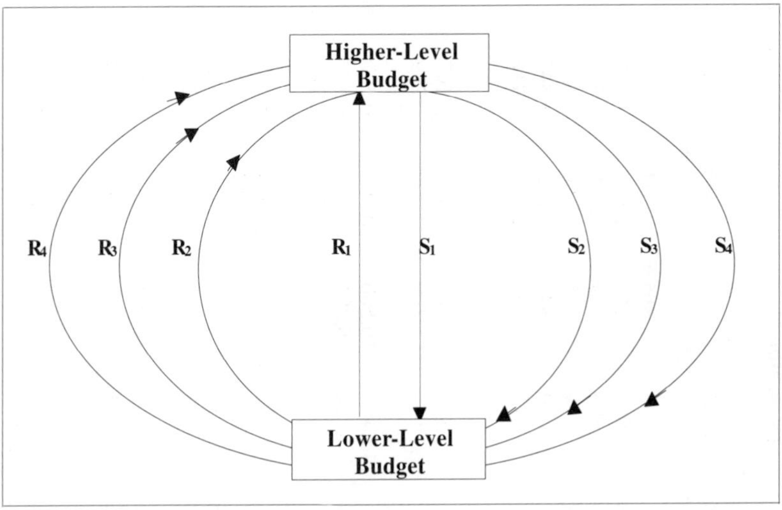

Downward Transfers:
$S1=$ quota subsidies under fiscal contracts
$S2=$ earmarked and other subsidies
$S3=$ compensatory payments for transfer of enterprise
$S4=$ final accounts subsidies

Upward Transfers:
$R1=$ remittances under fiscal contacts
$R2=$ special taxes
$R3=$ compensatory payments for transfers of enterprise
$R4=$ "loans" and contributions to central government

Table 1.3: Total Remittances and Quota Subsidies, by Province, 1985-1992
(Y million)

	1985	1986	1987	1988	1989	1990	1991	1992
Beijing	2,522	2,879	3,033	2,895	3,011	3,131	3,256	3,387
Tianjin	2,671	3,013	3,098	2,163	2,014	1,886	1,906	2,262
Hebei	1,324	1,348	1,505	1,587	1,658	1,733	1,811	1,892
Shanxi	60	68	79	425	500	530	554	571
Inner Mongolia	-1,783	-1,962	-2,060	-1,842	-1,842	-1,842	-1,842	-1,842
Liaoning[a]	3,890	1,945	3,077	2,257	2,336	2,418	1,606	1,682
Shenyang City	...	...	...	...	...	...	1,794	1,731
Dalian City	...	...	...	...	...	...	1,165	1,272
Jilin	-397	-397	-397	-107	-107	-107	-107	-107
Heilongjiang	305	-158	143	299	299	299	299	299
Harbin City	...	...	...	...	...	...	399	419
Shanghai	13,813	13,369	12,413	10,500	10,500	10,500	10,500	10,500
Jiangsu	5,085	5,506	5,924	6,201	6,511	6,592	5,412	6,757
Zhejiang	2,524	2,951	2,850	2,422	2,579	2,747	2,925	3,342
Ningbo City	...	...	...	...	...	...	904	952
Anhui	570	665	720	861	982	1,009	0.0	-444
Fujian	-235	-235	-235	0.0	-50	-50	-50	-50
Jiangxi	-239	-239	-239	-45	-45	-45	-45	-45
Shandong[a]	2,621	1,294	75	289	289	289	289	205
Qingdao City	...	...	...	...	...	...	1,547	1,594
Henan	886	989	731	1,206	1,266	1,329	1,396	1,381
Hubei	1,514	-385	0.0	0.0	0.0	0.0	0.0	-130
Wuhan City	...	...	...	...	...	...	2,024	2,431
Hunan	447	539	614	856	916	980	1,049	1,101
Guangdong	778	778	778	1,640	1,779	1,722	1,869	2,028
Shenzhen City	...	...	...	...	...	...	226	246
Guangxi	-716	-788	-827	-608	-608	-608	-608	-608
Hainan	...	...	...	-280	-437	-588	-571	-471

Table 1.3: Total Remittances and Quota Subsidies, by Province, 1985-1992 (cont'd)
(Y million)

	1985	1986	1987	1988	1989	1990	1991	1992
Sichuan	616	-400	0.0	0.0	0.0	0	0.0	-220
Chongqing City	...	...	...	...	...	...	1,093	1,375
Guizhou	-743	-818	-858	-742	-742	-742	-742	-742
Yunnan	-637	926	-972	-673	-673	-673	-673	-673
Tibet	-750	-825	-867	-898	-968	-991	-1,011	-1,071
Sha'anxi	-270	-270	-270	-120	-120	-120	-120	-120
Xian City								0
Gansu	-246	-246	-246	-126	-126	-126	-126	-126
Qinghai	-611	-672	-705	-656	-656	-656	-656	-656
Ningxia	-494	-543	-570	-533	-533	-533	-533	-533
Xinjiang	-1,450	-1,595	-1,657	-1,529	-1,529	-1,529	-1,529	-1,767
Line-Item Cities Total[b]	...	6,129	5,183	8,478	8,723	8,731[c]	9,737	12,899
Total Remittances[d]	39,625	40,529[e]	40,223	42,079	43,364	43,896	51,761	59,736[e]
Total Subsidies[d]	-8,571	-9,515	-9,904	-8,160	-8,436	-8,611	-8,614	-10,130
Net Transfers[d]	31,054	31,014	30,319	33,919	34,928	35,285	43,147	49,606

... Not available.

[a] In 1992, Liaoning Province remitted Y2,566 million while receiving a quota subsidy of Y884 million. Shandong Province remitted Y289 million while receiving a quota subsidy of Y84 million.

[b] Line-item cities refer to the nine prefectural cities in the table (Shenyang, Dalian, Harbin, Ningbo, Qingdao, Wuhan, Shenzhen, Chongqing, and Xian) that have fiscal relations with the central government.

[c] Derived as residual.

[d] Total remittances and subsidies include those of line-item cities. Net transfers are defined as total remittances less total subsidies.

[e] Totals are Ministry of Finance figures, which are slightly at variance with column sums.

Source: Ministry of Finance.

Table 1.4: Earmarked Grants from the Center,
1980-1993
(Y billion)

	Earmarked Grants	Quota Subsidies	Other Subsidies[a]	Total Subsidies
1980	7.2	5.9	1.0	14.1
1981	6.3	6.4	2.5	15.2
1982	7.1	6.9	5.1	19.1
1983	8.9	7.2	5.1	21.2
1984	10.2	7.8	7.4	25.4
1985	18.3	9.5	6.7	34.5
1986	25.7	8.6	12.1	46.4
1987	27.8	9.9	10.4	48.1
1988	27.3	8.2	18.3	53.8
1989	28.8	8.4	19.0	56.2
1990	29.6	8.6	20.3	58.5
1991	35.5	8.6	11.4	55.5
1992	37.8	10.1	11.7	59.6
1993	36.0	9.5	9.0	54.5

[a] Calculated as residual
Source: Ministry of Finance.

Table 1.5: Distribution of Central Earmarked Grants, by Use, 1993

	1993 (Y hundred million)	% of Total
Capital construction	24.6	6.8
Enterprise renovation	11.0	3.1
Makeshift building	1.5	0.4
Geological prospecting	0.1	0.0
Science and technology	4.3	1.2
Agricultural support	15.4	4.3
Agriculture, forestry, and fisheries	3.6	1.0
Industry and transport	1.9	0.5
Commerce	1.0	0.3
Urban maintenance	1.7	0.5
Culture, education, health	10.8	3.0
Science	0.2	0.1
Other administration	10.5	2.9
Welfare assistance	23.7	6.6
Administration	8.0	2.2
Law administration	4.8	1.3
Price subsidies	213.2	59.2
Aid to poor regions	7.2	2.0
Others	16.7	4.6
Education surcharge expenditure	0.3	0.1
Total	360.5	100.0

Source: Ministry of Finance.

Table 1.6: Central Earmarked Grants, by Province, 1985-1990
(Y million)

	1985	1986	1987	1988	1989	1990
Beijing	643	774	969	1,039	1,461	1,300
Tianjin	606	598	301	336	373	398
Hebei	710	963	1,114	1,128	1,199	1,288
Shanxi	820	850	856	745	772	834
Inner Mongolia	519	650	858	832	835	819
Liaoning	920	847	1,117	1,274	1,536	1,474
Jilin	689	1,135	1,456	1,438	1,384	1,202
Heilongjiang	866	1,449	1,324	1,299	1,351	1,391
Shanghai	289	304	541	660	720	767
Jiangsu	1,042	1,446	1,437	1,342	1,290	1,309
Zhejiang	522	762	857	787	831	888
Anhui	837	1,307	1,163	1,134	1,029	1,082
Fujian	320	487	606	612	586	697
Jiangxi	552	865	916	828	874	982
Shandong	930	1,356	1,413	1,471	1,604	1,627
Henan	981	1,503	1,261	1,230	1,227	1,360
Hubei	934	1,235	1,089	1,036	1,194	1,282
Hunan	629	1,058	1,042	982	1,038	1,145
Guangdong	717	1,392	1,622	1,371	1,375	1,241
Guangxi	491	817	935	907	785	782
Hainan	...	...	...	183	333	300
Sichuan	1,204	1,740	1,787	1,697	1,767	1,924
Guizhou	337	484	522	499	511	530
Yunnan	522	804	810	877	933	876
Tibet	279	134	141	119	235	235
Sha'anxi	560	753	741	720	678	756
Gansu	541	621	719	627	651	743
Qinghai	167	207	256	219	229	276
Ningxia	186	238	289	261	264	258
Xinjiang	485	647	682	718	708	741
Line-Item Cities	0	973	957	963	1,028	1,093[a]
Total	18,298	26,399	27,781	27,334	28,801	29,600

... Not available.

[a] Calculated as a residual.

Source: Ministry of Finance.

Table 1.7: Multistranded Fiscal Flows at the County Level, 1993
(Y million)

	Shandong		Guizhou	
	Qufu	*Penglai*	*Zunyi*	*Puding*
Collected revenues	140.76	101.59	140.47	13.78
Provincial subsidies	11.05	17.43	30.97	9.53
Quota subsidies	0.00	0.00	17.16	4.45
Earmarked subsidies	11.05	17.43	13.05	4.90
Other subsidies	0.00	0.00	0.76	0.18
Remittances to province	18.61	27.83	52.00	0.86
Contracted remittance	5.13	23.95	48.77	0.00
Special remittance	13.48	3.88	3.23	0.86
Net transfer[a]	-7.56	-10.40	-21.03	8.67
Available resources	133.20	91.20	119.44	22.45
Total expenditures	139.55	96.63	121.98	25.00
Per capita:				
Collected revenues (Y)	235	214	134	38
Available revenues (Y)	218	186	91	62
Expenditures (Y)	228	197	94	69

[a]A positive number indicates an inflow to the unit, and a negative number indicates an outflow.
Source: Fieldwork data.

central	34%
provinces	11%
prefectures/cities	29%
counties	16%
townships	11%

Within the local sector (excluding the central level), revenues were distributed as follows:

provinces	16.7%
prefectures/cities	43.9%
counties	24.2%
townships	16.7%

**Table 1.8: Distribution of Revenues and Expenditures,
by Administrative Level, 1993
(Percent)**

	PRC	Hebei[a]	Shandong	Guizhou
Revenues				
Province	16.7	9.3	8.2	7.0
Prefectures/Cities	43.9	49.9	34.9	37.3
Counties	24.2	22.6	36.5	33.2
Townships	16.7	18.3	20.4	22.5
Expenditures				
Province	23.8	24.0	16.6	25.2
Prefectures/Cities	31.7	32.1	28.1	23.4
Counties	30.2	33.5	38.2	34.8
Townships	12.7	10.4	17.1	16.6

[a] 1992 figures.
Sources: Ministry of Finance; fieldwork data.

The dominance of cities in revenue accrual is understated in these aggregate statistics in which the provincial share is inflated by the inclusion of Beijing, Tianjin, and Shanghai as provincial units: together the three municipalities accounted for 7 percent of total revenues in 1991. In contrast, the share of the provincial level ranges from 7 percent to 9.3 percent in the three provinces in our sample (Table 1.8).

During the 1980s, the provincial share of own revenues generally fell, as enterprises were largely transferred to municipal management. In Hebei, for example, after 151 SOEs were transferred to city/prefectural management in 1985, only 20 odd enterprises in the metallurgical, pharmaceutical, and chemical industries were still directly owned and managed by the province. Besides the shares of cities and prefectures, the share of counties also rose slightly, with the growth of TVEs, until townships were set up as a separate level of finance in 1986. After that, the township share grew at the expense of counties. The county share of total revenues fell from 26.2 percent in 1989 to 24.2 percent in 1993.

The distribution of expenditures by administrative level is shown in the lower half of Table 1.8. At each level, resources available to finance expenditures are equal to own revenues plus remittances from the lower level minus remittances to the higher level. Data in Table 1.8 show that within the local fiscal hierarchy, the province and county levels spend a greater share of revenues than they collect, while the inverse is true for prefectures/cities and townships. This vertical imbalance reflects, on the one hand, the tax system's reliance on industry and commerce to generate the bulk of revenues. Since industrial and commercial activities are concentrated in the cities (and increasingly in townships and villages), so also are revenues. On the other hand, it also reflects the special role assigned to the province and county levels in redistributing revenues among subordinate units.

Intergovernmental expenditure assignments in the PRC roughly follow international practice, with the central government responsible for expenditures related to national defense and external relations, and local governments responsible for day-to-day administration and the provision of social services such as health care and education (Wong, Heady, and Woo 1995). The central government, the only level empowered to borrow, also has sole responsibility for debt servicing.

As in most countries, for many major expenditures there is a high degree of overlap between levels of government, where financing is divided according to subordination relations. For example, education expenditures accrue to all levels of government. The general principle is that higher education is the responsibility of the central and provincial governments, while primary and secondary education are the responsibility of local governments. In practice, universities and research institutes are subordinate to either the central government or a provincial government, and their source of finance depends on the level to which they are subordinated. Likewise, primary schools in the cities are financed from municipal budgets, while those in the rural areas are financed from county or township budgets. Health expenditures are similarly divided among governments, with the central government financing key research hospitals, cities financing central hospitals and clinics, and counties and townships financing hospitals and clinics that serve local areas. This division of expenditure responsibilities is described in detail in Chapter 6.

In the pre-reform, centrally planned, system, the central government financed the bulk of capital investments as a core part of its program of economic management. In the reform period, as investments have been shifted out of the budget, the central share of the budget has declined. The expenditure burdens of local governments have grown, in contrast, as wage increases, which have exceeded the average rate of price inflation through the reform period, have pushed up the costs of day-to-day administration and service provision.

As a result of these shifts, the central share of total budgetary expenditure fell from 54 percent in 1980 to 40 percent in 1990-1991. The same decentralizing trend is seen at the subprovincial levels as well. In Shandong the provincial share fell from 34 percent in 1980 to 17 percent in 1993. The share of cities and prefectures rose from 16 percent to 26 percent during the same period, while the combined share of counties and townships rose from 50 percent to 57 percent. This shift to the subprovincial levels is driven by the same factors that are causing a decline in the share of central expenditures relative to local: the transfer of investment finance from the budget to enterprises and the banking sector, which reduced the outlays of the provinces disproportionately more than those of lower levels; the devolution of expenditure responsibilities for grain subsidies to the cities; and rising wages and the consequent rise in government service costs, which are borne predominantly by city, county, and township budgets. The growing burden of financing these services will be discussed in later chapters.

While provinces have substantial autonomy in assigning expenditures to lower levels, in practice the expenditure pattern is broadly similar across provinces. Table 1.9 shows the composition of expenditures by level of government for Shandong Province in 1992. It can be seen that, among the three major expenditure categories, current expenditures, including health and education, make up over three-quarters of local-government expenditures at the county level.

ROLE OF OFF-BUDGET FINANCE

Off-budget funds have been growing in importance in financing government, especially at the lower tiers. These consist of extrabudgetary

Table 1.9: Composition of Expenditures,
by Administrative Level, in Shandong Province, 1992
(Percent)

Use	Province	City	County
Investment	31.8	31.9	16.9
Current/Administrative	55.7	55.9	76.7
Subsidies	12.4	12.2	6.4

Source: Huang Kehua (1993), p. 22.

funds (*yusuanwai zijin*) under the control of local governments and administrative agencies, and "self-raised funds" (*zichou zijin*) at the county and township levels. Unfortunately, the reluctance of local governments to disclose all their available resources makes it difficult to ascertain the exact size and distribution of these funds. The problem of underreporting is likely to be most serious at the lowest levels of government, where monitoring is weakest. Aggregate data for the entire PRC show that in 1993 budgetary funds accounted for 74 percent of total revenues available at the township level, while extrabudgetary funds (EBF) made up 6.5 percent and "self-raised funds" (SRF) accounted for about 20 percent. In 1986, the share of EBF was 5 percent and that of SRF was 11.7 percent. On the expenditure side, EBF accounted for 7 percent and SRF for 25.4 percent of the total expenditures of townships.

Off-budget finance appeared to have a much larger role in our fieldwork sites. In Hebei, EBF totaled Y10.67 billion in 1992, exceeding the budget in size. Of this amount, Y4.14 billion belonged to local governments and administrative agencies. Adding this "fiscal" portion to the consolidated budget of the province increased its spending power by 40 percent. At the prefecture and city level it increased spending by 57 percent. In one township visited, SRF reportedly rivaled the size of the budget and financed as much as an additional 80 percent of township expenditures. In Shandong Province, SRF financed Y4.8 billion in expenditures at the township level in 1993, compared with the Y2.4 billion in the budget for that year.

Definitions of extrabudgetary funds and "self-raised funds" are vague. These are defined imprecisely as funds collected by governments and their agencies but not counted as budgetary funds.[9] They are often earmarked for specific uses (such as education and road maintenance) and, most importantly, are not subject to sharing with higher tiers of government. Conceptually EBF and SRF are indistinguishable. In practice EBF is the term usually applied to funds at the provincial and city levels, while SRF is commonly used at the county and especially township levels. The extent and implications of off-budget finance will be examined in Chapters 5-7.

---

[9] According to a Ministry of Finance directive, EBF at the township level are funds that by state regulations are not included in the budget, including various surcharges levied by the township government and administrative units, earmarked funds of SOEs and their supervisory departments, and "various other incomes." The same document defines "self-raised funds" as those collected by township finance bureaus that are "by state policy excluded from budgetary and extrabudgetary accounts." These consist mainly of profits remitted by township and village enterprises, and "unified levies" (*tongchou*) approved by the township people's congresses (Ministry of Finance 1992b).

Chapter 2

THE ROLE OF SUBNATIONAL GOVERNMENTS: THEORY AND INTERNATIONAL PRACTICE

by Christopher Heady

The role of local governments in a country is very strongly influenced by their power to levy taxes and to determine public expenditure. The assignment of tax and expenditure responsibilities to national and subnational governments affects the efficiency of government services and the degree of market distortion produced by the taxes that finance the services.

The theory that has been developed to help us understand the consequences of this assignment of responsibilities is often referred to as the "Theory of Fiscal Federalism."[1] But it applies just as well to unitary states, such as France and the United Kingdom (UK), as to countries with federal constitutions, such as Germany and the United States of America (US). The theory simply has to do with countries in which some government services are provided by a subnational level of government with some independent decision-making power. Almost all countries of significant size in the world fit this description.

ASSIGNMENT OF EXPENDITURE RESPONSIBILITIES

BASIC PRINCIPLES

Some government services, such as national defense and major transport systems (roads, railways), benefit the entire country. Decisions

---

[1] See Oates (1972), Bird (1986), and Bird (1992, Ch. 11).

about how much to spend on these items, and exactly how the services are to be rendered, have to be made by the national government. They cannot be left to local governments, which might well not consider sufficiently the effect of their decisions on the rest of the country.

On the other hand, garbage collection, street lighting, and similar services in a particular city affect only the residents of that city. The national government need not be brought into decisions about the provision of these services. Local government can decide the details of these services and the amount to allocate for each service.

These examples illustrate the basic principles behind the assignment of expenditure responsibilities. The national government is able to take into account the effects of public services that extend beyond a particular area. But where local public services are concerned, local government knows better the needs and wishes of the local people and can therefore make more suitable decisions.

Stated in this way, and in the light of the examples just given, the assignment of expenditure responsibilities seems straightforward. Local government should provide local services[2] and the central government should confine itself to providing nationwide services. However, there are two complications that must be considered. First, different local services cover localities of different sizes. Second, some services have both local and national components.

DIFFERENT AREAS OF SERVICE

First, regarding the varying coverage of different local services, compare garbage collection with public transport. Garbage collection has a very local impact. The efficiency of garbage collection in the northern section of a city has almost no effect on the residents in the southern section. However, the operation of a public transport system affects the city as a whole.

By implication, therefore, garbage collection should be organized by a level of government that is smaller than a city, to best reflect the

---

[2] This conclusion presupposes that local governments are able to provide the local services efficiently.

needs and wishes of those affected by the service, while the transport system should be organized by city government.

This statement would seem reasonable if only two public services were involved. But there are many public services and each one could best be managed by a local government of a different size—an obvious impracticality. The idea of, say, 20 different levels of local government, each with its own responsibilities, is an administrative nightmare.

Economies-of-scale considerations further complicate this issue of the best-sized unit for delivering particular services. Some services can be provided more cheaply if managed on a larger scale. For example, although garbage collection can be seen as very local, it may be cheaper to have a single organization collect the garbage for a large area.

In practice, compromises often have to be made regarding the size of the unit that should deliver each service. Some countries have more than one level of local government to accommodate variations in service coverage. The UK has counties with districts (in rural areas) and cities (in urban areas). The states in the US are subdivided into counties, where cities control certain services.

Because of the practical limits on the number of local-government levels, some of the services at each level could in theory be provided more effectively by a smaller (and therefore more responsive) unit or by a larger (and therefore more efficient) unit. Consequently, current assignments of expenditure responsibilities are the subject of argument within countries. Yet clear conclusions are often not possible. The UK, for one, in an effort to provide public services more efficiently, has reorganized the responsibilities and boundaries of local governments several times over the last 50 years.

SERVICES WITH BOTH LOCAL AND NATIONAL COMPONENTS

Some services with both local and national components are:

- Public parks, which are also used by visitors from the rest of the country.

- Locally provided education, which may also benefit other areas of the country as the local residents relocate and use their skills.
- Local police, who detain criminals and prevent them from operating elsewhere.
- Road building and maintenance, responsibility for which is split between the central and local governments in the UK. The central government is responsible for the major roads that link cities, since these roads serve the country as a whole. The responsibility for other roads which mainly benefit local residents rests within their boundaries.
- Poverty alleviation, which helps the poor people in a locality but also furthers the national goal of poverty alleviation.

Each of these services has a chiefly local impact and could be a responsibility of local government, which can be more responsive to the needs and wishes of local people. But giving complete control to local government may mean neglecting effects outside the local area. There must therefore be a tradeoff between meeting local needs and taking wider interests into account.

The balance of advantage between central and local control will differ with different services and, quite possibly, in different countries. Certainly, at least for some services, countries deal differently with this problem.

Many countries distinguish between national parks, which are the responsibility of the central government, and other parks, which are managed by local governments, although such a distinction does not completely solve the problem. National parks are still of greater benefit to those who live in their vicinity, while local parks are often major tourist attractions.

In education, practices vary widely. France is famous for its central control of education, a control that extended even to its colonies in Africa. At the other extreme, the Canadian constitution makes education a responsibility of the provinces, with no central-government control. The UK, among other countries, takes the intermediate position of dividing responsibility for education between the central and local governments. The central government finances university education, and counties spend for nursery, primary, and secondary schools, and schools for children with special needs, with some earmarked funding from the central government for such items as improvement of local school buildings and computer equipment. The underlying notion is that the education of children up to 18 or 19 years old is a service to the local community, whereas university education is a national service. Local education is nonetheless subject to standards set by the central government, which recently introduced a National Curriculum to raise the minimum educational standard.

Countries similarly show wide differences when it comes to responsibility for the police. France has a strong national police service. Subnational police forces in the UK cover large areas and are subject to central-government standards. The US has many local police forces, some of which cover fairly small areas, but responsibility for law enforcement is shared by federal, state, and local governments. The local police investigates crimes and enforces the law unless the violation spans more than one locality, takes place on a state or interstate highway (the jurisdiction of state highway patrols), uses the US postal system, or involves a federal enforcement concern (such as drug trafficking).

Countries likewise adopt different approaches to poverty alleviation. In the UK, it is exclusively a central-government responsibility. In the US, the federal government and the states both provide financial assistance.

This varied allocation of responsibility, with or without central-government regulation, is typical of a large number of public services that are primarily local but also significantly affect the rest of the country.

Some countries have a system of "matching grants" for local services that also have national benefits. Local-government expenditures on particular items (such as roads) attract a central-government grant which typically, but not always, covers half of the cost. The system is meant to encourage local governments to spend money on projects that benefit the country as a whole.

The matching grant is not automatic. It must be approved by the central government, which thus controls its total spending on matching grants and at the same time ensures that the projects do, indeed, provide a substantial national benefit. Such national benefits can, however, be difficult to measure in practice.

TAX ASSIGNMENTS

AVOIDANCE OF DISTORTIONS

Funds for public expenditure can come from taxes, service charges, loans, and asset sales. Taxes, the main focus of the fiscal federalism literature, are dealt with in this section. All four sources of revenue for local governments are discussed in the section entitled "Local Public Finance."

Much of the literature on tax assignments pertains to setting tax rates so as to avoid unnecessary market distortions. Its main concern has therefore been the extent to which tax rates should be allowed to differ within a country. In other words, the discussion has tried to settle the question of who has the power to set tax rates. It has not concerned itself with the issue of which level of government should receive the revenue of taxes whose rates are set by the central government, or which level of government should collect taxes.

Regarding the setting of tax rates, the first obvious question is, why not make the central government the sole rate-setting authority, instead of allowing local governments some control over tax rates. The answer is connected with the main reason for local control of expenditure: local governments can be more responsive to the needs and wishes of the local population. If the people in one area have a greater need or wish for public expenditure, they can exercise this wish either by setting higher rates of tax or by obtaining additional grants from the central government. As the central government will not be prepared to give more money to an area just because it asks for it, the local government can respond to local needs and wishes only if it is given power to choose at least one tax rate, and to receive the resulting revenue.

Accordingly, almost all countries give their local governments control over at least one tax rate, although sometimes the control is limited. In the UK, local governments determine the rate of the council tax (a tax on residential property), within an allowable range established by the national government for each locality.

The question now becomes: which tax rate (or rates) should the local government control? The answer has typically come from looking at some distortionary effects of different local governments setting different tax rates:

- Companies moving to areas with lower taxes on company profits.
- People, particularly the rich, moving to areas with lower personal income taxes.
- Enterprises moving to areas with lower taxes on production activity (such as China's product tax).
- People buying goods in areas with lower sales-tax rates.

These responses to different tax rates are distortionary because they can alter the allocation of resources without changing the real underlying social costs of production.

The only tax that would not produce some distortion of this sort is a tax on land—something that cannot be moved to another local-government area. In theory, a pure land tax has no distortionary effect because land is in fixed supply. A land tax will simply lower the purchase price of land such that the total cost of using land (purchase price plus tax) remains the same. This means that a land tax does not discourage land use.

In practice, many local governments all over the world derive a major part of their revenues from property taxes, a variant of the land tax. Most property taxes are not pure land taxes as they usually do not apply to all land (agricultural land is often exempted) and usually include other forms of property (frequently housing). Thus, these taxes are not completely nondistortionary. Nonetheless, they are generally regarded as less distortionary than any other tax (apart from the UK's theoretically nondistortionary community charge-poll tax which was withdrawn in the face of public opposition).

Despite this advantage of the property tax, there are also disadvantages (discussed in "Local Public Finance" below), and several countries do allow their subnational governments to choose the rates of other taxes. The Canadian provinces and the American states may choose their own rates of tax on company profits, personal incomes, and sales of goods. These taxes are levied in addition to the federal taxes on profits, personal incomes, and sales.

Subnational governments use distortionary taxes partly because property taxes alone cannot fully cover their expenditure responsibilities, and they see large transfers from the central government as undermining the distribution of powers in the federal system.

ADVANTAGES OF FISCAL COMPETITION

The discussion of tax assignment has so far concentrated on the distortions that can result from allowing subnational governments to set their own tax rates. However, a certain school of thought holds that having different tax rates carries some advantages.

In this view, governments at all levels do not try to meet the wishes of the populations for whom they are responsible. Instead, their sole interest is increasing their power and influence by collecting as much revenue as possible.[3] The tendency of taxpayers to move away from local-government areas with high tax rates and toward those with low tax rates is therefore seen as a good thing as it promotes fiscal competition. Local governments are encouraged to lower their tax rates to induce taxpayers to move into their area. According to this school of thought, everyone consequently benefits from tax rates that are lower than would otherwise have been set.

This theory stands in direct contrast to the conventional view. Instead of focusing on the distortions of the market that would result from different tax rates, it finds fiscal competition advantageous in that it leads to a general lowering of taxes, which are assumed to be too high.

Which view one thinks is more defensible depends on the extent to which one believes that local-government officials are concerned with meeting the needs and wishes of the local community or that they simply wish to increase their own importance. In other words, do the tax rates reflect the wishes of the people or the interests of the officials? It is difficult to determine which view is correct, and the answer may vary between countries. It is therefore also difficult to come to a firm view about the advantages of giving control over taxes to subnational levels of government.

However, this argument does not justify allowing local governments to set the rates of taxes that are used to finance the central government. These rates must be fixed by the central government; otherwise, fiscal competition will drive them down to zero especially since local officials will have no interest in maintaining central-government revenues.

---

[3] See Brennan and Buchanan (1980).

ALLOCATION OF REVENUES

Following the standard arguments of fiscal federalism, local governments should be made responsible for a large part of expenditure but should control only a small part of tax revenue (the property tax). The result is a mismatch between the revenues and expenditures of different levels of government.

This mismatch is common to almost all countries, and the typical solution is for the central government to provide grants to subnational governments. Local governments may also directly receive some or all of the tax revenues collected from their area, even if the central government chooses the rate of tax. This is the case not only in the PRC but also in Germany where the *Länder* receive some of the tax revenue that is collected in their area although the rates are determined at the federal level. However, the system in Germany does specifically provide for revenue to be redistributed among the *Länder* to compensate for differences in fiscal capacity.

Allowing local governments to use at least some of the tax revenues they generate has certain advantages over the other two methods of securing adequate resources for subnational governments:

- Compared with using central-government grants, subnational governments are given more autonomy, often regarded as fundamental in a federal system.
- Compared with allowing subnational governments to control major tax rates, it eliminates the distortions caused by differences in these rates. Thus, while Canadian provinces have different tax rates, Germany has uniform taxes on profits, incomes, and sales.

However, this system does create a variant of fiscal competition which might be thought wasteful. Subnational governments are induced to attract activities that will enlarge their tax base. For example, local governments might offer financial incentives for enterprises to move into their area.

This sort of fiscal competition can be seen as beneficial in that it promotes economic growth. But insofar as it simply draws activities from other regions of the country, it is wasteful competition: using scarce fiscal resources to redistribute a tax base with a fixed total size.

Whether the overall balance is good or not will depend on the extent to which genuinely new activities are created.

ALLOCATION OF TAX ADMINISTRATION

In countries where the central government receives the main revenue from income and sales taxes, it is usually also responsible for tax administration and collection. Typically local governments are then left with the task of administering and collecting local property taxes. In other words, taxes are administered and collected by the level of government that owns them.

This arrangement can also work in cases where different levels of government share the same tax base, as is true of the US and Canada. Those American states that levy their own income taxes administer them separately from the federal income tax (although both levels of government may use the same tax base to reduce administrative costs). However, in Canada, the federal government collects provincial income taxes on behalf of the provinces. This is seen as economizing both on administrative effort and on taxpayers' compliance costs.

Tax collection by one level of government on behalf of another needs to be considered carefully. Tax administration always involves some degree of discretion, and a tax authority can more easily exercise discretion in favor of a taxpayer if another level of government sustains the revenue loss.

Canada does not seem to find this a problem, presumably because provincial taxes and the federal tax have the same base and so tax concessions by the federal tax authorities would lower their own as well as the province's revenue. In Germany, the *Länder* collect taxes on behalf of the federal government, but strong central control of tax administration keeps the *Länder* from granting tax concessions in pursuit of fiscal competition. In the PRC, by contrast, lack of strong central control has allowed local governments to engage in fiscal competition by using administrative discretion, thus eroding the central government's tax base.

LOCAL PUBLIC FINANCE

The theoretical and practical implications of alternative methods of financing local government are outlined in this section. This issue is an important one, as local governments provide a very large proportion of public services. The methods used to finance these services clearly determine the level of the services and explain variations in service provision between different parts of a country.

Local governments can be financed from a range of sources: local taxes, charges for services, grants from higher levels of government, loans, and asset sales.

LOCAL TAXES

Local taxes are the most obvious source of finance for local governments, although in many countries they cover well under half the total level of local-government expenditure. Local taxes are also the main component of revenue that is controlled by the local government. As explained in the previous section, controlling the rates of these taxes allows local governments to accommodate the needs and wishes of the local population for particular levels of government expenditure. Usually, any expenditure increases that are not required by higher levels of government, in other words, increases requested by local people, must be met by increasing local taxes.

As explained in the section entitled "Tax Assignments," local taxes are usually property taxes. While the specifics vary between countries, these taxes are normally levied on residential property (land and buildings) and frequently also on commercial and industrial land and buildings.

To some extent, financing local-government services from property values is appropriate because many services—street lighting, garbage collection, public parks—contribute to the value of property. However, not all local-government services fall into that category. Also, property taxes have been variously criticized. Some say that if property taxes are a payment for service, the cost of, say, garbage collection from a valuable house should be clearly twice the cost of garbage collection from a house worth only half as much. As this is not always so, the taxes are seen as unfair.

Others argue that property values are not always a good measure of ability to pay. Pensioners, for example, may continue to live in a house that reflected their income while they were working, but their low pensions now make it difficult for them to pay the property taxes.

This is seen as another form of unfairness. In the PRC where most housing is owned by enterprises and they bear the burden of the tax, this argument does not yet have wide application but it will become increasingly important as the housing reform continues and more housing is owned by households.

From yet another point of view, it is argued that taxing house values discourages people from making house improvements that would raise the value of their houses and therefore also the tax liability. The criticism here is not one of unfairness, but of a distortion of incentives leading to economic inefficiency.

These different arguments combine to make property taxes unpopular among many people. But an alternative tax base is hard to find. One possibility is local income taxes. They have the advantage of not being inherently distortionary: areas with higher taxes can provide better local public goods and so people will be less likely to move away. However, having different rates in so many different areas could entail high administrative costs. This difficulty was avoided by the PRC tax reform of 1994, which allocated personal income taxes to local governments at a uniform rate set by the central government, but local governments were thereby denied the discretion to raise additional revenue.

Several countries, Canada and the US among them, do have local income taxes, reflecting the view that the extra administrative cost is warranted since local governments are better able to finance important local public goods and services. A similar argument could apply to the PRC, and the government should seriously consider extending the tax reform of 1994 to allow local governments to set their own rates of personal income tax.

Local governments in the PRC draw their funds from a much wider range of taxes than in most countries. Until the tax reform of 1994, local governments collected most of the country's taxes, remitted a part to higher levels of government, and kept the rest for their own expenditure. Property taxes are therefore not viewed as a major source of local-government finance in the PRC. Instead, to increase their revenues, local governments have tried to stimulate the growth of industries that would pay high rates of tax (such as alcoholic drinks and tobacco products).

SERVICE CHARGES

The unpopularity of property taxes has prompted local governments to look for other sources of revenue. These have frequently been in the form of service charges, which the public finds less disagreeable as they are seen as directly related to the service received. A fee for collecting unusually large quantities of garbage, for example, is considered quite reasonable.[4]

Some countries that had long been charging for services at part of their cost simply raised the fees to cover the full cost. In the UK, local governments used to provide housing at subsidized rents. Over the last 20 years they have raised these rents to nearer the free-market level and some local governments are making enough profits to pay for other services.

Obviously, service charges cannot be levied on all services. In many countries, basic education is provided free of charge. Also, some services, such as street lighting, are true public goods and cannot be charged for. Many local governments have nonetheless found service charges an attractive alternative to property taxes.

Criticisms against the setting or raising of service charges for local-government services have two underlying reasons. First, setting or raising charges for such "merit goods" as adult education and recreational facilities discourages the use of these socially beneficial services and is therefore harmful in this sense. Second, social charges make services more inaccessible to the poor and thus further exclude them from society.

The considerable force of such arguments has made local governments reluctant to set or raise charges for some of their services, but the increasing unpopularity of property taxes in many countries has left them with little alternative.

Closely related to the idea of service charges is the idea of benefit taxation: directly taxing the people who benefit from local-government expenditure. Many public services in urban areas, such as roads and drainage, raise the value of private land. Benefit taxation involves taxing some of that higher value to pay for the services. Designing such taxes requires detailed knowledge of each project and considerable skill. One

---

[4] A case for these charges is made in Bahl and Linn (1991) and Bird (1992, Ch. 12).

system of benefit taxation that has worked well is the "valorization" tax in Colombia,[5] which has financed a major part of public investment in the city of Medellin. A valorization tax is a tax on the increase in the value of land and buildings that results from improved public services.

When properly designed, benefit taxation does not suffer from the disadvantages of service charges. It is usually levied on landowners, who are generally not considered among the poor. Also, because it leaves the landowners with an overall benefit from the project, benefit taxation does not discourage their participation. This suggests that benefit taxation could be applied more widely to the financing of urban infrastructure projects.

Service charges are an important feature of local public finance in the PRC. They finance a range of services including health and education, particularly in the rural areas. These charges are not part of the standard budget of local governments. Instead, they are classed as extrabudgetary funds or self-raised funds and are held in separate accounts, for restricted use.

GOVERNMENT GRANTS

Grants from higher levels of government finance most local-government expenditure in many countries. Such grants are of three different types:

- Unconditional grants, which can be used for any purpose.
- Earmarked grants, which are fixed-amount transfers for specific purposes.
- Matching grants, which are provided by higher levels of government to finance a given proportion (typically half) of the cost of particular types of projects.

Unconditional Grants. Unconditional grants are intended to provide local governments with enough funds for necessary expenditures, as determined by the higher levels of government. These grants make up for the difference between the necessary expenditures and the revenue generated locally from taxes and service charges.

---

[5] Discussed in Bird (1992, Ch. 12).

To some extent, the difference exists because the main revenue-generating taxes are assigned to higher levels of government while many expenditures are assigned to the local level, as discussed above. But even if revenue and expenditure assignments matched on the average across the country, local governments with a smaller local tax base or greater expenditure needs would still require transfers from higher levels of government. In other words, these unconditional grants play an essential redistributional role, making it possible for all local governments to provide their residents with basic services.

Calculating how much each local government should receive is, however, difficult. The grant should close the gap between necessary expenditures and locally generated revenues, but neither one is easy to determine.

Necessary expenditures are estimated in two ways. One way is to look at the level of past expenditures of each local government and to make adjustments for cost increases and changed needs. This method has the advantage of taking into account particular local needs that, to the local government, justified extra expenditure in the past. But since past expenditure depended partly on past grants, local governments that were treated generously in the past will continue to be so treated.

A more subtle problem which is seen as important in some countries arises when local governments, realizing that past expenditure determines the size of their current grant, are encouraged to engage in excessive spending to attract larger grants in the future.

The second method of estimating necessary expenditures partly avoids these problems. This method involves assessing needs on the basis of objective characteristics of the locality. For example, educational expenditure will depend on the number of children of different ages. Expenditure on social services will depend on the number of people who are old or disabled, or have other social disadvantages. Expenditure on roads might depend on area and population.

A common formula with all the relevant characteristics is then applied to all local governments to calculate expenditure needs. The size of the coefficient for each variable—how much extra expenditure is needed when the measure of a given characteristic increases—now becomes the main issue. These coefficients can sometimes be obtained by, for example, investigating the cost of educating one more child or of helping one more disabled person.

Another approach is to use statistical techniques to arrive at an estimated equation that relates observed expenditures of local governments to the measures of relevant characteristics. The drawback is that current expenditures do not necessarily represent what is actually needed. On the other hand, these are actual expenditures, while the approach of investigating the costs of individual services (such as education) can sometimes appear arbitrary and too theoretical.

Despite these disadvantages, it is generally accepted that the amount of the grants must be based on some estimate of present needs and not merely on historical figures. This formula for calculating needs may never be ideal and may exclude special factors that affect needs in particular localities, but it is probably better than any alternative and must be used. Earmarked grants, discussed below, can deal with the special needs to some extent.

The other factor that determines the size of the gap that must be filled by the unconditional grant is locally generated revenues. These revenues clearly depend on the tax rates chosen by the local governments, but no local government deserves to have its grant reduced simply because it has set a higher tax rate. In principle, the PRC, where the tax rates are uniform and are set by the central government, should not have this problem. In practice, however, there are wide variations in tax effort, reflecting differences in enforcement and the granting of tax exemptions.

A usual solution to this problem is to adjust the current revenue figure by a measure of tax effort. In the UK, the government applies to the local governments a single local tax rate that it deems reasonable and, with its knowledge of the tax base of each local government, is able to calculate the resulting revenue. The size of the unconditional grant is then the difference between the expenditure needs calculated by formula and this expected local revenue.

The advantage of this system is that grants to local governments are not reduced when they raise extra revenue from higher rates of tax. On the other hand, neither does a shortfall in tax collection merit any extra grant. The system can therefore be seen as one that perfectly adjusts for tax effort.

However, many countries do not have similarly direct information about the tax base of each local government and cannot use the UK system. For example, until recently, the multiplicity of rates of indirect taxes in the PRC made it almost impossible to estimate the revenue that would be raised from a "reasonable" level of tax effort. Other indirect methods have to be used in such cases. One way would be to observe the current tax rate and revenue, and to estimate the revenue that would result from levying the "reasonable rate" of tax. This method, however, does not consider other aspects of tax effort, such as the varying levels of enforcement that are so common in the PRC. If this is thought to be a serious deficiency, the revenue figures must be adjusted by other measures of tax effort, such as the ratio of taxes to local total income, before the unconditional grant is calculated.

The simplified indirect tax rates, strengthened administration, and clearer revenue-sharing rules under the PRC tax reform of 1994 should aid in the calculation of the tax base of local governments. They should also help equalize the provision of services by permitting the introduction of a system of unconditional grants that conforms more to international practice.

Before the tax reform of 1994, unconditional grants were not a major source of funding for most local governments in the PRC. Instead, central-local transfers were made implicitly, in revenue-sharing arrangements. The flow of revenue was mainly in the other direction, with local governments collecting money that was used to finance central government. The upward transfers could theoretically have been calculated so as to ensure broadly equal provision of local public goods and services in each area, using the same information as is required for a grant formula. However, this was not done and, under the contract system, the money that was left with the local governments depended on a combination of "base figures" (past expenditures) and the recent rate of growth of local tax revenue.

Earmarked Grants. As mentioned earlier, earmarked grants can be used to finance particular needs of local governments that are not included in the general needs formula. If the sewers in a city need to be replaced, for example, the local government may be able to obtain earmarked funds from a higher level of government. Earmarked grants can also be used to persuade local governments to carry out projects that they would otherwise not choose to do, but which higher levels of government regard as being in the national interest, as discussed above.

Earmarked grants can therefore clearly play an important role in ensuring the appropriate provision of public services. However, they also have limitations.

First, the use of earmarked grants to persuade local governments to provide particular services to their residents goes against the principle that local governments are better at judging their people's needs and wishes than higher levels of government. This principle may not always hold, but grants of this type require careful justification. All extra funds needed to cover the costs of local public services should come through unconditional grants.

Second, earmarked grants may not actually increase the level of a service that is already being provided. The local government may simply use the funds to provide the same level of service and divert the funds that it previously used for the purpose to other uses. This scheme can be prevented only by imposing "additionality" requirements, which experience has shown to be difficult and costly to enforce.

Generally, particular services are most effectively encouraged through matching grants. Sometimes the grants are open-ended: the local government is allowed to choose the level of service it will provide and the higher level of government covers half of the resulting cost. However, some services can be overprovided as a result and, perhaps more importantly, expenditure control becomes difficult for the higher level of government. It is therefore more common for the matching grants to be limited to a specific total value.

Earmarked grants are widely used in the PRC both to encourage particular types of local investments and to ensure that local governments can meet certain expenditure requirements specified by the central government, mainly food subsidies to the urban population.

LOANS

Loans can be an attractive source of finance for any level of government. Because they allow the government to spend more without having to raise taxes immediately, loans can be seen as a way out of short-term budgetary difficulties. However, loans eventually have to be repaid, usually from future taxes. Local governments should therefore not take on so much debt that they have to raise taxes substantially in the future to repay the loans.

To keep shortsighted local governments from borrowing excessively, many countries regulate the amount of debt that local governments may contract. Some impose specific limits on a local government's total debt (which could be kept at zero); others confine loans to certain types of expenditure, such as capital investment.

In deciding which rules should apply in the PRC, the fundamental principle must be that the loan can be repaid without too much difficulty. The loan should therefore be used to finance an investment that will produce enough revenue to cover the repayments or that will yield benefits over the whole period of the loan, or the tax base should grow sufficiently so that the repayments can be made without raising tax rates.

If the projected revenue is enough to cover repayments, as in the building of toll roads, the loan is treated like any business loan. The only danger is that the revenue from the investment may be less than expected.

Loans that yield social, rather than financial, benefits are riskier, in that the money for repaying the loans does not come automatically. But if the community members find the benefits sufficiently valuable, they should be willing to pay higher taxes to cover loan repayments, especially while the benefits are still apparent. Governments should, however, guard against financing too many projects of this sort as the people would naturally oppose the substantially higher taxes. The period of the loan should also not outlast the benefits; otherwise, the people may refuse to pay taxes for a project that no longer shows perceptible benefits.

Loans based on projected growth in the tax base are the most risky, although they make perfect theoretical sense. Somebody who expects to become richer in the future can borrow on the basis of that expectation to buy things he needs now. The danger lies in the human tendency to overestimate the future rise in income. Therefore, such loans should perhaps be resorted to only for very important and urgent expenditures, such as disaster relief. Even then, the loans should not be so great as to use up all of the expected increase in revenue capacity.

It is impossible to estimate the extent to which loans finance the expenditures of local governments in the PRC, where such loans are not allowed for budgetary expenditures. However, loans increasingly finance such activities as road and bridge building, and are repaid from tolls or vehicle license fees. Both the loans and the money for their repayment are channeled through accounts separate from the main local-government accounts that are reported to higher levels of government.

ASSET SALES

Asset sales have become a significant source of revenue for both central and local governments in many countries. Mineral resources, public housing, and state-owned enterprises are among the assets being sold. Frequently, the sales are motivated by ideology or by a wish to improve market efficiency, besides the goal of raising money.

From a purely financial point of view, asset sales are very similar to loans with extended repayment periods. When a profitable state-owned enterprise is sold, the government receives a large lump sum, but also suffers the loss of the enterprise's profits for as long as the enterprise was expected to remain profitable. A government decision to increase public expenditure now must therefore be offset by higher taxes or lower public spending in the future.

The UK is a case in point. The sale of several large and profitable state-owned enterprises (and considerable oil extraction rights) during the 1980s allowed the government to increase public expenditure and lower taxes. However, since there are few state-owned enterprises left to sell, the revenue from these sales has dropped. Moreover, the profit income from the enterprises that have been sold is income forgone. This state of affairs partly explains the UK budget deficit—its largest ever—for which it has had to impose large and unpopular tax increases.

This does not mean that local governments should not sell assets, such as public housing, especially if the sales can improve the functioning of the market economy. However, it does mean that the proceeds from these sales should be used in the same careful way as the proceeds from loans. The money should be invested in projects that will either generate revenues or benefit the population over a long period of time such that the people will be willing to pay extra taxes. In the absence of such investment projects, the local government should repay existing loans or buy financial securities (possibly foreign) to generate money to replace the income lost from the assets that have been sold.

Asset sales do not appear in the main budgetary accounts of the PRC, and their importance as a source of local revenue is therefore unclear. For example, money from sales of municipal housing is normally put into a separate account, from which the local government draws for the construction of new housing. This may help balance the main budgetary accounts by reducing the need to finance new housing from the budget, but it is impossible to estimate the extent of the reduction because of changes in other factors that affect the allocation of budgetary expenditure.

Chapter 3

URBANIZATION AND URBAN INFRASTRUCTURE SERVICES IN THE PRC

by Kam Wing Chan

This chapter studies various policy issues related to urbanization and urban infrastructure development in the PRC. It also provides a background to the study of urbanization financing in Chapter 4. The chapter begins by examining the role of city governments in the PRC economy. The discussion includes an analysis of changes that took place in the administrative system in the reform era. Attention then turns to the urbanization trends in the nation and in two specific provinces. The last sections look into issues concerning urban planning, public housing, the land market, and the provision of urban infrastructure services, with examples drawn from our case studies.

ROLE OF CITIES IN ECONOMIC DEVELOPMENT

INTRODUCTION: GENERAL PATTERNS

Cities have long functioned as centers of administration (or governance) and commerce. In traditional China, county towns, many of which were walled for defense, were the main collection points for state taxes.

Most countries in the early stages of economic development undergo urbanization, or the concentration of the population into more and bigger urban centers, as they industrialize. Development engenders a systematic shift of labor and capital from agriculture-based activities to manufacturing and services which locate in urban centers to take advantage of "agglomeration" economies. Economies of scale and ease of communication and movement of people and goods allow greater division of labor and less wasteful use of land among firms in urban settings. Also, at a certain scale of operation possible only in major population centers, many public utilities such as piped water and electricity supply are provided more efficiently. Recent developments in international trade have helped make urban development more selective and concentrated because port facilities, expensive to build, can be installed in only a few locations. Modern urban centers produce manufactured goods and provide both public and business services, and contemporary economic development is intimately linked with their evolution.

ROLE OF CITIES IN THE ECONOMIC DEVELOPMENT OF THE PRC

As discussed in Chapter 1, cities in the PRC also function as local government units. They occupy different positions, depending on their level, in the government and the economic hierarchy where the administrative process is still important. This section describes the role of Chinese cities, especially in the pre-reform system, and explains how and why the administrative status of cities changed in the 1980s and 1990s.

Economic development based on modern industry developed in pre-1949 China was essentially urban and coastal. The PRC leadership, aspiring to join the industrial powers, has given overwhelming priority to industrialization since the early 1950s, and most industries are located in urban areas. A simple comparison of the population share of cities in the PRC with their output share underlines the importance of cities to the Chinese industrial economy. At the end of 1991, 479 cities (excluding the counties under them) produced 66 percent of the nation's industrial output (GVIO), generated 66 percent of passenger traffic, absorbed about 60 percent of foreign investment, and housed nearly 100 percent of all institutions of higher learning, despite their having only 30 percent of the country's total population.[1]

---

[1] SSB (1992, pp. 669-670).

More important, especially in relation to this study, is the near-complete dependence of the government of the PRC on revenues from state-owned industry. As "owner" of most manufacturing enterprises, the state has been able to tap industrial profits directly. Industry has accordingly become the main producer of state revenues (Chapter 1), and cities, where manufacturing largely takes place, have become direct "cash cows" for the government.

The push for industrial production, and for the revenues to be derived from it, led to the neglect of the "nonproductive" aspect of urban development in pre-reform China, as in most other traditional socialist economies. Given the goal of maximized industrial growth, investment in urban infrastructure such as housing, sewerage, and service facilities was deemed a diversion of resources which should be kept to the tolerable minimum (Ofer 1976; Chan 1994b). Urban infrastructure investment in the traditional system was therefore chronically underfunded. At the same time, the government restricted migration to cities to avert further strain on the overloaded infrastructure. Urbanization in Mao's China closely took this approach (Chan 1994b). Moreover, as the economy became increasingly demonetized and run by economic planners, there was no longer any need for the economic institutions that formed the core of urban economies in market regimes. Government bureaucracies took the place occupied by financial institutions, markets, and advertising agencies in market economies.

In short, Chinese cities in the pre-reform era were developed almost exclusively for industry, and in relative isolation of the rural sector. Industry generated huge resources for further industrialization, but many other aspects of modern cities were ignored, and investments were too meager to sustain long-run productivity, measured in broader terms. Urban infrastructure deteriorated rapidly as a result, the level of provision per capita dropped, despite the many urban services provided directly by enterprises, and urban productivity ultimately suffered. Equally important, the constricted, vertical economic system and the closed-door policy stripped many of the major urban centers of their accustomed role as centers of commerce (Solinger 1989), and the rigid bureaucratic boundaries sundered traditional economic ties between the cities and their hinterlands. Coastal cities also stopped being centers of international trade. Shanghai, the dynamic "Paris of the Orient" in the prewar era, came nowhere close to making the list of major trading and business centers on the western coast of the Pacific in the late 1970s. This situation was totally unconducive to a successful open-door policy and to the goal of speeding up economic development in a commodity economy.

CHANGING STATUS OF CITIES IN THE ADMINISTRATIVE SYSTEM

After the success of reforms in the countryside, the PRC leadership turned its attention in the early 1980s to reviving cities as centers of exchange. Major administrative reforms sought to improve the coordination of economic development at the local and regional levels which had been hampered by the vertical, bureaucratic channels of command and coordination in the previous system. Since market interactions are essentially horizontal and not vertical, the administrative changes were meant to facilitate market exchanges and horizontal or lateral links between nearby administrative entities and between the rural and urban sectors, by lowering the vertical barriers (see SESRC 1984). All the changes involve further empowering the cities and often raising their administrative status. Power has gravitated to major urban centers, especially coastal cities, also because market-oriented reform and the open-door policy have placed a premium on technology and savings from urban agglomeration economies and on the historical and commercial ties of cities with the outside world (Zhao 1982).

Since administrative change inevitably redistributes power over resource allocation, it is not surprising for governments of the next higher level to resist change, while pressure from below for faster change and more thorough reform builds up. This is most clearly seen in the struggle between provincial governments and line-item cities.

LINE-ITEM CITIES

As noted above, rigid, vertical administration dwarfed the economic role of major metropolises (mostly provincial capitals). The provinces, as the supervisory bodies, exercised direct power and control over the cities with scant regard for their interests and their development (Xiao 1991). The "line-item" (*jihua danlie*) reform in 1983 was introduced to free the key cities from the patronage and power of the provinces (Solinger 1993).

Attempted briefly without success in the 1950s and the 1960s, the program was reactivated in 1983, first in Chongqing and later in 13 other cities (Wuhan, Shenyang, Dalian, Guangzhou, Xian, Harbin, Qingdao, Ningbo, Xiamen, Shenzhen, Nanjing, Chengdu, and Changchun) (see Figure 3.1) (Association for Statistical Information Exchange 1993). As examined in Wong, Heady, and Woo (1995), the term *jihua danlie* means that these cities are singled out or listed separately alongside provincial units in the central plan. These cities thus report directly to the central government, bypassing provincial authorities in most economic matters. The economic management powers given to these cities equal to those of provincial-level units.[2] A full line-item city can approve foreign investment projects, issue state bonds, and dispose of funds appropriated from state finances and the central bank. When approving a project involving more than $10 million in foreign investment, a line-item city only has to apply to the appropriate departments of the State Council for approval and does not have to obtain the permission of the provincial government in advance (FBIS 1993a). Reflecting their relative autonomy, these cities also have quotas in some noneconomic matters (e.g., birth quotas) separate from those of the provinces.

However, while line-item cities enjoy provincial-level status in economic matters, in the government structure they are administratively subordinate to their respective provinces. This incongruence is often a source of conflict and tension between the center, the city, and the province. Line-item cities, moreover, vary in the extent of their independent powers. As of 1993, only nine such cities (including Qingdao) had fiscal powers separate from those of their governing provinces (see Wong, Heady, and Woo 1995). Guangzhou, Nanjing, and Chengdu, on the other hand, never acquired budgetary powers independent of their respective provinces.

According to the official literature, the State Council granted line-item status only to longtime keypoint cities with a solid industrial and

---

[2] The Chinese local finance system groups line-item cities with cities administered directly by the central government (see He 1992).

Figure 3.1: Line-Item and Open Cities

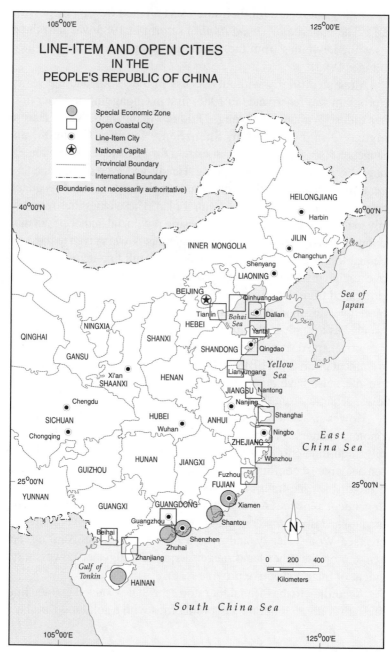

commercial base and technological capability, a population of at least 1 million in the city proper, a gross material product[3] of at least Y15 billion, a strategic role in promoting the PRC's open policy, and special importance in the PRC's economic development (Xiao 1993). The real test, one would suspect, lay in the political and economic powers of the cities vis-à-vis the provinces and the center. Of the 14 cities granted special status, ten are ports along the coast and Changjiang River. All except Shenzhen have a long history of development. The improved economic performance of most line-item cities since the upgrading of their status in the economic plan was reported in the Chinese press in the late 1980s.

This status upgrade has been welcomed by city governments but has understandably also caused resentment among many provinces at the breakaway of large cities from their jurisdictions. The loss of one or two economically developed large cities not only erodes the province's economic and administrative powers, but often also significantly diminishes provincial revenues, which rely heavily on the taxation of industry in cities. Especially with the continuing fiscal decentralization, a province that loses a large city can easily revert from revenue surplus to deficit, as happened in Hubei and Sichuan (Wong, Heady, and Woo 1995). The ongoing tug-of-war between provinces and line-item cities for administrative and economic management powers has also caused many problems in administration and economic planning as well as ill feelings between the parties involved (see Xiao 1993, pp. 310-318).

In an apparent inducement for the provinces to drop their opposition to the reform of the tax-sharing system, the central government in 1993 removed eight provincial capitals from the list of line-item cities, leaving only six nonprovincial capital cities (Qingdao, Dalian, Ningbo, Chongqing, Xiamen, and Shenzhen) on the list (FBIS 1993b). Although this change may herald the end of line-item city reform, major metropolises have already managed to gain prominence in the PRC administrative/economic system. The government also named 16 major cities (including all the "line-item" cities, except Ningbo, plus Jinan and Hangzhou) "deputy provincial-level" cities, with an implied administrative rank between that of a province and that of a prefectural city (*Zhongguo fangyue* 1994).

---

[3] Gross material product refers to the total value of society—the gross output of all material production sectors.

COASTAL OPEN CITIES

Following the establishment of four special economic zones (SEZs) in Shenzhen, Zhuhai, Xiamen, and Shantou in 1979 to attract foreign investors as part of the PRC's open-door policy, 14 coastal cities were declared "open" in 1984. These were Qinhuangdao, Tianjin, Dalian, Yantai, Qingdao, Lianyungang, Nantong, Shanghai, Ningbo, Wenzhou, Fuzhou, Guangzhou, Zhanjiang, and Beihai (Figure 3.1). Later Hainan, which became a province in 1988, also became an SEZ. One internal publication (Association for Statistical Information Exchange 1993) mentioned Weihai as the fifteenth coastal open city, although the latest volume of the *Statistical Yearbook of China* (1994) still refers to 14 coastal open cities (SSB 1994a).

The open cities and special economic zones offer tax concessions and other preferential terms to attract foreign capital and technology from abroad, and have greater autonomy in investment and trade matters. (For details, see State Council 1984c.) The SEZs and the coastal open cities enjoy only partial provincial-level status, except for Hainan and possibly Shenzhen. Qingdao, one of the places studied for this book, was named an open city in 1984, granted economic autonomy, and authorized to approve industrial projects with investments of not more than $5 million per project without having to seek the permission of the provincial authority (Zheng 1994). The State Council also grants higher foreign-exchange allocations to open cities and provincial status to enterprises in foreign trade (Zheng 1994; Lai, Zhao, and Liang 1992). Concessionary income taxes of 15 percent, the same tax rate applied in SEZs, are imposed on wholly foreign-owned firms and foreign-local collaborative ventures that invest more than $30 million in the urban areas of these cities or engage in high-tech industry or in the energy or transportation (including ports) sectors (State Council 1984b). Other investments in six broad designated sectors are charged income taxes 20 percent below the regular rate.

Furthermore, these coastal open cities may set up economic and technology development zones (ETDZs). The ETDZ in Qingdao, established in 1984 with an area of 15 km^2, will become a larger ETDZ after its expected merger with Huangdao District (fieldwork 1994). Like the SEZs, the ETDZs levy an income tax of 15 percent and grant tax holidays to foreign enterprises that locate in them.

Generally, the SEZs and coastal open cities have a relatively high degree of budgetary autonomy (He 1992). The status of many coastal open cities approximates that of line-item cities, especially in trade and foreign investment. As Wong (1990) points out, the softness of the Chinese tax system and the ease with which local officials can adjust tax rates as they see fit have gradually blurred the differences between SEZs and coastal open cities in their income tax rates for foreign enterprises.

COUNTIES UNDER CITIES

Horizontal linkages were also promoted through an expanded program of "putting counties under city administration" (*shiguanxian*). Introduced in the 1950s in a number of large cities mainly to overcome problems of vegetable supply (Fung 1980; Xiao 1993) and based on the successful experience in Liaoning, the program was broadened in 1983 and focused on building larger regional planning and administrative regions based on cities. From the start of the program in the 1950s to 1981, only 56 cities, almost all of which were large provincial-level and prefectural-level cities, had counties under them. These cities administered 173 counties, or 7 percent of the total number, for an average of only three counties under each city (Chan 1985). From 1981 to 1989, 114 cities of all sizes (including relatively small county-level cities that had been upgraded to prefectural-level cities) joined this category. As a result, by the end of 1989, 170 (provincial- and prefectural-level) cities were administering 701 counties and 78 county-level cities, or 40 percent of all counties and county-level cities in the PRC. By the end of 1993, 742 counties and 186 county-level cities were under city administration (computed from Ministry of Internal Affairs 1994).

Qingdao was already a prefectural city before 1983 with four counties within its jurisdiction. Two more counties came under it in 1983. Since then, one county has been converted into an urban district of Qingdao while the remaining five county-level units have become county-level cities, still under Qingdao.[4] Another city, Taian in

---

[4] Cities have thus come to administer other cities. See discussion below under the heading "Counties into Cities."

Shandong, was upgraded to a prefectural city in 1985. Currently it administers three counties and two county-level cities within its boundary. At the end of 1993, Shandong Province had 12 prefectural-level cities and 5 prefectures, while Guizhou Province had 2 prefectural-level cities and 7 prefectures (Ministry of Internal Affairs 1994). Interestingly, neither of Guizhou's two prefectural cities, Guiyang and Liupanshui, administers a county-level unit.

Shiguanxian has in effect raised the status of many cities from county to prefectural level, replacing the previous prefectures (see also Chapter 1), and unified the prefectural and city governments. Cities have been replacing prefectures since 1983. The newly upgraded prefectural-level cities and the counties they control now form larger regional planning and administrative units, presumably more conducive to rural-urban cooperation. The concern has gone beyond ensuring for the cities a steady supply of farm products from nearby counties to streamlining the administrative bureaucracy by removing the prefectural government, whose constitutional status is ambiguous.

So far, prefectures have ceased to exist in four provinces (Liaoning, Jiangsu, Guangdong, and the newly created Hainan). In these provinces, cities are the first level of subprovincial government. Four other provinces (Jilin, Heilongjiang, Zhejiang, and Fujian) are also close to replacing all of their prefectures with cities.

COUNTIES INTO CITIES

A relaxation since 1983 in the criteria for designating cities has likewise been introduced to promote lateral and rural-urban exchange. Only towns that were economically better developed and that met certain criteria could be reclassified as "cities" in the past. In 1986, the State Council ruled that a county with a population of less than 500,000 and a county-town with a "nonagricultural" population of at least 100,000 and an annual gross national product of at least Y300 million could also be designated as cities. What was different here was that the entire county, not just the town, was labeled "city." These county-level cities administer large expanses of rural areas and huge rural populations. The latest (1993) criteria for designating cities still used the same approach.

In essence, these administrative units are more than cities as we understand the term. Large stretches of rural areas were deliberately included as a means of achieving better coordination of the rural and urban sectors at the local level and as an administrative convenience. At the same time, by reclassifying the areas as cities, local governments also sought to promote industrialization and urban construction (Shandong Academy of Social Sciences 1992). Because it generally carries greater prestige and is more attractive to investors from outside, a city has more power than a county to collect taxes for urban construction from enterprises, even though a county and a county-level city share equal rank in the administrative hierarchy.

Counties have become county-level cities at a faster pace in recent years, despite the more stringent reclassification criteria issued by the central government in 1993. There were 115 new county-level cities between 1982 and 1988, 123 between 1988 and 1993, and 53 in the first eight months of 1994 alone (*Jingji ribao* 1994).

In 1986 Qufu County in Shandong became a county-level city under Jining, a prefectural city. In 1991 Penglai County became Penglai City under a prefectural-level city, Yantai. As stated earlier, all the five counties of Qingdao were made county-level cities, still under Qingdao, between 1987 and 1990. Anshun City in Guizhou has been a county-level city since 1958; in 1990 it annexed Anshun County.

The Constitution of the PRC does not provide for the administration of one city (county-level) by another (prefectural-level). The official handbook of administrative regions published by the Ministry of Internal Affairs (1994) lists county-level cities administered by other cities as "units directly under the province." Still, the fact remains that county-level cities are administered by prefectural cities (acting on behalf of the province). Many county-level cities have apparently also become prefectural "line-item" cities, reporting directly to the provincial administration and thus enjoying a higher status (Hu 1992), although this development still seems to hold a great deal of ambiguity and is being contested in many provinces.

TOWNSHIPS INTO TOWNS

An explosion in the number of towns has paralleled the rapid growth in the number of cities in the post-Mao era, starting in 1982 and 1983 when provincial governments were allowed more flexibility in approving town designations (Xu et al. 1985; Lee 1989, p. 779). The State Council in November 1984 issued a new, much more relaxed set of criteria for designating towns, further speeding up the process (Chan 1994a). As a result, the number of designated towns shot up from 2,819 in 1982 to 6,211 in 1984, and continued to rise steeply to about 9,000 in 1987; 11,935 in 1990; and 15,805 in 1993 (Table 3.1 and Chan 1994a).

It was thought that these newly designated towns, whose boundaries coincided exactly with that of the previous township (*xiang*), would "lead (administer) the development of the countryside." Like the cities that had been converted from counties, the new towns included large stretches of rural areas and a huge proportion of the rural population.

Table 3.1: Urbanization, 1982-1993

(a) Urban Population

	% of Total Population		Average Annual Growth Rate, 1982-1990 (%)	
	1982	1990	Urban Pop.	Total Pop.
PRC	20.6	26.4	4.5	1.5
Shandong	19.1	27.3	6.1	1.6
Guizhou	18.9	19.3	1.8	1.6

(b) No. of Urban Places

	1982		1990		1993	
	Cities	Towns	Cities	Towns	Cities	Towns
PRC	239	2,819	456	11,935	570	15,805
Shandong	13	97	33	856	33	...
Guizhou	5	93	8	397	14	...

... Not available.
Note: Data for 1982 and 1990 are midyear census figures while those for 1993 are year-end figures.
Sources: Yao and Yin (1994); Exhibition on Social Development in China (1994).

Also, such an arrangement, besides promoting rural-urban integration, was administratively expedient since township bureaucracies could become town bureaucracies without significantly changing their setup and the areas they administered.

ERA OF RAPID URBAN GROWTH AND MIGRATION

TRENDS

In most countries, urbanization has accompanied industrialization in the early stage of economic development. Noncomparability of data between countries and problems of definition have hampered the computation of average rates of urban population growth worldwide. The World Bank (1980) and the United Nations (1980) nonetheless estimated a high rate of growth, in the range of 4 percent per year, for the urban population of developing countries after World War II.

In the PRC as well, industrialization was largely behind the rapid urbanization of the 1950s. However, stringent migration controls since the early 1960s plus several massive campaigns to resettle urban residents in the countryside lowered urban growth rates to an average of only 1.4 percent annually between 1960 and 1977, in spite of high rates of industrial growth. In 1978, nonagricultural sectors already accounted for about three fourths of GDP, but the urban population was a mere 18 percent of the total (SSB 1989).[5]

The restrictions placed on rural-urban migration must be taken in the context of the overall development strategy of the PRC. As mentioned in "Role of Cities in Economic Development," the PRC's strategy treated its two separate economic and social subsystems and two populations differently. While the urban-industrial subsystem was given priority and resources, the rural-agricultural subsystem existed to supply raw materials at low cost to the industrial subsystem to maintain huge industrial profits. Administrative measures were thus necessary to contain the urbanization costs that went with rapid industrialization and to keep the two subsystems at an imbalance, especially to prevent movement from the countryside (Chan 1994b). State subsidies for food, clothing, housing, education, medical care, and other purposes were intended to help offset the low wages paid to urban workers.

---

[5] See Chan (1994b, Ch. 3) for an analysis of policies restricting urbanization in the Maoist era.

In banning outflows of population from the rural sector into the cities, the state safeguarded the welfare of the urban population and ensured political security in the cities, where almost all state-organized industrial activities were located. The state was thus able to tap the monopoly profits of industry for ambitious industrialization programs (Naughton 1995). To maintain profits in industry and contain the urban welfare burden, the rural population was kept out of the city and had to fend for itself in the countryside. The principal means of restricting mobility was the household registration (*hukou*) system.

Unlike the restricted urbanization and tightly controlled migration of the post-1961 Maoist era, when households registered as "agricultural" could not easily be reclassified as "nonagricultural," the urban population has grown at a steadily high rate since the economic reforms of the late 1970s. Based on broadly comparable official intercensal data (see Chan [1994a] for a rundown of the difficulties involved in defining the urban population figure in the PRC), the urban population (including both agricultural and nonagricultural populations in urban areas, or *shizhen zongrenkou*) rose by about 40 percent between 1982 and 1990, from 208 million to 297 million. During the same period the urban population also jumped from 20.6 percent of the total population to 26.4 percent (Table 3.1). The 4.5 percent average annual growth rate of the urban population means an average of 11 million more people in the urban areas each year. A similar average annual gain was maintained in the 1990-1993 period. The latest (end of 1993) official figures place the size of the urban population at 334 million, or 28.1 percent of the nation's total (SSB 1994a).

High urban inflows and extensive enlargement of the urban areas bolstered this sustained urban growth. Between 1982 and 1993, more than 9,000 new small towns were created and the number of cities doubled from 239 to 570 (Table 3.1). According to Chan (1994a), net rural-urban migration, including urban reclassification between 1983 and 1990, reached 64 million, or about three-quarters of the urban population increase. Of these 64 million, about 30 million came from the roughly 9,000 new towns.[6] The remaining

---

[6] The reclassification component identified here represents mostly physical expansion of the urbanized areas and is therefore part of urbanization. Migration from villages had also swelled the populations of many of these new towns prior to their designation.

34 million can be classified under (net) migration that involved a change of residence.

More importantly, the above estimate of net rural-urban flows based on official statistics excludes a large portion of the so-called "floating" or "mobile population" (*liudong renkou*), which has become prevalent in big cities since the mid-1980s. The "floating population" refers loosely to the population staying in places where they are not permanently registered (Li and Hu 1991). This category includes tourists, people on business trips, traders, sojourners, peasant workers contracted from other places, and vagrants and other unemployed people (Table 3.2). Floating populations, as the term suggests, are elusive and seasonal. Within any given year, their size tends to be larger during winter when there is low demand for work on the farm, and usually reaches its peak in February or March immediately after the Spring Festival. Their period of stay ranges from a couple of days to a few years. Therefore, some of them are short-term visitors or seasonal workers.

Based on data from an 11-city survey by the Ministry of Urban Construction (Table 3.2), Chan (1994a) and Sha and Cai (1994) estimated the size of the urban floating population in the late 1980s to be around 70 million. Recent estimates put the size of the floating population in the range of 80-120 million (fieldwork 1994), indicating a rising trend after a dip in 1989 and 1990 due to an austerity program. The median figure, 100 million, is roughly 30 percent of the total urban population (SSB 1994a). Applying ratios derived from the 11-city survey, one can infer that half of the floating population, or 50 million, stay longer than six months. These floaters can be considered "permanent" migrants. Sixty percent of these, or 30 million, come from rural areas. They are mostly concentrated in major cities such as Shanghai, Guangzhou, Wuhan, and Beijing, and coastal provinces like Guangdong, Hainan, and Jiangsu. Their numbers were expected to raise the overall urban population size in 1993 by 8 percent and the average annual growth rate of urban population between 1982 and 1993 to 5.0 percent. Whether short-term or permanent, floaters have put tremendous pressure on major cities and their infrastructure.

The picture at the national level described above inevitably masks significant regional variations in the PRC. Without comparable provincial urban population figures, firm evaluations are not possible, but

Table 3.2: "Floating Population" in the PRC

(a) Size of Floating Population in Selected Cities (Millions)

City	Year	Size	City	Year	Size
Shanghai	1988	2.09	Beijing	1988	1.31
Guangzhou	1989	1.30	Wuhan	1990	1.20
Chengdu	1989	0.42	Hangzhou	1989	0.50
Taiyuan	1989	0.36	Zhengzhou	1989	0.37
Harbin	1989	0.23	Anshan	1989	0.16
Jilin	1989	0.07			

Note: Total population of these cities in 1989 was 33.79 million. Total floating population was 8.01 million. Floating population as a % of population of cities was 23.7%.

(b) Floating Population: Reasons for Move

	%	Average Reported Length of Stay (No. of days)
Seeking employment	48.3	
Nannies	9.0	307
Technicians	0.6	302
Construction workers	14.6	297
Other employment	10.5	236
Self-employed vendors	10.7	225
Self-employed repairers	2.9	207
Visiting family/friends	10.4	
Seeking support from relatives	2.4	324
Visiting relatives and friends	8.0	224
Using urban facilities	33.6	
Study and training	4.0	210
On medicare	3.2	136
On business	11.7	66
Attending meetings	1.8	16
Tourists	3.4	10
In transit	9.5	3
Others	7.9	
Vagrants	0.5	173
Unclassified	7.4	133
Total	100.0	

Source: Li and Hu (1991).

the two provinces studied show significantly different rates of urban population growth. The data in Table 3.1 indicate that the more economically advanced province, Shandong, is urbanizing much faster than Guizhou. The urban population of Shandong grew by an average of 6.1 percent per year from 1982 to 1990 while Guizhou grew by a mere 1.8 percent per year, a rate only slightly higher than the overall rate of population growth of Guizhou during the same period. This contrast may not be totally surprising in view of the great differences in the economic development of the two provinces. Migration figures also show that in the five years before 1990, Shandong absorbed more than it lost to other provinces while Guizhou lost more than it gained (State Council and SSB 1993). A substantial portion of the increase in urban population in Shandong was due to more annexations by cities and the creation of more new cities in Shandong than in Guizhou, as can be seen in Table 3.1.[7] Still, the urbanization trend has taken root in Guizhou: according to the Guizhou Provincial Statistical Bureau, 52 percent of the 470,000 who migrated within the province in 1985-1990 did so from rural to urban areas and only 4 percent migrated from cities and towns to the countryside.

POLICIES FAVORING URBANIZATION

Policies favoring urbanization and migration resulted largely from a change in the leadership's view of urban development, as described earlier. More than 300 cities and about 13,000 towns have been designated since 1983, contributing to rapid urban population growth. Equally fundamental were agricultural reform and decollectivization, which brought out previously disguised rural unemployment and produced tens of millions of footloose rural laborers. This rapid expansion has been fairly well matched by the urban-industrial economy, especially the nonstate sector.

The shift was also made easier by relaxed controls on migration and employment as the government came to realize the value of cheap labor to the economic boom that was taking place mostly in urban and peri-urban areas associated with the growth in the township and village

---

[7] Five of the six counties that were formerly administered by Qingdao have recently been converted into cities.

enterprise (TVE) sector. Most urban construction workers, garbage collectors, street sweepers, maids, and bootblacks are peasant migrants; so are most of the factory workers in such coastal boom towns as Shenzhen. Measures allowing different kinds of migration, as described below, and a rapid erosion in social control through urban residence permits, foodgrain ration tickets, employment quotas, neighborhood watch systems, and similar means have made the country more mobile since the mid-1980s.

Together with the decollectivization of the farm sector in the early 1980s, restraints on migration were first relaxed in an ad hoc manner by local governments in small towns, where the state's urban social welfare commitments were lowest (Chan 1994b). The State Council in 1983 formally allowed peasants doing nonagricultural work in towns and with secured accommodations to obtain resident status but with no claim to state-supplied benefits including food grain (hence the category "households with self-supplied food grain"). Furthermore, the government legalized migration to urban centers by "temporary residents" as early as 1983 in some provinces and finally nationwide (Solinger 1985; *Renmin ribao* 1985). This opened an important, previously closed, gate to unorganized, "spontaneous migration" (*ziliu renkou*) and out of poverty for those with labor or other skills to sell to the city. The ban on hiring in the countryside was lifted at about the same time (Tang and Jenkins 1990). Peasants could also now be self-employed or set up their own shops in small, undesignated towns while retaining their rural household registrations (State Council 1983, 1984a). Construction workers, craftsmen, shoe repairers, and the like were thus able to enter many urban locations and find work.

Formal rural-urban migration has likewise been made easier, particularly for intellectuals and cadres who are separated from their families, and as many as 2 per thousand of the nonagricultural population may now convert their household status from "agricultural" to "nonagricultural" (*nongzhuanfei*) (Liu 1992). Besides, the decentralization of administration has given provincial and other local authorities more powers or enabled them to approve conversions of household status from agricultural to nonagricultural by exploiting loopholes in the system. The resulting rapid growth in the number of the nonagricultural households has been described in the Chinese official press as "out of control" (*Guangmin ribao* 1989).

About half of the *nongzhuanfei* population in the 1980s were approved under measures passed by local authorities, presumably not totally in line with the objectives of the central government. Some local officials were quick to capitalize on the opportunity to raise badly needed funds for urban administration, including infrastructure development, and to enrich themselves by selling urban residency rights. One source noted that 3 million urban resident registers (*hukou*) had been sold to peasants by early 1994, generating a revenue of Y25 billion (*Sing Tao Daily* 1994). Similar practices are found in Anshun and Qufu (examined later).

Many of the new "nonagricultural" householders, however, have little or no access to subsidies (and so do not cost the government as much as full-status urban residents), while those without local household registration (the floating population) can claim no state benefits at the destination. The Chinese urban population is being differentiated based on entitlement, and a dualistic social structure of "haves" and "have-nots" has emerged in recent years (Chan 1995).

In general, the scrapping of many administrative controls has pushed the economy further toward urbanization. The society created by the post-Mao marketization and the erosion of state powers is more diverse and complex and, admittedly, harder to monitor and control. Many migrants now depend on jobs outside the state's practical control, including those in the "hidden" economy. The household registration system is no longer as effective in limiting the movement of the population. Indeed, many people do not even bother to register their stay with the authorities. The drop in migration in 1989 and 1990 proved to be short-lived. A new round of market-oriented reform starting in 1991 set off a bigger economic boom and vigorous property development which found favor among many local governments. Migration and urbanization have accordingly increased further in the last three or four years.

URBAN DEVELOPMENT AND INFRASTRUCTURE PROVISION

URBAN PLANNING IN A PLANNED ECONOMY

Urban infrastructure can be generally defined to include public utilities (such as power, piped water supply, sewerage, and garbage disposal), municipal works (mainly roads and drains), parks, and transit systems. In the PRC, most of these urban infrastructure services are under the jurisdiction of urban construction (*chengshi jianshe*) authorities, who oversee the planning, construction, and management of infrastructure in cities. The precise areas they cover are municipal housing;[8] municipal works (roads, sewerage, and wastewater treatment, collectively referred to as *shizheng gongcheng*); public utilities (tap water supply, buses, and piped gas supply, or *gongyong shiye*); parks; and solid waste treatment. Electricity, considered a directly productive activity, is under the Ministry of Electric Power.

Until the late 1970s, the government devoted little attention and few resources to urban construction. In this study, we concern ourselves largely with those areas of urban infrastructure in the PRC that are classified under "urban construction."

In the first place, as has been pointed out, the government adopted a straightforward but shortsighted socialist industrialization strategy in its zealous attempt to achieve high industrial growth. Consumption and infrastructure investment, both considered "nonproductive," were not priorities. Before reform, urban construction had very limited funding. It appeared to depend heavily on "urban maintenance and construction funds" (UMCF) and some small central budgetary allocations, plus a variety of ad hoc and changing levies and fees, mainly on enterprises and users. There were separate budgets for "public" housing run and managed by state-owned enterprises and for urban infrastructure such as roads serving certain enterprises.

According to Hua (1993), vice director of the policy research center of the Ministry of Construction, in the three decades before 1979 investment in urban construction totaled Y12 billion—about 1.43 percent of the nation's total fixed investment and about 0.23 percent of GDP. Hua points out that these figures are very low compared with urban construction's 10-15 percent share in total fixed investment and its 3 percent share in GDP in many other countries. The UMCF averaged about Y1.07 billion per year between 1973 and 1977,[9] or roughly Y10 per urban resident. Before 1979, funds for urban construction,

---

[8] A large portion of public housing is owned and administered by individual enterprises (see next section).

[9] For comparison, the figure for 1992 in nominal terms is Y39.35 billion.

including capital investment, were determined mainly by the central government, which not only drew up investment plans but also set the rates for urban construction taxes and fees. Local municipal authorities had limited power to raise funds for infrastructure investment and infrastructure maintenance (Editorial Committee of *Dangdai Zhongguo* Series 1990).

Secondly, before reform, urban construction had no strong "advocate" in the administrative setup. The high priority given to industry meant that decision making was dominated by the industrial ministries. Service facilities were funded and built often as part of the package of industrial projects determined by industrial planners. In 1954, for instance, the State Economic Planning Commission required most new industrial enterprises to provide their workers with housing and basic service facilities such as shops and barber shops. The larger ones, such as Baotou Steel Plant and Wuhan No. 1 Machinery Factory, even had to build major infrastructure such as water channels and port facilities (Editorial Committee of *Dangdai Zhongguo* Series 1990).

This was typical in the Soviet-type economy where investment for infrastructure was mostly allocated along with industrial projects and funds were decided by individual ministries and channeled vertically. City mayors were primarily responsible for industrial output and not for urban public services. The urban planning and construction branches, with limited power and financial resources, were totally subordinate to economic planning (Bater 1980). In the radical era in the PRC—the entire 1960s—the city planning profession and bureaucracies were considered superfluous and disbanded. The city planning that did exist in the 1950s mostly functioned to assist in finding sites for projects already decided upon by economic planners and to design the layout for industrial and related projects. As a consequence, infrastructure was more likely to benefit specific projects and output than to serve the interests of a larger population. One Chinese commentator in 1980 summed up the pre-reform situation quite well: "For many years, urban development has been regarded as nothing more and nothing less than the industrialization of a city" (*Guangmin ribao* 1980, cited in Kirkby 1985).

In macro urban development, the policy was to locate new industrial enterprises in smaller cities, mostly inland. This policy was apparently related to the planned construction of new industry centers in the resource-rich interior under the extensive industrialization program, to the lower infrastructure funding requirements of the smaller, generally less well provided cities (which tied in with the government's attempts to reduce its urban infrastructure outlays), and to the greater security afforded by the inland provinces.

CHANGES SINCE 1978

At the start of reform, inadequate urban housing and commercial facilities (e.g., shops and, perhaps more importantly, supply of consumer goods) were two of the most urgent urban concerns. To redress the past neglect of urban infrastructure development and in the process regain popularity, the early post-Mao leadership began trying to raise urban living standards by channeling more funds into urban housing and other infrastructure. This change in attitude, as well as the leadership's better appreciation of the central role of cities in market-oriented regional economic activity, became even clearer when the government publicized in 1984 its blueprint for a more market-responsive urban sector. Among the new policies were a higher administrative rank and some autonomy for many cities, as described earlier.

The importance of municipal planning vis-à-vis economic planning was also generally recognized. The National Conference on Urban Planning, held in 1980, placed mayors in charge of planning, constructing, and managing urban infrastructure within their jurisdictions. All cities and towns were asked to draw up master plans for their physical development. By the end of 1986, 339 of the 353 cities at the time and 1,675 of the 1,980 county towns had prepared their master plans, most of which had been approved by the respective authorities (Editorial Committee of *Dangdai Zhongguo* Series 1990). Once reestablished, urban planning concerned itself with salvaging the historical relics in the cities from the damage wrought by the Cultural Revolution decade and by haphazard urban construction. Twenty-four cities of historical-cultural value, including Qufu, were identified in 1982, and another 38 were added to the list in 1986. These cities received special central grants from the Bureau of Cultural Relics, as seen in the case of Qufu in the discussion below.

The 1980 conference also reiterated the previous national policy of developing urban settlements and signified the government's continuing intent to "control the growth of large cities, rationally develop medium cities and actively promote the development of small cities." As officially interpreted, this strategy denoted a need to restrict the number of large urban centers and the size of their (nonagricultural) population, based on the notion of "optimal" city size espoused by many centrally planned economies. In this view, large cities were overcrowded, costly, and inefficient, while smaller urban centers were more productive. Considerable debate on this issue has raged among academics in the PRC since the 1980s. Critics (such as Zhou, Y., 1988 and Bao 1995) take the side of large cities, contending that they are generally more productive than smaller cities.

Together with the return to urban planning, the PRC has moved to systematize legislative-administrative framework for urban construction. The Regulations of Urban Planning promulgated by the State Council in 1984 specified procedures for approving and coordinating urban projects. Cities could regulate their own planning within the national framework. The Law of Urban Planning, hailed by many Chinese planning professionals as a major milestone in formalizing city planning in the PRC, was finally approved by the National People's Congress in 1989. In 1991 the first national urban land-use classification and planning standards were issued.

Investment in urban housing shot up in the late 1970s and the 1980s. About 85 percent of housing built since 1959 was built between 1979 and 1993 (fieldwork 1994). Before 1986, housing reforms were focused on increasing the supply of housing; since then, they have dealt with the more fundamental question of market allocation of housing, especially through higher rents and privatization. These measures are examined in the next section.

Funds for urban construction also received a big boost. Total investment in urban construction in the first half of the 1980s soared to Y18.1 billion, about 3.4 percent of the nation's total investment in fixed assets (Hua 1993) and larger in nominal terms than the total investment in the previous three decades. New sources of revenue made the increase possible. A new urban construction levy of 5 percent of the industrial and commercial profits of domestic enterprises was introduced in 47 cities in 1979 and then applied in a total of 150 cities in 1984. Following the conversion of enterprise profits to taxes (*ligaishui* reform), the levy was replaced by the urban maintenance and construction tax (UMCT) in 1985. The UMCT rate was 7 percent of the combined value of the product tax, VAT, and business tax (the so-called "three taxes") for domestic enterprises in cities, 5 percent in towns, and 1 percent elsewhere (Editorial Committee of *Dangdai Zhongguo* Series 1990). The relative stability of the three taxes made the UMCT a steady source of revenue for urban construction. In 1987 the UMCT generated Y6,192 million, or 38 percent of the total urban maintenance and construction funds (UMCF). This broad pattern continued through 1991. In 1994 the UMCT was revamped and given a new name, "urban and rural maintenance and construction tax," along with other major changes in the PRC's tax system. The financing aspect is examined in detail in Chapter 4.

Some cities in the 1980s tried charging fees for the use of urban infrastructure, especially major municipal works. Wastewater treatment fees began to be collected in more than 30 cities in 1984. In the mid-1980s Guangzhou and Foshan started requiring toll payment for vehicular use of their bridges (Editorial Committee of *Dangdai Zhongguo* Series 1990). "Infrastructure connection" fees on new construction and new in-migrants (the so-called *zengrong fei*, or fees for expanding capacity) were also allowed by the State Council in some cities in 1984. The fees eventually covered all municipal works and many public services throughout the country. Indeed, taxes and mostly unregulated fees on urban land development have proliferated, perhaps to an unacceptable level. The fees and taxes levied on new development in urban Shandong are given in Table 3.3.

Another popular way of raising revenues for local governments is the sale of urban residency rights. The 3,000 new household registers issued by Qufu to in-migrants at Y3,000 per head raised Y9 million, half of which reportedly went to the UMCF account. Anshun has sold 500 urban *hukou* since it started selling them in 1993, and most of the Y1.5 million it has raised was to be used to finance urban construction. By early 1994, as mentioned earlier, 3 million urban resident household registration books had been sold to peasants throughout the country, generating a revenue of Y25 billion.

**Table 3.3: Costs, Fees, and Levies
on New Urban Land in Shandong: An Illustration, 1994
(Figures taken from Qingdao)**

Comprehensive Construction Costs (A)–about Y1,000/m²
-including site formation and land resumption (Y600/m²) and compensation for loss of vegetable land and agricultural work (Y400/m²)

Land Development Fee (B)–about Y200-Y250/m²
-the so-called *"da peitou"* fee for the construction of road, water supply, and electric power systems

Urban Infrastructure Connection Fees (C)–about Y200/m²
-mainly payments for water and drainage connections and other urban infrastructure

Other fees charged by city departments (D)–totaling about Y200/m²
-including civil air defense (*renfang*) fee (Y13/m²); retail network fee (Y14/m²); gas connection (Y3,000 per unit); central heat supply fee (Y100/m²); telecommunications fee (Y14/m²); electricity capacity expansion fee (Y900/KW); and tap water capacity expansion fee

Tax for Regulating the Direction of Investment in Fixed Assets (E)–collected by the central government
-5% of investment amount for housing, 15-30% for hotels, and 0% for public facilities

Other taxes and levies (F)
-arable land use tax; agricultural land protection tax; new vegetable land development tax; basic arable land protection funds; road construction surcharge for nonagricultural development; and land differential rent (*jicha dizhu*)

Land sale (*churang,* or conveyance) price = A + B + C + F

Perhaps more important to urban development in the long run, both in promoting efficient use of urban land and in financing urban infrastructure, were reforms creating an urban land market. All land used to be administratively allocated and could be used for free. The reforms introduced such market mechanisms as bidding, auction, and negotiation to set a price for the use of land for a period of 40 to 70 years (State Council 1990), on the premise that land-use rights can be transferred, unlike land ownership, which remains in the hands of the state. This practice is modeled on the relatively successful experience of Hong Kong and, to some extent, driven by the opportunity to cater to the Hong Kong and overseas markets. Land-use fees were first tried out in 1981 in Shenzhen on projects funded by foreign sources.

A broader program for the sale of land-use rights was tried in six cities (Shenzhen, Shanghai, Tianjin, Guangzhou, Xiamen, and Fuzhou) in 1987 (fieldwork 1994) and the first land-use right was auctioned off in Shenzhen that same year (*China Daily* 1994). In 1988 the transfer of land-use rights was legalized and written into the revised PRC Constitution (Zhuang et al. 1993). Other cities could now also transfer land-use rights to individuals, foreign joint ventures, and domestic companies (Dowall 1993). By 1994, land-use rights were being sold in all provincial units except Tibet (*Ta Kung Pao* 1994). However, as many de facto "land sales" regulations, like the two temporary sets announced by the State Council in 1990 (Zhuang et al. 1993), are still quite rudimentary and experimental, the transfer of land-use rights varies in practice from place to place.

By one estimate, 44,000 land sales had been transacted and 79,000 ha of land had changed hands by the end of 1993 (*Economic Information Daily* 1994). While this amounted to only about 10 percent of the nation's new urban land supply, the percentage went as high as 50 percent in Guangdong and even higher in Zhuhai, and was close to 100 percent in Shenzhen (fieldwork 1994). In Shandong, this percentage increased from about 4 percent in 1992 to about 20-25 percent in 1993 (fieldwork 1994). Guizhou, on the other hand, has been less successful in attracting land sales. Guiyang earned Y20 million from land sales in 1993 and expected to earn Y70 million in 1994, while Anshun has not yet begun selling land.

As in Hong Kong (see Box 3.1), land sales can be a significant source of public revenue (Schiffer 1991; Yeh and Wu 1994). The *Economic Information Daily* (1994) reports that local governments in some coastal open cities derived 80 percent of their total revenue from land sales. In many other cities, a share of 20 percent is more common (Bao 1995). The speculative real estate boom that began in 1991 especially in the ETDZs and coastal cities, combined with the urge of many local governments to make "quick bucks," has sent land sales and property development soaring. Up to the end of 1992, land sales generated an accumulated total of Y50 billion (*China Daily* 1993), and a year later this figure had more than doubled to Y123 billion.[10] But only 10 percent of the transactions were done through the market; the remaining 90 percent were still bureaucratically allocated (*Ta Kung Pao* 1994).

Much of the land was sold at discount prices: if the figures reported are accurate, the implied average price of land was only Y156 per m², a real bargain. At first, the central government was supposed to get 60 percent of the receipts and local governments, 40 percent. The sharing was later changed to 40 percent for the central government and 60 percent for the local governments (Liu 1993), with the latter having to set aside 20 percent of its share for urban construction and land development. Even at this 40:60 split, ample opportunities for rent seeking and profit sharing between developers and local officials made the scheme hard to enforce. Also, local governments, which absorbed most of the land development costs, resented the large share of the central government. The sharing of the land sales proceeds has since increasingly favored local governments. After a change in the central- and local-government shares to 32:68 and then to 5:95,[11] local governments, under the new tax system of 1994, now get to keep all the proceeds—potentially a major source of revenue for them.

Of all the taxes in the PRC, the one closest to the property tax in the West is the urban land-use tax introduced in 1988. The tax, which covered all commercial land, ranged in 1991 from Y0.30-Y6.00 per m² in small cities to Y0.50-Y10.00 in large cities. These rates have since been raised quite drastically and now range from Y0.90-Y18.00 in small cities to Y1.50-Y30.00 in large cities. Before 1994, the revenue from this tax was shared equally by the central and local governments. The local governments thus had little inducement to implement the tax, which, as of 1992, had still not been applied in a full one-third of cities and towns (Li 1992).

The urban land use tax was changed into a local tax in 1994, perhaps to stimulate local tax efforts. A tax on the appreciated value of

---

[10] The Y123 billion figure came from Zhou Yuechuan, director of the State Land Management Bureau (reported in *Wen Wei Pao* 1994). Other reports placed land sales revenue in Shanghai in 1992 at Y10 billion plus and in Guangdong in 1987 through 1994 at Y40 billion (*Ming Pao* 1994; *Sing Tao Daily* 1995). These figures far exceeded the reported land sales revenues collected by the central and local governments in various yearbooks published by the Ministry of Finance (e.g., MOF 1992, 1993). Land sales earned for the government only Y288 million in 1991 and Y999 million in 1992, excluding the proceeds from land sales in Pudong, Shanghai (Y368 million), and a large part of the proceeds has not yet reached the state coffers.

[11] The actual shares of the central and local governments, as reported in the various financial yearbooks of the MOF, were 51.6:48.4 in 1990, 51.8:48.2 in 1991, and 38.2:61.8 in 1992.

Box 3.1: Financing Urban Development—The Case of Hong Kong

By most economic standards, Hong Kong in the 1950s and 1960s was a "Third World" city. Today, Hong Kong is a thriving modern metropolis of six million people and a world-class financial center on the Pacific rim. Much of its success has to do with a well-constructed and well-maintained infrastructure that has supported economic growth of 7 percent per annum in real terms over the last three decades.* Hong Kong is well-served by a communications system that has supported the city's emergence as a financial and telecommunications center for the Asia-Pacific region. It also has a well-functioning public transport system which operates underground and an extensive system of roadways to move millions of people in and around one of the most densely populated urban centers in the world. The city is also efficiently supplied with water and power. All this has been provided by an efficient public administration which has quietly managed the transformation of the city state to world-class status.

Major infrastructural development includes a public housing program begun in the 1950s and several large-scale reservoir projects in the 1960s. These were followed by an ambitious, and still ongoing, newtown program and the construction of an underground subway in the 1970s. The 1980s were marked by a significant expansion of the road networks, including the building of several tunnels and expressways. Currently, Hong Kong is enhancing its infrastructure capacity through so-called "rose garden" projects which are centered on ports and an airport project in Chek Lap Kok, which will handle 35 million passengers a year starting in 1997. The provision of more infrastructure facilities has become necessary to satisfy increasing demand generated by population increases and rising living standards. Likewise, continuous development of facilities is crucial today as Hong Kong competes for the position of leading business service center in the Asia-Pacific region.

A comparatively high percentage of urban infrastructure services is financed by user charges and private-sector participation. The government has taken the view that it should not undertake activities that can be carried out by the private sector. Only certain, perhaps more strategic, infrastructure services are provided by the government, but even these are often charged at full cost, including services provided by the Transport Department, the Civil Aviation Department, the Postal Services, and the Water Department, and the operation of public parks and tunnels. It is estimated that user charges and quasi-user charges (excluding rents collected from public housing) make up about 12 percent of total government revenue.

Many infrastructure services, especially internal transportation, are operated by the private sector on commercial principles. These include the rail systems and one cross-harbor tunnel (they are run as "public corporations"), a wide range of other transport modes, from franchised buses, ferries, and trams to public light buses, and utilities like gas and power supply. By their very nature, the delivery of many of these services gives rise to monopolies and oligopolies; hence, their operations need to be and are under varying degrees of government and public scrutiny.

---

*Most statistics used here are from official sources, such as the Hong Kong government (1995).

To meet occasional large capital outlays for infrastructure projects, the government also borrows (from the Asian Development Bank and other development lending institutions) and issues bonds. The amounts have never been large, especially compared with fiscal reserves. To finance the multibillion-dollar container port projects and the airport project at Chek Lap Kok, the government has issued bonds in several rounds since 1991, with the full consent of the PRC government. Some of the bonds will mature after the sovereignty changeover on 1 July 1997.

A distinctive feature of the Hong Kong budget is the large share of nontax sources in total revenues, a significant portion of which comes from land sales. By virtue of its ownership of practically all the land, the Hong Kong government has generated significant incomes from land and related property sales. Land is "sold" (actually leased) to the private sector by public auction and tender, bringing in sizeable incomes for the government and encouraging efficient use of land. In 1994, some $2.4 billion, or about 11 percent of total revenue, came from land transactions. In some years in the 1980s, this percentage was as high as 30 percent. In 1995, the average price of urban land sold was about $12,500 per square meter (*Sing Tao Daily* 1995)—no doubt among the highest in the world. Land for public projects, schools, and the like is, however, made available at a nominal premium.

The high land prices inevitably translate into lofty property rentals and purchase prices which force a large segment of the population out of the private housing market. The public or government-subsidized housing program has provided a way to deal with this problem (see Schiffer 1991). Started as an emergency shelter program for the people displaced by a major fire in 1953, Hong Kong's urban public housing program has become one of the largest of its kind in the world. About 45 percent of the population, or about 2.7 million, live in public housing. Subsidies for the program accounted for some 12-13 percent of the government's annual expenditure in the 1990s. It has been argued that low-cost public rental housing has contributed significantly to Hong Kong's low cost of labor, especially of the semiskilled and unskilled type, thereby enhancing the competitiveness of its export industry.** The largest component of the program, public rental housing, is heavily subsidized through the provision of free land so that tenants pay only a fraction of the market rents. Rentals collected mainly cover maintenance costs. Since 1978, the government has exacted higher rents from those who can afford to pay and has sold off a portion of public housing to create an ownership program for better efficiency and social equity in the provision of housing.

Rapid infrastructure development in Hong Kong appears to be related to several factors: recognition by the government of the economic importance of infrastructure; rapid economic growth, producing more financial resources; prudent fiscal management, including careful selection of projects and financing; emphasis on the efficient use of infrastructure, partly through management and privatization; and a multitude of sources of financing for infrastructure, including substantial participation by the private sector. The heavy reliance on land sales revenue, especially in the past, has, however, exposed the fiscal base to a significant degree of uncertainty and the emphasis on efficiency has given rise to equity issues. Access of low-income groups to reasonable housing and public services remains a major issue that must be dealt with.

** For example, despite the very high (private) housing costs, housing accounted for only 19 percent of average household expenditure in 1984 (compared with 22 percent in the US). This low share was attributed to the low consumption of housing space and low rents paid by tenants in public housing apartments.

land, publicized in late 1993, had been mothballed in many provinces, including Guangdong, apparently on account of opposition from coastal provinces and overseas property investors (Knight-Ridder 1994; Ming Pao 1995). Most recently, the government in July 1994 issued regulations concerning the management of urban real estate, to soft-pedal the effects of the boom of 1992 and 1993 on the property market.

Still another source of funds for urban infrastructure, besides fees and taxes, is foreign private-sector investment, especially of the build-operate-transfer type. Under such a scheme a private company finances the investment, provides working capital, builds the project, runs it long enough to repay debts and achieve a return on equity, and then transfers the project back to the host government. Foreign investors began funding urban infrastructure in the PRC in the mid-1980s. Among the early examples was the development by Hopewell Hong Kong of power stations and a toll road in Guangdong (Hong Kong Government 1995). Foreign investments have broadened in recent years to encompass many inner-city redevelopment projects in Wuhan, Guangdong, Beijing, and Tianjin. In these projects, private developers renovate a certain part of the old city in return for permission to develop certain more profitable commercial land.

HOUSING DEVELOPMENT AND REFORMS

REFORM PROGRAMS

Housing reforms in the 1980s and early 1990s are described in Wong, Heady, and Woo (1995). To summarize, the government concentrated on increasing housing supply in the first stage (1981-85). Experimental reform programs in a few cities were primarily intended to increase the supply of housing by inviting new sources of finance, including private investment. The second stage launched in 1986 was concerned with the more complicated problem of adjusting rents on the huge stock of public housing. Four cities (Yantai, Bengbu, Tangshan, and Changzhou) were chosen as test sites for the comprehensive housing reform, which involved raising rents and providing state employees with partially offsetting wage subsidies. The government also tried to sell off some of its public housing.

From the experience gained in these test cities, the Leading Group for Housing Reform (LGHR) of the State Council issued

"The Proposal to Implement Nationwide Urban Housing Reform by Groups and by Stages" in 1988. That proposal laid out a plan to commercialize urban housing by: disclosing the extent of housing subsidies granted to urban employees, reforming the investment system so that housing construction is treated as commodity production, setting up a house financing fund, and readjusting the production structure to stimulate the development of a real estate market. Partly due to the macroeconomic adjustments of 1989 and 1990, rent reform made little progress but some public housing was sold to individuals at heavy discounts.

The reforms proposed in 1988 got a renewed push in 1991 after the second national meeting on urban housing. The State Council again called for a reform of the rent system and for the sale of public housing. The municipalities of Beijing, Shanghai, and Tianjin, along with coastal cities, were expected to lead the way. Again, the cities made little progress in raising rents. The average rent on public housing in 1993 was still only Y0.30 per m² (compared with Y0.13 in 1980), although some cities like Shenzhen managed to raise the average rent on public housing to Y4.9 (fieldwork 1994). Today, housing rents account for about 1 percent of the average urban household expenditure, the same as in 1985 (SSB 1994a).

However, especially in coastal provinces like Guangdong, there was no slowdown in sales of public housing at huge discount prices, most of which were below the bottom price of Y120 per m² proposed by the State Council in 1988.[12] By the end of 1993, 20 percent of the housing stock (including those owned by enterprises) had been sold to individuals, according to the MOF.[13] This massive transfer of state property to individuals at bargain prices prompted the State Council in late 1993 to declare a temporary ban on the sale of public housing pending further review of the program.

CURRENT SITUATION

The production of housing has progressed rapidly, especially in 1992 and 1993 (Table 3.4). The average per capita urban housing floor area

---

[12] In Beijing public housing that had cost an estimated Y800 to build was being sold at an average of Y188 per m².

[13] The corresponding LGHR figure was only 10 percent (fieldwork 1994).

(living area) jumped from 3.6 m² in 1978 to 6.9 m² in 1991 and further to 7.5 m² in 1993. At this rate, the PRC can almost certainly achieve its target of 8 m² per capita for the urban population by the turn of the century. However, urban housing is unequally distributed and the allocation system is fraught with problems, as Wong, Heady, and Woo (1995) have observed. As of 1994, 4.4 million households (down from 5.3 million in 1991) were still living on less than 4 m² of floor area per capita. This figure, of course, totally excludes the housing needs of the "temporary" population in cities and towns and related problems, an issue that the PRC government has not yet faced squarely.

The sale of public housing with partial property rights resumed in the first half of 1994 in some cities and especially after the State Council directives pushing housing reform in July of that year. The current objective is to sell public housing to workers at "standard price,"

Table 3.4: Urban Housing Suppy, 1991-1993

		New Housing		
	Per Capita Floor Area (m²)	*Total Investment[a] (Y billion)*	*Floor Area Added (million m²)*	*Implied Costs (Y/m²)*
Annual Average, 1979-1993			135.3	
1991	6.9	52.3	142	368
1992	7.1	75.1	178	422
1993	7.5	162.8	205	794

[a]Prices in current year.
Source: Materials from LGHR (fieldwork 1994).

which consists largely of the construction cost and a small compensation for expenses incurred in removing the original structures (not the land price itself). An MOF official said that the market price of a unit consists, on the average, of three roughly equal costs: construction, the land itself, and other infrastructure services (in the form of taxes and fees).

Cities are selling off their public housing at a varied pace and at different prices, reflecting differences in location and the quality of housing. In Qufu, sales of public housing at an average of Y200 per m^2 were well underway in the summer of 1994, and the city expected to sell off all its public housing by the end of 1994. In Qingdao, sales were to begin in late 1994, at the standard price of Y670 per m^2. The program in Guiyang and Anshun in Guizhou began in 1993. The standard price in Guiyang was Y220 in 1994 and in Anshun was Y207 in 1993 and Y460 in 1994. Discounts, typically 30 percent off the standard price in Guiyang, were often given to city residents, existing occupants, and those who paid cash.

Twenty-five provincial-level governments and 110 prefectural-level cities (57 percent of all prefectural cities at the time) had established housing provident funds by the end of 1993. Such funds made up 40 percent of the Y11 billion in housing funds that had been accumulated by the end of 1993 by one group of 49 cities. Modest progress has been made in raising the rentals for public housing, at least judging from the experience of those cities. Qingdao raised rents from Y0.18 per m^2 in 1992 to Y0.53 in 1994 and planned to increase them further to Y1.3-Y1.4 (about the costs of maintenance) in 1995 and finally to Y3.3 (roughly 15 percent of the average income of a double-worker family) in 2000. Guiyang in 1994 was renting out public housing at Y0.40 per m^2 and planned to raise rents to Y0.80 shortly. Rents in Anshun were Y0.25-Y0.70 in 1994, compared with the previous year's level of below Y0.10. Temporary price controls imposed by the State Council in the summer of 1994, in the face of rising inflation, forced city governments that had been gearing up for bolder rent reforms to stop or at least defer these moves. Because of the continuing low rents, renting an apartment is a more attractive option than owning one.

URBAN INFRASTRUCTURE SERVICES

LEVEL OF PROVISION

This section examines the current level of provision of urban infrastructure. The financing aspect is discussed in the next chapter. Table

3.5 presents the most recent figures available for the five cities studied. National and provincial averages, where available, are also included. These figures were taken directly from reports provided by the Chinese urban construction authorities. Following official practice, the population base used in computing "per capita" averages and coverage was the "nonagricultural" population of the cities, i.e., "per capita of nonagricultural population." As explained before, this population figure is smaller than the actual resident population of the cities. The real per capita provision will therefore be lower than the figure in the table.

Quantitative comparisons of the level of provision in the cities in the PRC with world "averages" are impossible because, unlike many other economic statistics, cross-country urban infrastructure statistics are not systematically collected and standardized for that purpose. Even where international statistics exist for certain sectors (e.g., World Bank 1994a; World Resource Institute and International Institute for Environment and Development 1994), these are not directly comparable with Chinese statistics.

From scattered information, the per capita figures in Table 3.5 appear to place the PRC broadly in the category of lower middle-income countries when it comes to providing urban infrastructure.[14] This slightly higher position in comparison with the PRC's overall economic position is perhaps not too surprising, given the construction boom in the PRC in the last 14 years and the higher priority accorded to the urban sector in the overall development strategy. Although the very high percentage of the population with access to piped water would put the PRC in the group of upper middle-income countries, half of the cities in the PRC are classified as water-deficient by the government and about 110 of these are judged to be in "serious water deficit." Compared with many major cities in the world, the urban sector of the PRC also ranks low in per capita water consumption and is probably the equal of cities in low-income or lower middle-income countries in Asia in most other respects. These include public transportation and waste treatment, as shown in Table 3.5, and telecommunications and electricity for domestic use.

---

[14] Although the level of per capita availability of major urban infrastructure service is closely related to per capita income, it also reflects the geography of the cities (e.g., whether inland or coastal) and their climate.

Although Shandong and Guizhou are far apart in the provincial ranking based on per capita GDP, their cities differ only slightly in the level of provision of many, perhaps basic, infrastructure services including housing floor area, piped water consumption and coverage, and density of sewers. These services, except for piped water supply, are provided at levels that approximate national averages. In fact, Shandong and Guizhou are not far from the national averages in their per capita revenues from the two urban maintenance and construction levies (i.e., urban maintenance and construction tax, or UMCT, and public utilities surcharge, or PUS), although Shandong's per capita revenues from all sources are close to twice those of Guizhou's. The likely reason is the protection given by central allocations to basic services in the urban sector, especially the cities, where regional income disparities tend to be narrower than in the rural sector.

But even at this broad level there are noticeable differences in some sectors, apparently as a result of variations in per capita income and city size, as well as geographic factors. More definitive assessments will have to be based on detailed information about the spatial configurations of the cities as well as the manner in which these statistics are defined, especially in view of the enormous complexity of the definition of Chinese urban boundaries. Shandong's cities are significantly better provided with paved roads, garbage and night soil treatment, and gas supply than cities in Guizhou. Except for the higher gas consumption in Shandong, which is attributable to the need for indoor heating in winter, this difference may be related to the higher per capita revenue for urban construction in Shandong. On the other hand, the average urban resident in Guizhou has better access to tap water, buses, wastewater treatment, and public green areas. Shandong's urban construction authorities have identified shortfalls in tap water supply and wastewater treatment (both of which are below national averages), paved roads, and centralized heating. For their part, urban construction officials in Guizhou emphasized the age of most of the urban infrastructure of the province, and the need for renewal and new investment.

Among the three cities in Shandong surveyed, Qingdao, the most developed, provides the highest average level of access to tap water, piped gas, buses, sewers, and treatment of garbage and night soil. Qufu, the smallest city in the Shandong sample, has the lowest average level of provision of housing, tap water, buses, paved roads, and green

Table 3.5: Urban Infrastructure Service Revenue and Level of Provision in Selected Cities, 1992 and 1993

(a) Population and Revenue for Urban Construction

	Total Population (10,000)	Nonagri. Population (10,000)	City Area (km²)	Population Density (persons/km²)	Per Capita Tax Revenue NP (Y)	Per Capita Tax Revenue TP (Y)	Per Capita Revenue NP (Y)	Per Capita Revenue TP (Y)
	1	2	3	4	5	6	7	8
All Cities in PRC	30,748.2	15,459.4	969,728.5	317.0	75.9	38.2	254.5	128.0
Shandong	4,071.1	934.7	63,611.0	639.0	85.4	19.6	212.0	48.7
Qingdao	209.3	137.9	1,102.4	1,899.0	106.7	70.3	281.6	185.5
Taian	143.7	27.4	2,088.6	688.0	41.8	8.0	259.2	49.4
Qufu	60.9	6.7	895.8	680.0	31.2	3.4	162.8	17.9
Guizhou	718.1	234.3	24,081.0	298.0	69.8	22.8	128.8	42.0
Guiyang	158.6	106.4	2,436.0	651.0	93.6	62.8	195.1	130.9
Anshun	68.4	17.8	1,710.1	400.0	24.2	6.3	45.5	11.8

5: Per capita tax revenue (UMCT and public utilities surcharge combined) of nonagricultural population (NP)

6: Per capita tax revenue (UMCT and public utilities surcharge combined) of total population (TP)

7: Per capita revenue for urban construction of nonagricultural population

8: Per capita revenue for urban construction of total population

(cont'd)

Table 3.5: Urban Infrastructure Service Revenue and Level of Provision in Selected Cities, 1992 and 1993 (cont'd)

(b) Level of Provision (Based on NP)

	Housing UA	Housing LA	Tap Water (vol)	Tap Water (%)	Buses	Gas	Paved Roads	Density of Sewers	Wastewater Treatment	Green Areas (m²)	Green Areas (%)	Garbage/Night Soil Treatment
	1	2	3	4	5	6	7	8	9	10	11	12
All Cities in PRC	10.7	7.3	186.0	92.5	5.9	52.4	6.2	4.5	17.3	4.2	21.0	25.1
Shandong	12.2	7.9	138.5	87.8	5.1	52.3	12.1	4.8	6.0	4.5	27.1	39.6
Qingdao	10.4	7.4	118.9	96.5	12.0	60.0	6.1	7.0	3.4	3.7	25.9	94.0
Qingdao (1993)	10.8	7.5	117.3	99.1	14.0	63.1	6.7	7.3	4.5	3.9	26.5	92.2
Taian	13.3	8.7	143.6	90.5	3.7	54.4	25.4	2.8	0.0	4.0	31.8	0.0
Qufu	8.6	5.1	126.2	71.6	0.4	25.4	15.4	3.8	0.0	6.0	25.1	0.0
Guizhou	9.2	6.6	132.6	93.1	10.7	5.4	3.7	4.9	22.9	7.3	21.4	12.7
Guizhou (1993)	9.6	7.1	135.8	91.6	7.6	16.2	3.9	4.4	23.7	7.2	18.5	4.2
Guiyang	9.4	7.1	182.0	92.5	16.2	5.3	2.0	4.4	12.8	13.3	31.4	16.7
Guiyang (1993)	9.6	7.3	178.2	93.3	9.7	32.5	2.4	4.7	9.1	13.3	31.4	5.5
Anshun	9.8	7.7	40.8	89.9	4.9	0.0	2.8	5.7	0.0	1.6	7.5	42.9
Anshun (1993)	9.6	7.9	47.3	88.4	4.6	0.0	2.6	5.4	0.0	1.0	6.1	13.8

1: Housing, usable floor area (UA) per capita (m²)
2: Housing, living floor area (LA) per capita (m²)
3: Tap water, household consumption per day per capita (liters)
4: Tap water, % of population with access to
5: Buses (standard cars) per 10,000 persons
6: Gas, % of population with access to
7: Area of paved roads per capita (m²)
8: Density of sewers (km/km²)
9: % of wastewater treated
10: Public green area per capita (m²)
11: Green area as % of built-up area
12: % of garbage and night soil treated

Sources: Ministry of Construction (1993); fieldwork (1994).

areas. Qingdao officials raised problems similar to those cited by provincial officials.

In Guizhou, the average level of provision of housing, paved roads, sewers, and tap water is similar for the cities of Guiyang and Anshun. But in Anshun per capita water consumption is extremely low (only 22 percent of the national average in 1992). There is low coverage of public green areas, and no gas supply or wastewater treatment whatsoever is provided. Water supply per capita is extremely low largely because of the low availability of water from surrounding rivers. Anshun officials talked at length about serious shortfalls in tap water supply and the lack of wastewater, garbage, and night soil treatment systems.

In general, large cities within the same province tend to be better provided with infrastructure services than smaller cities, for most sectors except for housing and perhaps paved roads.[15] A positive correlation similarly appears between per capita availability of funds for urban construction and size of city (Figure 3.2). It is therefore not too surprising to hear officials of small cities such as Qufu expressing eagerness to catch up with the level of provision of big cities.

URBANIZATION ISSUES IN THE PRC

As pointed out earlier, many of the urbanization and urban construction issues examined above are complex and multifaceted. The complexity of those issues is compounded by significant regional variations and the seemingly ever-changing rules and practices of the last few years.

The following preliminary observations and suggestions regarding urbanization and urban infrastructure service policies are based on limited field visits and relevant materials provided. The financial aspect is treated in the next chapter.

---

[15] This is opposite to what Zhou (1994) has argued. However, Zhou makes his point on the basis of paved roads per capita, using questionable urban population figures. The higher level of provision of paved roads in some smaller cities could be due to the excessively large stretches of rural areas and roads and the few "nonagricultural" householders.

Figure 3.2: Per Capita Revenue for Urban Construction and Size of Cities, 1992

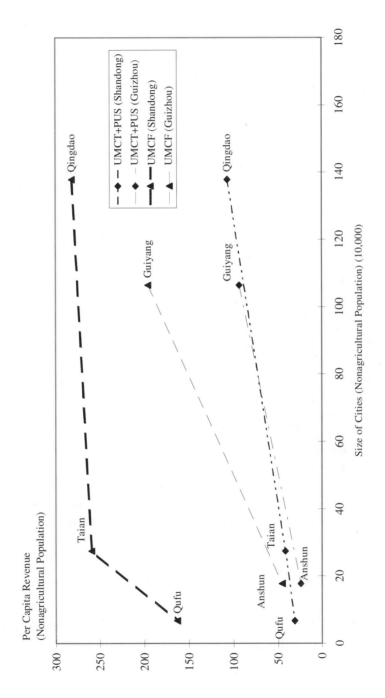

LOCAL ADMINISTRATIVE SYSTEM

The present system of local governments (province, prefecture, county, township) has too many layers by international standards. Since various levels of government in the PRC are heavily involved in running the economy, the multiple layers only lengthen the chain of command and increase response time. The reforms described above have given more powers to cities, but have also made the administrative structure even more cumbersome. The "line-item" city program has made revenue sharing more difficult to manage centrally. Finally, the setting up of "line-item" cities does not appear to conform to the provisions of the Constitution.

The problems caused by the incongruence of the vertical and horizontal systems constitute a larger issue that requires further study, but from an efficiency standpoint it may be useful for the PRC leadership to begin by more clearly defining the jurisdictions of cities as local governments and keeping the system unchanged over a period of time. Many of the administrative changes in the last decade appear to be ad hoc and not well thought out, possibly encouraging unproductive behind-the-scenes negotiations and fostering unequal competition between urban governments.

In market economies, private entrepreneurs are the primary operators of enterprises. This is not so in the PRC where there is a preponderance of state-owned enterprises with close administrative ties to different levels of government. Many conflicts between the vertically organized administrative system and the horizontal system of market-based economic interaction are inevitably generated. Administrative reforms described earlier have attempted to resolve some of those conflicts, but until there is a clear separation of enterprises from governments, these measures are likely to have very limited effect. Administratively determined strictures still dominate much of the economic interaction between major cities today.

As some analysts have pointed out, the effort to free these cities through what are still basically administrative means, as in the *jihua danlie* reform, has muddled the issue of who is the ultimate authority, since administrative power and economic power are nearly impossible to differentiate (Solinger 1993). Administrative power often entails final approval of supposedly "economic" decisions made at lower levels. Moreover, the cities have a tenuous hold on their new economic powers, none of which is legally binding (Wang, Cui, and Zhang 1987). In fact, new strains have emerged between the provinces and the line-item cities, and the rivalry between these two sides has often been contentious.

URBAN DEVELOPMENT STRATEGY

For more than three decades the PRC has implemented an urban development strategy of "promoting the growth of small and medium-sized cities and controlling that of large cities." This strategy is based on a simple, perhaps questionable, notion of optimal city size which is difficult to define. Given the present stage of development and the scarce capital resources of the PRC, development must still be selective. It is, however, premature to limit the growth of large urban centers, where large agglomerations still engender many scale economies. Many of the so-called "big city" problems in the PRC today, such as traffic congestion, inadequate water supply, and environmental deterioration, are due mainly to underinvestment and inefficient management, rather than to urban size.

URBAN INFRASTRUCTURE SERVICES: DEMAND AND SHORTFALL

The PRC has undoubtedly made great strides in expanding urban infrastructure services in the last 15 years. This can be inferred from Table 3.6 which traces the growth in per capita provision of most types of service in almost all of the cities between 1987 and 1992, the period for which comparable data could be compiled. Growth has been fastest in gas supply and bus services, both nationwide and in the five cities studied. However, despite these improvements, there are still evident shortfalls in the provision of urban infrastructure service, notably in water supply, public transportation, and electricity supply. Many other aspects of urban infrastructure services not covered in this study, such as telecommunications, sanitation, and fire services, may also need substantial improvement.

These shortfalls will worsen as urbanization proceeds apace. In the past ten years, actual urban population growth rate averaged about

5 percent per year. If this trend continues, as expected, the urban population will more than double, from the present 343 million to about 750 million by the year 2010, making the PRC predominantly urban. Rising per capita income, especially in the cities, will also heighten the demand for better urban infrastructure services. These pose a critical problem of financing infrastructure maintenance and investments, necessary for economic growth and a better quality of life. The PRC will need to set up a fair and efficient system of financing urban services, as well as source funds for new investments. The Asian Development Bank has estimated that to meet the increased demand, the PRC would need to invest more than $500 billion over the next ten years to improve its transportation and communications infrastructure alone (SCMP 1995). Most of these investments will have to be in the urban centers.

While all levels of government, including those visited by the study team, recognize the importance of financing, management is equally crucial and should not be overlooked. The neglect of management, traditionally a weak point in most socialist economies, is a legacy of the conventional physical planning mentality in which expansion (construction) overshadows efficiency (better management). Management includes regulating demand; otherwise, excessive and wasteful use will prevail. Piped water is underpriced in most cities in the PRC, and consumption is excessive in many places, even in the face of general water shortages in the urban sector. There is a strong case for the PRC to raise urban water rates, especially considering today's actual, not official urban incomes (see Hong Kong Government 1995). Similarly, better management can increase the efficiency of use of most urban facilities. An obvious case is the use of urban roads and the lack of any effective traffic management. In fact, among the five cities visited in Shandong and Guizhou, only one (Guiyang) has created a separate entity to look after the day-to-day maintenance of infrastructure services. In other cities, this task falls to the urban construction authorities, who at times seem more interested in building facilities than in making them work.

Urban planning in the PRC is still dominated by "master planning" based on a set of relatively static blueprints which often cannot keep pace with changes in the urban economy. The result has often been inefficiency in the provision of urban infrastructure and services. Furthermore, the urban planning apparatus must be made better able to deal with the rapid encroachment of farmland at the urban fringes and the haphazard development that followed the property boom of 1992 and 1993.

EQUITY ISSUES

Furthermore, as pointed out earlier, the average growth rates in urban infrastructure service are all overstated because they do not take into account the growing segment of urban residents registered as "agricultural" households. This group includes the "floating population," whose size has grown from a few million in the early 1980s to about 100 million in 1994. While not entitled to government-provided urban services, these people cannot be totally excluded from sharing some of the services, such as roads, public transportation, and water supply. In any case, dividing the population within cities into those with urban entitlements and those without is bound to exacerbate social conflict. This discrimination against new migrants from the countryside reflects a strong urban bias in the overall approach.

Per capita service provision varies significantly between cities (even considering only the "full-status" urban population). Economic forces, often differences in revenue, tip the balance in favor of larger centers. Besides being inequitable, this systematic bias is also inefficient because it distorts fair competition between urban centers and regions, and underlies the significant hierarchical brain drain from the countryside to small centers and to larger metropolises, as has happened in many Third World countries. The depletion of well-educated human resources in areas outside major metropolises is detrimental to the long-term national development of the PRC. Urban development will ultimately have to be decentralized for the nation's potential to be fully exploited.

Finally, the same service costs differently to different users. Residents in new projects and those in existing structures pay different fees. The marginal costs involved in developing new facilities may warrant charging higher fees and taxes, but as old users pay no fees or only nominal ones for practically the same facilities and services, the new rates would seem excessive and unfair. Moreover, this differential treatment of different groups further complicates the system of charging.

Chapter 4

MUNICIPAL PUBLIC FINANCE

by Christopher Heady

This chapter examines the way in which cities in the PRC finance the public services that determine the quality of life of their inhabitants and further economic growth. The chapter starts by considering the ways of financing urban growth. Attention then turns to the budgetary position of the four cities studied and to the provision of basic services. The next section discusses the financing issues that have arisen from the recent establishment of citywide social insurance schemes. Finally, the chapter ends with a summary of the main points raised.

THEORY AND PRACTICE OF URBANIZATION FINANCING

The mode of financing of the municipal services that accompany urban growth is dealt with in this section. These services are related to the provision of infrastructure such as roads, sewers, public housing, and water supply. The discussion has three parts: the relevant economic theory; the financing of urban growth in other countries; and the financing of urban growth in the PRC.

After considering the nature of the infrastructure services provided by municipalities, this section proceeds to demonstrate the importance of distinguishing between "private" and "public" goods and goes into the appropriate form of financing for each category of service.

THEORY OF URBANIZATION FINANCING

General Principles. In looking at the financing of the various aspects of urbanization, it is important to distinguish between "public" and "private" goods.

The consumption of a private good by one person or household prevents its consumption by another person or household. A house occupied by one household cannot be occupied by other households, and a liter of water consumed by one person cannot be consumed by anybody else. Garbage collection is also a private good as the use of the service by one household reduces the extent of service that can be provided to other households, at a given level of resources. Charging people for the use of private goods is therefore both possible and desirable.

In contrast, a single unit of a public good can benefit many people at the same time. Charging individuals directly for the use of the good would therefore be impractical because people can gain access to the good without paying, or undesirable because its use by one more person entails no extra cost, or both. For example, charging people for the use of an urban road is usually not practical; besides, unless the road was congested, charging would not be desirable as it would discourage people from using the road although the use would not add to the cost of the service.

This distinction between private and public goods can be made clearer by going over the main categories of urban construction:

- Housing construction: the production of a private good, as explained above.
- Urban roads and bridges: generally public goods, except where congestion would make it desirable to reduce access by charging a toll.
- Public transport: a private good unless excess capacity allows more people to be transported at no extra cost—an unlikely situation in PRC cities, where full use of buses and other public transport is common.
- Water supply and household sewage treatment: private goods, although the water mains and sewers, whose cost depends on the area covered rather than on the volume of water or sewage

carried, can often be regarded as public goods.

- Garbage collection: a private good, as discussed above.
- Parks and other public amenities: like roads, public or private depending on their state of congestion. A park is usually a public good, but a communal swimming pool or a busy airport should be regarded as a private good, because its use by more people causes inconvenience to present users.

The Financing of Private Goods. As stated above, it is both practical and desirable to charge people for the use of private goods. Normally, people should be charged the full cost of producing a good to encourage its prudent use and to conserve the scarce public funds of the city government.

This leaves the issue of financing the investment to produce private goods. In the case of housing, households should pay the full cost, but usually cannot do so by the time they move in. They either borrow or the city government pays for the housing and charges rent, effectively lending to the households which amortize the loan and pay interest through rentals. In terms of economic efficiency, these alternative arrangements are about the same, provided that the rent charges reflect the full interest and amortization costs.

If the city government pays for the housing out of its revenue budget, it may have to cut down on its other current services, but it can expect rent income to pay for additional services in the future. As less service is generally not an option, however, the city could also get a loan or sell its assets to raise the needed funds—essentially similar approaches, since both entail finding more income in the future to repay the loan or to replace the income that the assets used to generate for the city. Renting the houses at full cost will take care of the loan, as required for prudent borrowing (see Chapter 2).

In summary, therefore, the city may borrow (or sell its assets) to finance the building of houses, provided that it charges rents that cover the entire loan plus interest. This same principle of full charging applies to investments the city makes in other private goods that it provides.

It is possible to argue against individuals paying the full cost of publicly provided private goods in two cases: when the full cost is too high to be borne by the poor without subsidies, and when the goods benefit society as a whole, as when wider use of public rather than private transport eases traffic on the roads.

However, as they divert scarce city revenues from good alternative uses, subsidies must be applied with caution, only in the absence of an alternative and in expectation of major benefits.

While the poor would be helped by subsidizing goods they consume, the subsidy would be of more benefit to the rich who consume more of the good. For this reason, direct, "targeted" payments, rather than subsidies for goods are the preferred means of helping the poor. In any case, city residents typically have above-average incomes and so do not really qualify for government subsidy.

Likewise, rather than subsidizing public transport, the government can achieve the same effect and raise revenue besides by taxing the use of private cars. Subsidy is therefore justified only if taxing cars is impractical and the subsidy can be shown to decongest traffic substantially.

The Financing of Public Goods. The financing of public goods is more difficult because charging directly for the good is either impracticable or undesirable or both. Some other form of funding, whether city tax revenue or special charges, must be used.

If the public goods benefit a wide range of the city's population, as public parks do, they can be funded from tax revenue. However, other public goods benefit only a small group. So, for example, building a good road or extending a main sewer to a new area of the city might benefit mainly the property development companies which can now demand higher prices for the houses or commercial buildings that they are putting up. Using city resources to fund such projects would be untenable. Instead, as discussed in Chapter 2, the city could use benefit taxation—levy a charge on the development companies based on the resulting increase in land value.

As in the financing of private goods, any loan incurred to produce public goods that will be subject to benefit taxation is amortized and the interest on it paid out of future benefit taxes. Projects for which no fee will be charged present a difficulty here. As explained in Chapter 2, loan finance would not be suitable in the absence of revenue with which to repay the loan. Small projects of this type should generally be funded from current tax revenue. Large projects which would not recur for a number of years allow the costs of loans (or property sales) to be spread out, although the loans must be repaid from future general tax revenue. Prudence therefore dictates that borrowing for such projects be carefully controlled to obviate service cutbacks when repayments have to be made.

EXPERIENCE OF OTHER COUNTRIES

Urbanization is expensive. The difference in cost between urban development and rural development lies mainly in infrastructure or urban public service costs. The private sector in many countries had an important role in infrastructure provision in the 19th century and until the governments and parastatals took over that role in the mid-20th century (World Bank 1994b). This pattern of development applied equally well to urban public services. Of their very nature (their status as public goods and the externalities and economies of scale involved in providing them), such services lend themselves to provision by the different levels of government, agencies, and semipublic bodies in many market economies. The tendency since the early 1980s to place greater reliance on the market has, however, revived private participation in financing urban infrastructural projects.

Widely dissimilar government structures, preferences, and accounting systems in different countries make it almost impossible to arrive at universally relevant generalizations about urban services of all types. However, one can look at the way they are funded by local governments, which in many countries are responsible for urban public services. The following brief summary of the literature, based mainly on Prud'homme (1987) and Bahl and Linn (1992), will help establish "average" revenue patterns which may not necessarily be the most efficient.

From a study, done mostly in the early 1980s, of the revenue statistics of local governments in nine Western industrial countries (excluding nongovernment entities in the utilities and other urban service industries) Prud'homme (1987) concluded that local taxes are the most important source of financing, apart from borrowing. The International Monetary Fund data he put together indicate a median share of 41 percent for local taxes, with a range of 11.2 percent to 69.2 percent. Grants and subsidies come next, with a median share of 35 percent. Other sources, largely user charges, account for the remaining 17 percent. Prud'homme suggested that if nongovernment entities providing urban services were included, user charges could well emerge as the most important source of financing, followed by central-government grants and subsidies (since many utility companies received transfers and grants from the central and regional governments), and finally local taxation.

While its precise "average" share is difficult to generate from the current data, borrowing to finance urban public services is certainly prevalent in industrial countries, particularly among local governments whose spending makes up a large share of the public debt. To fund capital-intensive infrastructure, local governments often have to borrow from the market or from higher-level governments to supplement current government revenues.

The financing pattern, according to Prud'homme, is thus: those services that are easy to price, such as electricity and piped water, are generally covered by user charges; other services are supplied by local governments and financed with local taxes or with borrowing or transfers from other levels of government. The central or regional governments may also provide urban public services directly.

The developing countries are a more diverse lot. Countries vary greatly in government structure, local-government responsibilities, and local urban population, and hence also in financing patterns and preferences. For lack of comparable data on urban revenues in developing countries that would allow a systematic analysis of the revenue structure and trends, Bahl and Linn (1992) studied the revenue patterns of about 40, not necessarily representative, cities in developing market economies in the 1970s and 1980s.

Table 4.1 gives the financing shares of local public expenditures by type of revenue, based on the median. Locally raised revenues are distinguished from external revenues (including borrowing). According to the table, local sources finance a median share of 70-80 percent of local expenditure; a share of 60 percent to 90 percent is typical for most cities. In other words, local resources are the major sources of financing for urban public services. This share of local financing, however, tends to diminish as local governments take on broader expenditure responsibilities and turn more to external sources, typically transfers from higher-level governments. Overall, the locally financed share declined in the 1980s.

Table 4.1: Percentage Shares of Financing
of Local Public Expenditure, by Type of Revenue,
for 37 Cities in Developing Countries

	Up to 1979[a]	*After 1979*[a]
Locally raised revenue	78.5	70.1
Local taxes	46.2	38.8
Self-financing	13.4	17.6
Other	7.9	7.8
Revenue from external sources	21.5	29.1
Grants and shared taxes	11.2	22.0
Net borrowing	8.7	7.0

Note: Data given are median values for each type of revenue.
[a] Only 12 of the cities were the same in the two periods.
Source: Bahl and Linn (1992).

Taxes account for over half of locally raised revenues in the "average" city, but again there is a wide variation. Cities providing more "general" services (such as education and public health services), which do not readily lend themselves to benefit-related charge financing, rely on local taxes to a great extent. As in Western industrial countries, benefit and user-charge financing is more important in cities where urban governments are heavily involved in water and electricity supply and other public utilities. User charges have grown in importance since the late 1970s.

Among the local taxes, the property tax exists in almost all the cities surveyed, and often dominates the revenue structure, with a median share of above 40 percent of the local-tax total. Other common taxes are levies on motor vehicles and on entertainment, industry and commercial taxes, and the sales tax. Although these are not significant as a whole, nonproperty taxes of one kind or another do provide the bulk of resources for some cities, and consumption-based taxes, rather than property taxes, have been gaining currency since the 1970s. Less common are local income taxes and property-transfer taxes.

On the average, the cities sampled raised about 30 percent of all their local revenues in the 1980s from external sources, mostly from grants and shared taxes. This low share of external funding indicates a relatively high degree of self-sufficiency among urban governments in developing market economies. Loan financing, with less than 10 percent of total financing, is generally the smallest revenue source for cities in developing countries, in marked contrast to their counterparts in advanced Western countries, which for the most part borrow to fund their capital outlays.

Bahl and Linn (1992) also found highly diverse patterns of change in a smaller sample of 21 cities for which time-series data were available. But, in general, locally raised resources determined the ability of urban governments to spend for urban services. These resources contributed most to increased per capita expenditure in some cities during the 1970s, and conversely were the greatest constraint on those cities that spent less per capita.

Bahl and Linn concluded that many urban governments in developing countries do not yet fully utilize their revenue capacity. Property taxes, motor vehicle taxes, betterment levies, and user charges seem to be the most underutilized revenue instruments. The possibility of raising local taxes is, however, limited in Western industrial countries, but user charges could be applied more widely.

URBANIZATION FINANCING IN THE PRC

As discussed in Chapter 2, local-government financing in the PRC is fundamentally different from the practice in most other countries. The difference is particularly striking in municipal government. Whereas cities in most countries require grants from higher levels of government to supplement local tax revenues, cities in the PRC collect more in taxes than they spend, on the average, and are able to remit substantial funds to higher government. In theory, the tax revenues remitted either belong to the central government or are shared between the central and local governments. Yet continual renegotiation of the basis for sharing destroys any real concept of tax-revenue ownership and means that, in the PRC, "locally raised revenue" cannot readily be distinguished from "revenue from external sources" as was done in Table 4.1.

Another difficulty in presenting PRC data to correspond with those in Table 4.1 is the absence of consolidated municipal accounts. Municipal activities are variously funded from budgetary and extrabudgetary revenues, as well as from special accounts that serve to accumulate house and land sales revenues and the like. The data relating to these different municipal funding sources are not gathered together in a way that allows a clear overall picture to be drawn. Tables 4.2 and 4.3 nonetheless provide data on the urban construction financing in the PRC. This definition of expenditure, while narrower than that in Table 4.1, is more closely related to the topic of this section.

The first column in Table 4.2 shows the average pattern of financing sources for all cities in the PRC in 1991. Like the cities covered in Table 4.1, the cities in the PRC derived their funding principally from local taxes (in this case, the urban construction tax), grants, loans, and user charges. Although, as explained above, meaningful comparisons of the share of local and other taxes in Tables 4.1 and 4.2 are not possible, it is worth noting that the PRC relies somewhat less on user fees (referred to as "self-financing revenues" in Table 4.1) and more on "other" sources (including the land sales and infrastructure connection fees discussed in Chapter 3). The other four columns of figures show widely varying shares for the different funding sources in the cities studied.

Table 4.2 indicates the changing pattern of finance between 1991 and 1993. The cities in the PRC raised only slightly more than double from the urban construction tax, Y58 billion in 1993, compared with Y27 billion in 1991, but finance from "other" sources almost quadrupled, to Y25.5 billion in 1993 from Y6.5 billion in 1991, perhaps reflecting a surge in sales of land and housing.

This increased reliance on revenue from sales of land and housing is worrisome. Such sales can provide much-needed finance for urban development, as discussed in Chapter 3, but also mean rent revenue foregone, as explained in Chapter 2. Although the rents may now be very low, as is the case for housing, they could become a significant revenue source following rent reform, if the assets have not all been sold by then. Moreover, selling the assets also raises the problem of where the revenue is to come from later when there are no assets left to sell. For these reasons, asset sales should by no means be seen as a costless way of raising funds.

Table 4.2: Sources of Urban Construction Funds, 1991 and 1993
(Percentages)

	All Cities		Guiyang		Anshun		Qingdao		Taian	
	1991	1993	1991	1993	1991	1993	1991	1993	1991	1993
Urban construction tax	36	23	77	45	66	76	55	28	13	26
Other budgetary funds	3	4	6	0	0	0	1	0	0	1
Central grants	1	1	0	0	0	0	0	0	0	4
Local grants	10	10	1	0	22	2	3	5	1	5
Water charges	1	1	1	1	0	0	0	0	1	2
Domestic loans	9	8	0	0	0	0	5	28	43	11
Foreign loans	4	2	0	0	0	0	0	0	22	0
User charges	11	8	6	8	8	16	22	15	3	7
Others[a]	24	44	10	46	3	7	15	24	18	45

Note: Figures in columns have been rounded off and may therefore not add up to 100%.

[a] Includes revenues from land sales, land-use fees, and infrastructure connection fees.

Source: Ministry of Construction (1992).

It can, of course, be argued that selling these assets increases the role of the market and allocates them more efficiently. However, urban governments should still use the revenue from such sales carefully, making sure that investments yield future financial returns, so that no severe cuts in the municipal budget become necessary. Some of the funds could be invested in financial assets that yield a proper rate of return.

Comparing Tables 4.1 and 4.2 gives rise to another cause for concern: the small, and slightly falling, share of user charges in urban construction financing. As explained in Chapter 2, such charges have considerable advantages and many countries have raised substantial funds through them. PRC municipalities need to look more closely at the proper application of user charges.

To give substance to these summary figures, the rest of this section examines some aspects of urbanization in greater detail. Three major urban infrastructure services—roads, water supply, and public housing—are considered, together with the manner in which they are financed by the cities studied.

ROAD FINANCING

Road construction financing through user charges is particularly well developed in the PRC. Higher revenues from vehicle license fees are financing the construction of elevated roads in Guiyang. In Anshun, toll revenues will finance some road improvements.

Municipal governments clearly find user charges an attractive alternative to scarce budgetary sources. Besides, as the road improvements are evident, the charges are easy to justify. This case therefore strengthens the arguments in favor of user fees outlined in Chapter 2. However, the issue of whether user charges are an ideal method of finance is worth raising. As suggested in the theoretical discussion above, a road must first be defined as a private or a public good to determine whether or not user charges are appropriate. An uncongested road should be regarded as a public good, for which no toll fees should be charged; otherwise, vehicles would be discouraged from using the road although such use does not add to its cost. License fees, which do not discourage the use of the road, would be more appropriate. But for congested roads, where the presence of more vehicles would inconvenience other users, toll fees are appropriate.

From casual observation in the cities studied, the choice between toll fees and license fees does not always follow from the level of traffic congestion. For example, there were uncongested roads for which toll fees were being charged. The point here is that, despite their general desirability, user charges are not to be used indiscriminately. Their applicability in any particular situation should be carefully evaluated.

WATER SUPPLY FINANCING

Water is a private good that is usually provided by the public sector. Because it is a private good, charging users the full cost of collecting, purifying, and distributing water is justified. Water charges in the PRC have nonetheless never been enough to cover costs, and substantial subsidies have had to be granted to the water companies from general revenue to make up the difference. In the past few years, water companies in both Guiyang and Anshun have raised their water charges to cover their operating costs at least. Whether the charges also cover interest and amortization for the very large capital costs is harder to determine. Certainly, the difficulty that Anshun has been having in raising money for an urgently needed dam suggests that its full cost is not expected to be covered by the revenue from the additional water supply. If so, water charges should be increased further.

The case of Anshun shows how reluctance to charge full-cost user fees can harm consumers. The shortage of water in the city regularly prevents the water company from supplying piped water to all city residents. As a result, the residents have to pay local farmers to carry water to their houses from the countryside, at a cost that is 60 times higher than the charge for piped water. This manifest willingness to pay for water at much higher rates suggests that consumers would be better off paying higher charges for piped water in the first place.

HOUSE CONSTRUCTION FINANCING

The failure to charge full costs is much more extreme in urban housing. Like water, housing should be thought of as a private good and full costs should be charged for it. The failure to charge fully for housing in the

PRC has led to seriously inefficient allocation of housing stock and to allegations of corruption. As discussed in Chapter 3, housing rents have gone up recently in all four of the cities studied, but are still well below the level required to cover the maintenance costs, let alone the capital costs.

Charging full economic rents (including maintenance, management fees, and capital costs) would enable urban housing operations to finance the building of new houses as the old ones become unusable. Instead, the cities in the study sample are selling off public housing to finance new building or are resorting to other means. As described in Chapter 3, while such moves have substantially increased urban living space, soon nearly all the public housing will have been sold and no funds will be left to finance new housing. In other words, sales of public housing are just postponing the time when city governments will have to raise rents rapidly to finance continued house building. It is better to raise the rents more rapidly now before there is a crisis in housing finance. In addition, higher rents will allow the government to realize higher revenues from the sale of public housing units that are deemed desirable.

ASSESSMENT OF MUNICIPAL BUDGETS IN THE PRC

This section analyzes the factors that determine the revenue and expenditure patterns of cities in the PRC and therefore also the nature and quality of the public services provided.

MUNICIPAL BUDGETS IN GUIZHOU PROVINCE

Neither Guiyang (the provincial capital) nor Anshun—the two cities in Guizhou Province that were included in the sample—has counties under it. The budgets of these cities will be analyzed later in the section; for now, a discussion of the provincial revenues and expenditures will help in seeing these budgets in context.

Guizhou Province. A province in deficit, Guizhou spent more than it earned in revenues every year between 1980 and 1993. However, the deficit decreased in proportion to expenditures over the period (Table 4.3). The alcohol and tobacco tax revenues remitted to the center have been outweighed by the subsidies received from the center, which include special assistance to Guizhou's minorities. These make up 34 percent of the population of the province. Most of the subsidies are quota subsidies, which have been fixed in nominal terms since 1988, but earmarked subsidies are also substantial. Table 4.4 shows that real public expenditure per capita has increased almost every year since 1980, despite the declining importance of central subsidies.

The relationship between the province and its prefectures mirrors Guizhou's deficit position (see Table 4.5). Only in 1992 and 1993 did the prefectures remit to the province more than they received from it in subsidies. In 1980 revenues exceeded expenditures in only two cities. As with the quota subsidies from the center, the quota subsidies to the prefectures have been fixed in nominal terms since 1988. However, in contrast to their large share in central subsidies, quota subsidies form only a small proportion of subsidies to prefectures, implying that the provincial government exercises far greater control over the levels of government under it than does the central government.

**Table 4.3: Guizhou Province - Fiscal Relations
with the Central Government, 1980-1993
(Y million)**

Year	Revenue	Expenditure	Total Subsidies	Quota Subsidies	Remittance to Center
1980	604.6	1,209.4	654.5	525.8	20.82
1981	559.7	1,256.0	742.2	578.4	23.93
1982	372.9	1,413.9	829.8	636.2	38.02
1983	872.3	1,554.6	870.2	656.4	60.52
1984	1,097.3	2,114.1	1,000.5	722.1	76.39
1985	1,717.0	2,387.6	1,154.1	743.3	43.99
1986	1,754.9	3,038.7	1,440.7	817.6	59.50
1987	2,154.0	3,160.0	1,524.6	858.5	63.48
1988	2,595.6	3,614.4	1,359.7	742.3	119.27
1989	3,213.8	4,589.2	1,359.3	742.3	82.78
1990	3,607.6	4,858.1	1,399.2	742.3	126.70
1991	4,562.1	5,587.8	1,290.2	742.3	180.39
1992	4,727.6	6,063.3	1,370.4	742.3	86.22
1993	5,650.1	6,738.9	1,192.6	742.3	23.36

Source: Guizhou Finance Bureau.

Table 4.4: Guizhou Province - Real Government Expenditure Per Capita, 1980-1993

Year	Expenditure (Y million)	Price Level (1950=100)	Real Expenditure	Population (million)	Per Capita Real Expenditure (Y)
1980	1,209.4	146.9	823.3	27.77	29.7
1981	1,256.0	150.4	835.1	28.27	29.5
1982	1,413.9	153.3	922.3	28.75	32.1
1983	1,554.6	155.6	999.1	29.01	34.4
1984	2,144.1	160.0	1,340.1	29.32	45.7
1985	2,387.6	174.1	1,371.4	29.68	46.2
1986	3,038.7	184.5	1,647.0	30.08	54.8
1987	3,160.0	198.0	1,596.0	30.51	52.3
1988	3,814.4	234.6	1,625.9	31.44	51.7
1989	4,589.2	276.4	1,660.3	31.84	52.2
1990	4,858.1	282.2	1,721.5	32.37	53.2
1991	5,587.8	290.4	1,924.2	32.71	58.8
1992	6,063.3	311.9	1,944.0	33.01	58.9
1993	6,738.9	358.0	1,882.4	33.32	56.5

Sources: Table 4.4; SSB (1994a); Guizhou Statistical Bureau (1994).

Table 4.5: Guizhou Province - Financial Flows to and from Prefectures and Prefecture-Level Cities, 1980-1993 (Y million)

Year	Prefecture Remittances to Province	Total Subsidies to Prefectures	Quota Subsidies to Prefectures	Net Flow from Prefectures
1980	214.6	375.1	162.0	-160.5
1981	288.7	415.6	187.5	-126.9
1982	361.8	458.0	203.1	-96.2
1983	457.8	515.9	209.7	-58.1
1984	495.1	584.0	231.6	-88.9
1985	536.3	761.2	161.6	-224.9
1986	553.7	776.3	224.8	-222.5
1987	700.2	1,146.5	240.6	-446.3
1988	926.0	1,164.6	216.0	-238.6
1989	1,108.4	1,547.4	216.0	-439.0
1990	1,286.2	1,558.3	216.0	-272.1
1991	1,433.7	1,470.1	216.0	-36.4
1992	1,365.0	1,332.5	216.0	32.5
1993	1,610.6	1,342.7	216.0	267.8

Source: Guizhou Finance Bureau.

Table 4.6 shows how Guizhou allocated budgetary expenditure among its various functions from 1980 to 1993. The major items were investment (including capital construction, technical renovation, makeshift building, and science and technology), agriculture and fisheries (including agricultural support), culture, education, and health (CEH), general administration, and "others" (a category which presumably includes food subsidies). The share of investment expenditure has substantially gone down since 1980, but mostly before 1988, probably on account of the transfer of the responsibility for industrial investment from the government to individual enterprises. However, the continuing decline in this item, which also includes urban infrastructure in-

**Table 4.6: Guizhou Province - Percentage Distribution
of Budgetary Expenditure, 1980-1993**

	1980	*1984*	*1988*	*1990*	*1992*	*1993*
Capital construction	20.2	16.3	10.2	9.5	9.1	8.4
Technical renovation	6.9	8.3	3.5	3.6	3.8	6.2
Makeshift building	1.8	0.7	0.4	0.3	0.3	0.3
Science and technology	0.6	1.0	0.7	0.6	0.6	0.6
Working capital	1.6	0.2	0.0	0.6	0.6	0.9
Agricultural support	4.4	5.2	6.0	6.7	6.0	6.3
Agriculture and fisheries	12.8	6.1	4.8	4.5	4.8	4.8
Industry and transport	1.7	1.9	1.9	1.4	1.5	1.3
Commerce	0.0	0.2	0.3	0.2	0.2	0.3
Urban maintenance	1.4	3.7	3.6	3.6	4.4	3.7
Urban employment	0.8	0.6	0.2	0.1	0.1	0.1
Culture, education, health	24.5	25.3	24.9	23.4	23.8	23.9
Science	0.4	0.7	1.3	1.1	1.0	1.0
Other administration	0.0	3.4	4.0	5.1	5.0	5.1
Welfare assistance	3.3	2.9	2.7	2.6	2.1	2.2
General administration	12.6	12.6	11.3	11.1	12.8	13.3
Law administration	0.0	3.2	3.7	4.1	4.2	4.3
Aid to poor regions	0.0	0.0	3.1	2.4	2.6	1.7
Others	7.0	7.9	17.4	19.1	17.1	15.8
Total expenditure	100.0	100.0	100.0	100.0	100.0	100.0

Source: Guizhou Finance Bureau.

vestment, indicates that budgetary funds are not keeping pace with the demands of rapid urbanization mentioned in Chapter 3. For this and other reasons municipalities have resorted to selling off their assets to finance urban infrastructure, as discussed above.

Table 4.6 also shows a considerable reduction in the share of expenditure on agriculture and fisheries, again occurring early in the period and possibly as a result of economic reform. The share of CEH spending in the budget has been almost constant, while the share of administrative expenditures has been increasing after an initial decline. A sharp rise in the share of other expenditures, on the other hand, preceded its fall in recent years, partly reflecting the pattern of expenditures on food subsidies, although other items are included here as well.

The distribution of expenditure by administrative level in 1993, as given in Table 4.7, reveals investment to be mainly a provincial responsibility; agriculture and fisheries, a county responsibility; urban maintenance, a responsibility of prefectures and counties (some cities are classed as prefectures, others as counties); and CEH, a lower-level responsibility. These and the other areas of responsibility shown in Table 4.7 are broadly consistent with the principles discussed in Chapter 2. For example, public capital construction is now centered on infrastructure, which could have significance throughout the province, while agricultural support and much of education usually affect only the immediate area. However, as we observed during our fieldwork, cities generally expect to take major responsibility for urban infrastructure and have recourse to alternative funds such as those generated by asset sales when they find their budgetary resources insufficient. The division of responsibility for infrastructure investment could therefore justifiably be reexamined.

The data in Table 4.7 have to be interpreted carefully because of the large volume of earmarked subsidies, which enable the provincial government to control lower-level expenditures. Such provincial control undermines one of the main arguments for local government: its ability to respond flexibly to the needs of the local people.

Finally, Table 4.8 shows the levels of extrabudgetary revenue for the province as a whole. These data afford interesting comparisons with those in Table 4.3. For example, extrabudgetary revenues in 1992 were almost half of budgetary revenue, but since more than half of these extrabudgetary revenues belonged to enterprises they cannot be considered available for public expenditure. Governments are able to provide public service because of the supplemental funds from local departments of finance and public service organizations. But even here, there is an important distinction. Local finance-department funds, like additional tax revenue, can be used for any purpose. The funds of public service organizations, on the other hand, are typically earmarked for specific purposes, such as road maintenance.

Guiyang City Budget. Table 4.9 summarizes the main features of Guiyang's budget from 1986 to 1993. The city was in clear surplus throughout this period, making upward remittances that far exceeded

**Table 4.7: Guizhou Province - Percentage Distribution
of Budgetary Expenditure, by Administrative Level, 1993**

	Province	*Prefecture*	*County*	*Township*
Capital construction	71.2	18.6	8.1	2.1
Technical renovation	27.2	48.1	23.4	1.2
Makeshift building	54.7	19.0	26.3	0.0
Science and technology	65.5	21.4	13.1	0.0
Working capital	71.7	17.2	11.1	0.0
Agricultural support	20.6	16.9	54.0	8.4
Agriculture and fisheries	18.7	19.4	42.1	19.7
Industry and transport	58.0	17.6	23.2	1.2
Commerce	65.8	19.4	14.9	0.0
Urban maintenance	2.3	50.2	44.0	3.5
Urban employment	18.1	26.9	55.0	0.0
Culture, education, health	14.0	16.7	34.6	34.7
Science	71.0	20.5	8.5	0.0
Other administration	52.0	6.7	24.4	16.9
Welfare assistance	5.1	15.8	68.6	10.5
General administration	10.8	18.7	39.6	31.0
Law administration	15.5	22.8	57.2	4.4
Aid to poor regions	3.2	9.9	71.3	15.6
Others	26.4	37.2	31.4	5.0
Total expenditure	25.2	23.4	34.8	16.6

Source: Guizhou Finance Bureau.

Table 4.8: Guizhou Province - Extrabudgetary Revenues,
1980-1992
(Y million)

	1980	*1984*	*1988*	*1992*
Total	547.1	948.6	1,856.4	3,024.0
Fiscal departments (1)	41.0	43.6	39.4	83.5
Administrative agencies (2)	105.2	221.3	450.7	1,099.4
State-owned enterprises	400.9	683.7	1,366.3	1,841.1
Fiscal extrabudgetary funds (1+2)	146.2	264.9	490.1	1,182.9

Source: Guizhou Finance Bureau.

the subsidies it received. Nominal revenues have experienced strong growth, but real revenue actually declined in 1993. Expenditure has outpaced revenue since the conclusion of a revenue-sharing agreement with the province which allows the city to keep 70 percent of any increase in revenue. Real expenditure per head has soared as a result, although it fell back slightly in 1992 and 1993.

More than 80 percent of the city's revenue throughout the period came from the three main indirect taxes (product tax, value-added tax, and business tax). This distinctive feature of Chinese local-government finance discussed in Chapter 2 makes large increases in public expenditure affordable to cities like Guiyang, with their strong industrial growth. But it also renders local expenditure vulnerable to reductions in tax revenues, as was the case in 1993.

Table 4.9 also shows the shares of major expenditure items in Guiyang's budget. The share of investment fell sharply from 1986 to 1990, but has since partially recovered. Expenditure on agriculture has been modest (as would be expected of a city) but shows an upward trend. Urban maintenance occupies a high but quite variable share, while the share of CEH is slightly lower than for the province as a whole and has stayed nearly constant. Administrative expenditure has increased its share significantly, for no obvious reason. Price subsidies grew rapidly until 1990, but have since

Table 4.9: Guiyang City - Budgetary Revenue
and Expenditure, 1986-1993

	1986	1988	1990	1992	1993
Revenue (Y million)	663	873	1,248	1,408	1,550
% Increase over 1986	...	32	88	112	134
Price increase over 1986 (%)	...	27	53	69	94
Real % increase over 1986	...	4	23	25	21
Turnover taxes as % of total revenue	84	88	90	88	85
Total subsidies (Y million)	93	196	209	195	316
Earmarked subsidies (Y million)	50	100	122	68	55
Total remittances (Y million)	463	646	862	945	1,041
Expenditure (Y million)	279	379	620	678	766
Real expenditure (Y million)	279	298	405	401	395
Real % increase over 1986	...	7	45	44	42
Population (million)	1.4	1.5	1.5	1.6	1.6
Real expenditure per head (Y)	199	205	265	253	246
Expenditure shares (%):					
Investment	24	15	11	12	19
Agriculture	4	4	5	6	6
Urban maintenance	17	15	14	20	14
Culture, education, health	21	20	17	19	20
Administration	7	8	7	10	11
Price subsidies	14	18	21	8	4

... not available
Note: Figures in this table were rounded off, hence, the apparent inconsistencies. All calculations were, however, performed on data before they were rounded off.
Source: Guiyang Finance Bureau.

plunged, as they have done all over the country—a welcome change in the pattern of expenditure.

Anshun City Budget. Table 4.10 gives the main features of Anshun's budget from 1986 to 1993. Like Guiyang, Anshun is a city in surplus, with remittances exceeding subsidies every year. However, the size of its surplus is very much smaller than Guiyang's. The total

**Table 4.10: Anshun City - Budgetary Revenue
and Expenditure, 1986-1993**

	1986	*1988*	*1990*	*1992*	*1993*
Revenue (Y million)	37	52	80	86	87
% Increase over 1986	...	38	115	130	134
Price increase over 1986 (%)	...	27	53	69	94
Real % increase over 1986	...	9	41	36	21
Turnover taxes as % of total revenue	53	66	68	66	73
Total subsidies (Y million)	17	14	16	16	14
Earmarked subsidies (Y million)	14	10	12	11	11
Total remittances (Y million)	19	23	33	30	30
Expenditure (Y million)	32	47	62	75	74
Real expenditure (Y million)	32	37	40	45	38
Real % increase over 1986	...	18	28	41	21
Population[a] (million)	0.22	0.22	0.67	0.68	0.69
Real expenditure per head (Y)	146	167	60	65	55
Expenditure shares (%):					
Investment	7	6	7	7	3
Agriculture	5	4	4	6	6
Urban maintenance	12	7	8	8	4
Culture, education, health	34	29	28	31	33
Administration	17	12	16	19	19
Price subsidies	6	13	4	4	2

... Not available
Note: Figures in this table were rounded off, hence the apparent inconsistencies. All calculations
were, however, performed on data before they were rounded off.
[a]The absorption of surrounding areas caused a sharp increase in the population of Anshun in
1990.
Source: Anshun Finance Bureau.

remittances shown in Table 4.10 have two parts. The basic remittance
is set at Y16.3 million per year, plus 20 percent of any increase in
revenue over the previous year's figures. In addition, the city remits 40
percent of increases in revenue from the product tax on alcoholic drinks

and other special taxes such as the tax on cigarettes, and keeps the remaining 60 percent.

A comparison with Table 4.9 shows that Anshun did not benefit as much from its revenue growth as did Guiyang. Revenue increased more rapidly in every year except 1993, yet expenditure grew more slowly in both 1990 and 1992.

Such comparisons are, however, imprecise. A substantial part of the increase in the revenue of Anshun from 1988 to 1990 probably resulted from its absorption of the surrounding, mostly rural areas, causing the population in 1990 to swell to about thrice its former size. The lower revenue potential of rural areas explains the less-than-proportional increase in revenue relative to the increase in population. More remarkable was the slower growth in expenditure compared with revenue from 1988 to 1990, and the consequent plunge in real expenditure per head, reflecting the much lower level of public spending in rural areas. The absorption of surrounding areas is not likely to have produced a significant shift in expenditure away from the original city area. The figures for average expenditure per capita after 1990 therefore considerably underestimate expenditure on the original residents of the city.

Even before the population increase of 1990, Anshun was spending substantially less per head than Guiyang, whose status as provincial capital perhaps prompted it to spend more. But it is also a fact that the less economically developed Anshun collected only about one-third of the revenue per head of Guiyang in 1986, and a still lower one-eighth in 1993. The smaller difference in expenditure per head compared with the difference in revenue demonstrates the redistributive effect of the system of subsidies and remittances. The differences in expenditure between two cities in the same province are nonetheless remarkable.

This lower level of expenditure per head probably accounts for the most part for the different patterns of expenditure of the two cities. As a measure of the vital role of education and health, Anshun allots a higher proportion of its budget to CEH than does Guiyang. Anshun also spends a higher proportion on administration, too high, in fact, to be justified solely by the requirement to provide a minimum level of administrative services. Spending so much on administration when other vital public services are severely underfunded certainly seems such a waste.

The lower proportions set aside for price subsidies, urban maintenance, and investment offset the higher proportions spent on CEH and administration. Less price subsidies may mean less waste, but the low levels of expenditure on investment and urban maintenance are cause for concern. A city that does not spend enough on urban infrastructure can hardly hope to develop its industry and so raise extra revenue in the future. Table 4.2 shows that Anshun has not raised enough from asset sales to supplement its budgetary funds for urban construction. The resulting difference in the quality of urban infrastructure between Anshun and Guiyang is obvious to any visitor.

MUNICIPAL BUDGETS IN SHANDONG PROVINCE

Both Qingdao and Taian, the two cities in Shandong Province that were covered by the study, are prefectural cities, with counties under them. As most of the available financial data pertained to entire prefectures, it was difficult to analyze the cities themselves and particularly to compare them with the two cities in Guizhou, which have no counties under them. Data for Qingdao and Taian cities, covering a more limited period, helped in making the comparisons.

As with the cities in Guizhou, some knowledge of the provincial context is essential.

Shandong Province. Shandong, unlike Guizhou, has alternated between surplus and deficit. According to Table 4.11, revenue exceeded expenditure in 1980 and 1985, but then lagged behind from 1988 to 1992. The province came back into surplus in 1993. The figures for subsidies from and remittances to the central government are incomplete, but, as suggested by the data in Table 4.11, the difference between earmarked subsidies from the center and provincial remittances of tax revenue determined the net flow of resources.

The pattern of financial flows between the province and the central government is made more complex by the fact that Qingdao became an independent "line-item city" in 1987. Table 4.11 and subsequent tables present data for the whole province, including Qingdao, to provide a consistent time series. But in reality, Qingdao in 1992 accounted for Y1,678 million of the remittance figure of Y2,427 while receiving only Y551 million of the Y2,847 in total subsidies. Therefore, without

**Table 4.11: Shandong Province - Fiscal Relations
with the Central Government, 1980-1993
(Y million)**

Year	Revenue	Expenditure	Total Subsidies	Earmarked Subsidies	Remittance to Center
1980	4,811	3,007	...	...	...
1985	6,753	5,130	...	930	...
1988	8,643	9,782	...	1,471	...
1990	10,911	12,385	...	1,627	...
1991	12,852	13,206	2,373	...	2,249
1992	13,932	14,570	2,847	...	2,427
1993	19,440	18,837	...	...	...

... Not available.
Note: Data for Shandong include those for Qingdao throughout the period.
Source: Shandong Finance Bureau.

Qingdao, Shandong has been in substantial deficit, which is covered by a surplus of central-government subsidies over remittances.

Table 4.12 shows that Shandong (including Qingdao) more than doubled its real government expenditure per capita from 1980 to 1993. The increase was partly due to the 1986 agreement with the central government binding Shandong to hand over all of its tobacco tax revenue to the center in exchange for a guarantee to keep its contract remittances at a constant level until 1993.

An interesting comparison can be made between Shandong and Guizhou in terms of the growth of per capita government expenditure. Tables 4.4 and 4.12 show that per capita expenditure grew somewhat more slowly in Guizhou. Shandong in 1980 spent slightly less per capita despite being in surplus, but by 1993 it had overtaken Guizhou. This rapid increase in expenditure could not have been due to faster growth of revenue, as, based on Tables 4.3 and 4.11, Guizhou's revenue grew substantially faster (1993 revenue was more than nine times the 1980 value) than Shandong's (1993 revenue was only about four times the 1980 value). The 1986 agreement between Shandong and the central government may have made up for the slower revenue growth of the province.

**Table 4.12: Shandong Province - Real Government
Expenditure Per Capita, 1980-1993**

Year	Expenditure (Y million)	Price Level (1950=100)	Real Expenditure	Population (million)	Per Capita Real Expenditure (Y)
1980	3,007	146.9	2,047	72.96	28.1
1985	5,130	174.1	2,947	76.95	38.3
1988	9,782	234.6	4,170	80.09	52.1
1990	12,385	282.2	4,389	84.24	52.1
1991	13,206	290.4	4,548	85.34	53.3
1992	14,570	311.9	4,671	85.80	54.4
1993	18,837	358.0	5,262	86.42	60.9

Sources: Table 4.12; SSB (1994a); Shandong Statistical Bureau (1994).

Yet the difference in per capita expenditure between Shandong and Guizhou was less than that between Guiyang and Anshun, even before the increase in the population of Anshun.

Table 4.13 shows how Shandong allocated budgetary expenditure among its functions from 1980 to 1993. The pattern is fairly similar to Guizhou's (Table 4.6), although Shandong spent more on CEH and less on investment. Over time, the allocation of expenditure in the two provinces also changed in similar fashion: progressively less went to investment and to agriculture and fisheries.

Table 4.14 gives the distribution of expenditure by administrative level in 1993. As in Guizhou (Table 4.7) this distribution conforms broadly to the principles discussed in Chapter 2: the responsibility for investment falls mainly on the provinces; that for agriculture and fisheries, on the counties; and that for CEH, on the lower levels of government. On the other hand, the provinces control too high a proportion of investment expenditure, as was pointed out in the discussion concerning Guizhou.

Unfortunately, for lack of data on the amount of earmarked grants made by Shandong to lower levels, it is impossible to judge the extent

**Table 4.13: Shandong Province - Percentage Distribution
of Budgetary Expenditure, 1980-1993**

	1980	1985	1988	1990	1992	1993
Capital construction	15.6	10.8	6.1	6.3	5.9	6.1
Technical renovation	7.8	2.5	1.1	0.8	1.3	4.1
Makeshift building	1.5	0.5	0.2	0.2	0.3	0.4
Science and technology	0.9	1.0	0.6	0.7	0.9	0.8
Working capital	3.5	0.0	0.1	0.0	0.0	0.1
Agricultural support	12.8	3.6	4.1	5.1	5.5	4.8
Agriculture and fisheries	0.0	4.7	3.9	3.9	4.3	3.8
Industry and transport	1.5	1.4	1.1	1.2	1.3	1.2
Commerce	0.0	0.1	0.2	0.2	0.2	0.2
Urban maintenance	3.1	7.0	6.5	6.2	6.1	5.6
Urban employment	0.8	0.4	0.1	0.1	0.1	0.1
Culture, education, health	28.9	32.7	27.4	27.7	30.5	28.5
Science	0.0	0.0	1.1	0.9	1.0	0.8
Other administration	0.0	2.7	2.9	4.1	4.2	3.9
Welfare assistance	5.2	4.8	3.5	3.9	3.8	3.8
General administration	13.0	13.6	8.1	8.6	10.9	11.0
Law administration	0.0	0.0	3.6	4.1	4.2	4.0
Aid to poor regions	0.0	0.0	0.2	0.1	0.1	0.1
Others	5.4	14.2	29.2	25.9	19.4	20.7
Total expenditure	100.0	100.0	100.0	100.0	100.0	100.0

Sources: Shandong Finance Bureau; Shandong Statistical Bureau (1994).

to which the province might be keeping its subordinate governments from responding to local wishes and needs.

Finally, the level of extrabudgetary revenue for the province as a whole is shown in Table 4.15. In both 1988 and 1992, this level almost equally matched budgetary revenue (Table 4.11). However, as was noted with regard to Guizhou, only the "fiscal" extrabudgetary funds are available for public expenditure, although enterprise contributions for education and other local services were perceived to be more likely in Shandong than in Guizhou. Shandong also has substantially more fis-

**Table 4.14: Shandong Province - Percentage Distribution
of Budgetary Expenditure, by Administrative Level, 1993**

	Province	*Prefecture*	*County*[a]
Capital construction	76.8	21.7	1.4
Technical renovation	11.9	50.5	37.6
Makeshift building	6.0	60.3	33.7
Science and technology	34.7	36.4	28.9
Working capital	0.0	6.8	93.2
Agricultural support	10.4	15.0	74.6
Agriculture and fisheries	14.5	23.7	61.7
Industry and transport	33.0	40.4	26.6
Commerce	79.7	19.6	0.8
Urban maintenance	0.0	43.9	56.1
Urban employment	34.0	44.2	21.8
Culture, education, health	13.2	17.0	69.8
Science	59.8	23.3	16.8
Other administration	14.4	27.0	58.6
Welfare assistance	3.4	12.7	83.9
General administration	5.7	19.6	74.7
Law administration	10.4	27.1	62.4
Aid to poor regions	25.0	0.8	74.2
Others	18.7	38.7	42.6
Total expenditure	17.0	26.2	56.8

[a] County data include township expenditures.
Sources: Shandong Finance Bureau; Shandong Statistical Bureau (1994).

cal extrabudgetary funds. In 1992 they were only slightly less than half of budgetary revenue, versus Guizhou's less than a quarter. This advantage is likely to be more important in explaining differences in service provision than the very slight differences in budgetary expenditure per capita that were mentioned above.

Qingdao City Budget. Table 4.16 summarizes the main features of Qingdao's budget from 1986 to 1993, based mainly on data for the prefecture. In substantial surplus throughout the period, the prefecture remitted over half its revenue directly to the central government and

Table 4.15: Shandong Province - Extrabudgetary Revenues, 1980-1992
(Y million)

	1980	*1984*	*1988*	*1992*
Total	2,506.8	4,234.9	9,171.8	13,700.6
Fiscal departments (1)	314.9	349.2	280.5	697.2
Administrative agencies (2)	434.3	794.6	3,011.7	5,378.2
State-owned enterprises	1,757.6	3,091.1	5,879.6	7,625.2
Fiscal extrabudgetary funds (1+2)	749.2	1,143.8	3,292.2	6,075.4

Source: Shandong Finance Bureau.

received comparatively small subsidies, about half of which were ear-marked. The 41 percent growth in real revenue since 1986 resulted mainly from strong growth in turnover tax revenues, whose share in total revenue has increased.

Until the reform of 1994, Qingdao's revenue-sharing contract with the central government allowed it to keep the revenues from any increase in turnover taxes beyond 5 percent. Remittances have there-fore grown more slowly than revenue, such that real expenditure has far outstripped real revenue.

Expenditure per head of the city population can be calculated only for 1990, 1992, and 1993, the years for which data on the expen-diture of the city itself could be obtained. These data show expenditure per capita in Qingdao to be substantially higher than in Guiyang and Anshun. Differences in extrabudgetary funds probably heighten these differences, as mentioned above. Qingdao had Y982 million in fiscal extrabudgetary revenues in 1992, more than half of the prefecture's budgetary expenditure. No equivalent data for Guiyang and Anshun are available, but the figures are unlikely to be as large since Guizhou's extrabudgetary funds were so much smaller than Shandong's.

There have been substantial changes in the shares of some major expenditure items for the prefecture, most notably, in the share of

Table 4.16: Qingdao City - Budgetary Revenue and Expenditure, 1986-1993

	1986	1988	1990	1992	1993
Revenue (Y million)	1,464	2,124	2,423	2,805	4,017
% Increase over 1986	...	45	66	92	174
Price increase over 1986 (%)	...	27	53	69	94
Real % increase over 1986	...	14	8	13	41
Turnover taxes as % of total revenue	61	73	77	73	76
Total subsidies (Y million)	257	306	533	551	468
Earmarked subsidies (Y million)	125	157	229	159	195
Total remittances (Y million)	1,137	1,176	1,657	1,678	2,241
Expenditure (Y million)	616	1,035	1,339	1,607	2,177
Real expenditure (Y million)	616	815	875	951	1,122
Real % increase over 1986	...	32	42	54	82
Proportion of expenditure that applies to the city (%)	...	...	0.73	0.72	0.77
City population[a] (million)	1.27	2.01	2.06	2.09	2.12
Real expenditure per head (Y)	...	...	310	327	408
Expenditure shares (%):					
Investment	9	7	7	17	31
Agriculture	4	4	5	5	4
Urban maintenance	15	13	1	13	9
Culture, education, health	24	19	19	21	18
Administration	8	8	8	10	8
Price subsidies	25	22	26	9	4

... Not available

Note: Figures in this table were rounded off, hence the apparent inconsistencies. All calculations were, however, performed on data before they were rounded off.

[a]The absorption of surrounding areas caused a sharp increase in the population of Qingdao in 1988.

Source: Qingdao Finance Bureau.

investment, which has increased dramatically. At the same time, the shares of urban maintenance, CEH, and price subsidies have fallen. The fall in price subsidies reflects the nationwide reduction in subsidies, while the relatively fixed expenditure needs for urban maintenance and CEH, both considered necessities, probably account for their lower share in the total expenditure of the prefecture.

Qingdao's expenditure shares for 1993 show that the city allocated 14 percent of its budget to CEH, less than Guiyang's 20 percent (Table 4.9). However, on account of its higher total budget, Qingdao managed to spend more, Y57 per capita as compared with Guiyang's Y49 per capita (in 1986 prices). This expenditure pattern coincides with the view, illustrated by Guizhou as well, that CEH is a necessity.

Taian City Budget. Table 4.17 gives the main features of Taian's budget from 1986 to 1993, based mainly on data from the prefecture. Prefecture revenue increased by 61 percent. The slight fall in turnover taxes as a proportion of revenue indicates that other factors—state-enterprise profits and miscellaneous charges—were primarily responsible for the increase in revenue.

The prefecture was in deficit throughout the period, as subsidies from the province exceeded remittances. Earmarked subsidies gained in relative importance and total subsidies decreased, as did remittances at the start of the period, before they increased in compliance with the terms of a contract setting an 8 percent remittance growth for the province. The fall in subsidies despite a substantial cut in the contract remittance in 1993, to offset the loss of a large revenue city from the prefecture, meant that real expenditure was not rising as fast as real revenue.

Data on the city's own expenditure were available only for 1992, when the city spent Y288 million against Y752 million in prefecture expenditures. The city's share of 38 percent was applied to prefecture expenditures in 1993 to get an estimate of its expenditure in 1993. Real city expenditure per head in 1993 was thus estimated to be Y113, a much lower figure than the corresponding figures for Qingdao and Guiyang, and higher or lower than Anshun's, depending on whether one looks at Anshun's figures before or after its population increase. Differences in extrabudgetary funds between Taian and Qingdao were even more marked. Taian's fiscal extrabudgetary revenue of Y149

Table 4.17: Taian City - Budgetary Revenue and Expenditure, 1986-1993

	1986	1988	1990	1993
Revenue (Y million)	241	407	520	753
% Increase over 1986	...	69	115	212
Price increase over 1986 (%)	...	27	53	94
Real % increase over 1986	...	33	41	61
Turnover taxes as % of total revenue	75	66	64	73
Total subsidies (Y million)	167	108	134	109
Earmarked subsidies[a] (Y million)	96	121	136	106
Total remittances (Y million)	89	34	46	48
Expenditure (Y million)	336	477	620	832
Real expenditure (Y million)	336	375	406	429
Real % increase over 1986	...	12	21	28
Proportion of expenditure that applies to the city (%)	...	...	...	0.38
City population (million)	1.34	1.38	1.42	1.44
Real expenditure per head (Y)	...	...	...	113
Expenditure shares (%):				
Investment	4	3	2	3
Agriculture	8	8	11	10
Urban maintenance	8	6	6	7
Culture, education, health	32	31	31	28
Administration	14	11	11	14
Price subsidies	19	19	16	6

... Not available
Note: Figures in this table were rounded off, hence the apparent inconsistencies. All calculations were, however, performed on data before they were rounded off.
[a]Earmarked subsidies exceeded total subsidies in 1988 and 1990 because of negative figures for other subsidies.
Source: Taian Finance Bureau.

million in 1992, less than a quarter of its budgetary expenditure, contrasts with the more than 50 percent share reported above for Qingdao.

Expenditure allocation in Taian is substantially different from that in Qingdao and Guiyang, but fairly similar to that in Anshun. Taian spends a higher proportion on CEH and administration than Qingdao (with its higher level of expenditure per head) and a lower proportion on urban maintenance and investment. As was pointed out when comparing Anshun with Guiyang, Taian's relatively higher expenditure on CEH and administration probably reflects in part their status as necessities. As with Anshun, such a level of administrative spending seems out of place, particularly when investment and other categories of expenditure are so seriously underfunded.

PROVISION OF URBAN SERVICES

The foregoing analysis of the budgetary revenue and expenditure of the four cities in the study brought out considerable differences in the levels and rates of growth of revenue and expenditure per capita. The present section analyzes the manner of funding and the adequacy of provision of the services that these expenditures are supposed to finance. Fortunately, most of the data, except for the level of funding per pupil in education, apply to the cities themselves, rather than to entire prefectures.

The analysis in this section will concentrate on two areas of service provision: public health and education (at the primary and secondary levels). These were chosen for their vital importance to all communities. Differences in the level of service are therefore unlikely to represent differences in the need for these services; rather, they represent differences in the extent to which common needs are being met and, for this reason, are matters of major concern to the public.

One important question suggested by the previous section is whether cities that spend higher per capita also provide better service. While a yes answer might be expected, differences in costs of provision, in the use of extrabudgetary funds, and in the efficiency of the service organizations may dictate otherwise. Measures of the level of service provided, as presented in the rest of this section, are therefore important.

PUBLIC HEALTH

Hospitals, clinics, and immunization stations dispense public health care. The immunization stations are funded by governments at the municipal, district, or township levels, while hospitals and clinics are provided both by government and by enterprises. Even patients in government hospitals have to contribute toward the cost of their care, although a large part of their contribution will come from their employer. Thus, the cost of health care is met by a combination of patients, enterprises, and government.

Not surprisingly, in view of the complexity of the funding and service delivery arrangements, estimates of total expenditure on health care in the four cities studied have been impossible to obtain. Information about the levels of service provision is nevertheless given in Table 4.18. The data exhibit a very striking pattern. Qingdao and Guiyang provide about the same level of service, above the national urban average, in terms of the ratio of beds, doctors, and medical personnel to the population. Anshun and Taian, on the other hand, provide approximately equal service at a substantially lower level than Qingdao's and Guiyang's and below the national urban average.

Table 4.18: Public Health Provision in Selected Cities, 1993

	Guiyang	*Anshun*	*Qingdao*	*Taian*[a]
Beds per 1,000 population[b]	7.0	3.2	8.1	3.0
Doctors per 1,000 population[c]	5.0	1.8	4.1	1.9
Medical personnel per 1,000 population[d]	13.6	4.0	9.2	4.3
Immunization rate (%)	95.5	...	100.0	100.0

... Not available.
[a]Taian data are for 1992.
[b]National urban average for beds per 1,000 population (1991) = 4.7.
[c]National urban average for doctors per 1,000 population (1991) = 3.3.
[d]National urban average for medical personnel per 1,000 population (1991) = 7.4.
Sources: Interviews with city officials; Qingdao People's Press (1994); statistical yearbooks of Guiyang, Anshun, and Taian.

This is broadly what might have been expected from the budgetary analysis in the section entitled "Assessment of Municipal Budgets in the PRC" earlier in this chapter. Qingdao and Guiyang are the two cities with the highest city expenditure per capita, while Anshun and Taian lag some way behind. Qingdao, with its higher income level, might have been expected to provide better medical services than Guiyang. However, as discussed previously, Qingdao's lower CEH expenditure share implies a fairly small difference in per capita CEH expenditure between the two cities. When it is also noted that the salaries of health workers in Shandong are higher than in Guizhou (Y3,339 in Shandong as against Y2,514 in Guizhou, according to the *1994 Statistical Yearbook of China*), the similarity between the two cities is not surprising.

PRIMARY AND SECONDARY EDUCATION

Like public health, education is funded with a combination of individual fee payments, enterprise contributions, and local-government allocations. Table 4.19 gives data on total expenditures for the four cities studied, except for the figures for Qingdao and Taian, which relate to the prefecture rather than the cities themselves. In general, government finance (general revenue plus education surcharges) funds at least two-thirds of expenditure, fees cover a very small proportion of costs, and other sources (including enterprise expenditure on schools, as well as donations and other self-raised funds) make a minor but significant contribution.

The figures for education surcharges cover both the urban education surcharge, on enterprises' turnover tax payments, and the rural education surcharge, on rural households. Essentially a tax rather than a service fee, as they do not directly relate to the attendance of particular children at school, these surcharges yield too little revenue to cover the full cost of education. This means that, although nominally earmarked for education, the surcharges are simply another financial resource for the municipality, allowing the latter to use less of its general revenue to support schools. In other words, these surcharges do not determine the amount of resources devoted to education and, from an allocative point of view, have no reason for continuing as separate taxes.

Table 4.19: Provision of Education in Selected Cities, 1993

	Guiyang	Anshun	Qingdao[a]	Taian[a,b]
Overall pupil-teacher ratio	15.2	32.3	20.6	14.9
Primary pupil-teacher ratio[c]	18.4	33.5	21.4	14.9
Secondary pupil-teacher ratio[d]	11.1	30.3	19.5	14.8
Ratio of secondary to primary school students[e]	0.46	...	0.69	0.53
Expenditure per student (Y)	696	169	534	437
Funded from:				
General revenue	465	142	249	225
Education surcharges	103	7	133	75
Fees	25	5	31	33
Others	103	15	121	104

... Not available.
[a]Expenditure figures for Qingdao and Taian are for the prefectures, not just the cities.
[b]Taian data are for 1992.
[c]National average for primary pupil-teacher ratio (1991) = 22.0.
[d]National average for secondary pupil-teacher ratio (1991) = 14.7.
[e]National average for secondary-primary school student ratio (1991) = 0.43.
Sources: Interviews with city officials; Qingdao People's Press (1994); statistical yearbooks of Guiyang, Anshun, and Taian.

Expenditure per pupil varies widely among the four cities, and the expenditure pattern does not seem to fully bear out the discussion in the section "Assessment of Municipal Budgets in the PRC." Despite spending less per capita overall, Guiyang spends more per pupil than Qingdao, whose spending for the educational needs of surrounding counties in addition to its own possibly reduces its average expenditure.

Another unexpected piece of information from Table 4.19 is that Qingdao has a worse pupil-teacher ratio than either Taian or Guiyang (and these figures relate to the cities alone, excluding surrounding counties), despite a substantially higher per capita urban expenditure and despite spending more per pupil than Taian. Qingdao's secondary school pupil-teacher ratio is even higher than the national average. Other than higher wages for teachers or inefficiency, no explanation suffices.

Entirely expected is the information that Anshun, which spends least per head overall, has the worst pupil-teacher ratios, well above the national average. This shows that Anshun has been unable to provide adequate education, despite the relatively high proportion of its budget for the sector.

CITYWIDE SOCIAL SECURITY SCHEMES

The move toward citywide social insurance schemes in the PRC started in 1984 when some cities began to reform the financing of retirement pensions. Regulations issued by the State Council in 1986 formalized the change in these five areas of social insurance:

- Pensions
- Unemployment insurance
- Medical insurance
- Industrial accident insurance
- Maternity insurance

Progress in some of these areas has been slow, but all the four cities studied had established pension schemes. The present analysis will focus on pensions, the area of social insurance that involves by far the largest amount of money.

Except for unemployment insurance, which is needed to cover a risk previously unheard of in the PRC, these areas of social insurance used to be provided by enterprises. The transition to a market economy made the transfer of this responsibility to the government necessary, for two reasons. Without such a transfer, the new possibility of enterprise bankruptcies would deprive employees of their pensions. Moreover, enterprises funded their pensions on a "pay as you go" basis, that is, pensions for current pensioners were paid out of current revenue and considered a cost of production. Older enterprises with more pensioners thus faced higher costs and so could not compete with newer enterprises, with their smaller pension costs. The citywide schemes were intended to allow enterprises to pool these costs so that they could all compete on equal terms.

The second argument suggests that pooling should be carried out over as large a number of enterprises as possible over as wide an area as possible; otherwise, enterprises in areas with more established industries (and therefore more pensioners) would be at a disadvantage. There has, in fact, been some move toward pooling across wider areas than cities. Shandong, for example, implemented in July 1994 a scheme that transfers money from those cities with insurance schemes in surplus to those cities with insurance deficits. But only 4 percent of surplus is transferred under this modest scheme. Guizhou similarly pools unemployment insurance, but not pensions, causing severe hardship in some poor, insufficiently funded, areas. In 5 percent of Guizhou's counties, pensions are only Y40 per month, versus the provincial average of Y180.

Designing pension and other social security systems involves many other issues, which deserve a separate study. This section limits itself to a discussion of how these funds relate to city finances.

In all the cities, the schemes are administered by the labor department, which collects the contributions from the enterprises and then arranges for the pensions to be paid. The funds are held and managed outside the municipal budget. As most retired workers still receive their pensions through their employers, the money passing between an enterprise and the labor department is simply the difference between the contribution obligation of the enterprise and the cost of its pensions. The contributions comprise the contribution of the enterprise (usually between 15 percent and 30 percent of its wage bill) and the contribution of the individual worker (usually between 2 percent and 3 percent of the worker's wage) which is withheld from the worker's pay.

Both of the cities in Guizhou that were studied have separate schemes for permanent workers (those hired before 1986) and contract workers. In Guiyang and Anshun, the contributions on behalf of the permanent workers are calculated to be about equal to the pension obligations. However, the same approach could not apply to contract workers, so few of whom have been retiring. Their contributions are accumulating in a fund which is invested in bank time deposits and government bonds. However, the scheme for permanent workers in Guiyang is now operating at a small deficit, which is being financed from the scheme for contract workers. Both Guiyang and Anshun plan to combine the two schemes eventually. The continued subsidy from the contract workers will therefore keep the pensions for permanent workers affordable for several more years with no need to cut benefits or raise contributions. But as more and more contract workers retire, the subsidy will no longer be available and a difficult choice will then have to be made whether to reduce benefits, increase contributions, or obtain subsidies from general government revenue.

It is not only Guizhou that can hardly afford pensions without continually increasing contribution rates. Officials in Qingdao reported that their pension reserves could run out before the end of 1994. For the PRC as a whole, pension insurance revenue was Y49.7 billion and expenditure was Y45.1 billion in 1993, and there was an accumulated balance of Y26.8 billion. But the annual surplus and the accumulated balance could quickly disappear as the contract workers, whose retirement rates are currently low, start retiring in large numbers. This worldwide phenomenon has been documented at length by the World Bank (1994b). The basic problem is the increasing proportion of the world's population that is above retirement age. The problem is particularly acute for the PRC because of its plummeting rate of population growth.

The obvious implication for municipal finance is that pension fund authorities, hard put to choose between cutting benefits and raising contributions, may instead seek the support of general government revenue to finance the payment of pensions at the current level. The financing involved is so large that it could come only from a substantial increase in taxes. A better solution is to come to grips with this urgent problem of pension financing now, as argued in World Bank (1994b), rather than to postpone having to deal with the problem for a few years by enrolling new groups of workers. The retirement age may have to be increased (at least for new entrants to the scheme) and other ways of saving for old age may have to be found. The pension funds will also have to be managed more efficiently to reduce administrative expense and ensure higher returns from investments.

These improvements can be achieved only if the central government plays an important coordinating role, preferably by merging the individual schemes into a national social security system. Besides conforming to international practice, such a system would simplify pension management for workers who move between cities during their working lives.

URBAN FINANCE ISSUES IN THE PRC

This chapter has analyzed the key components of municipal finance in the four cities studied and raised issues that are typical of many cities in the PRC.

The first section, "Theory and Practice of Urbanization Financing," showed that user-fee revenues must be increased to finance urban infrastructure, particularly public housing, but that some municipal governments are resorting excessively to certain types of user charges. They are also selling assets (land-use rights and housing) instead of applying proper user fees. As explained in Chapter 2, asset sales are similar to loans and so they should be contracted only after their impact on future municipal budgets has been carefully considered. It is better to increase the proper user charges now, to avert a financial crisis when there are no assets left to sell.

The next section, "Assessment of Municipal Budgets in the PRC," went into the very large differences in expenditure per capita on local services resulting from variations in revenue capacity, revenue growth, and contracting arrangements. It also suggested that much less is spent in peripheral areas of cities than at the center, and that extrabudgetary funds are amplifying the differences in budgetary expenditures. A fundamental change in the operation of the system of subsidies and remittances is indicated.

The third section, "Provision of Urban Services," brought out the equally large variations in service provision between cities, reflecting, to a considerable extent, the differences in expenditure analyzed in the preceding section. However, the significant deviations from this pattern of provision imply that city governments differ widely in the efficiency with which they are able to translate financial expenditure into service. Issues of equity and managerial efficiency must therefore be resolved before the PRC can deliver adequate public services to all its citizens.

The final section, "Citywide Social Security Schemes," showed that, despite their important contribution to the move toward a market economy, citywide social insurance schemes do not have a sufficiently sound financial base to last more than a few more years without major reform. If the issues arising from an aging population are not dealt with soon, these schemes will start to place a heavy financial burden on the cities that are responsible for them. The problems are best addressed by merging the individual schemes into a national social security system.

Chapter 5

RURAL PUBLIC FINANCE

by Christine P. W. Wong

R ural public finance has received relatively little systematic examination despite officials' frequently expressed concern that
county and township budgets are hard pressed and often in deficit. In fact, since over 70 percent of the PRC's population resides in
rural areas (including county-level cities and lower-level towns), the
ability of rural governments to provide needed social services and infrastructure significantly affects the well-being of some 800 million
people as well as the country's prospects for growth and social stability. The assessment of the financial health of the county and township
governments begins in this chapter, which examines the expenditure
responsibilities of the county and township levels and compares these
with available revenues. Chapter 6 will complete the assessment by
looking at how rural governments provide basic services.

Rural finance in the PRC today shows strong continuity with the
pre-reform past. The dualistic development strategy of "walking on
two legs" spawned policies in the 1960s and 1970s that called for a
self-reliant rural sector. The countryside had to take care of itself and
not impose financial burdens on the modern sector or government.
Under the system of collectivized agriculture, all rural services (health,
education, and social welfare) were funded from collective accumulation, an implicit tax on rural income. About 10 percent of the state
budget each year was invested in rural infrastructure. Supplementary
funding came from the profits of light industries run by communes and
brigades, consistent with the slogan "letting industry support agriculture" (*yigong yangnong*). To encourage rural savings and investment,

the countryside was left largely untaxed, and rural enterprises were exempted from virtually all direct and indirect taxes (Wong 1988, 1990). This concept of local self-reliance still guides rural finance today, along with its corollary of "letting industry support agriculture" *in situ*.

Compared with urban governments, rural governments have relatively simple expenditure responsibilities. In the PRC, rural governments provide few of the infrastructure services listed in Chapter 4 as typically provided by urban governments, such as housing, public transport, water and household sewerage, and garbage collection, or public amenities such as parks. Even rural roads and bridges are often a responsibility of the province, along with most capital construction except in agriculture. Broadly speaking, the breakdown of expenditures in Guizhou and Shandong provinces presented in Tables 4.7 and 4.14 shows that the rural sector (counties and townships) accounts for most of the expenditures in agricultural investments, education and health care, administration, welfare assistance, and aid to poor regions.

Self-reliant rural finance left a legacy of fluid and murky expenditure assignments, with a high degree of overlap in the services provided at the county, township, and even village levels. This is because each administrative unit was called on in principle to provide as much as possible for itself to minimize "dependence" on aid from higher levels. As resource endowment determined what each unit (or level) could do, the regions came to have differing expenditure responsibilities. In education, for example, even though primary education was provided mainly by production brigades, and middle schools were run by communes and senior middle schools by counties, a good deal of variation emerged. Some primary schools in richer areas were run by production teams, some middle schools by brigades, and some senior middle schools by communes. The running of medical clinics and hospitals similarly varied between regions. These differences still exist.

The first section gives a brief overview of the role of rural governments and their expenditure assignments. The next four sections deal with the status of government budgets in the counties covered by our fieldwork, with township finance at the fieldwork sites and public finance at the village level, and with off-budget finance and the efficiency and equity implications of relying on off-budget funds. The chapter ends by summarizing rural public finance issues.

ROLE OF RURAL GOVERNMENTS AND EXPENDITURE ASSIGNMENTS

COUNTY

Counties have redistributive fiscal functions, as noted in Chapter 1. They play a role in the vertical redistribution of funds by channeling resources from higher to lower tiers of rural administration—they are nodes for the distribution of funds from the central and provincial governments earmarked for agriculture, disaster relief, and poverty alleviation. By collecting remittances from rural townships and, at least in theory, redistributing these downward, counties likewise play a role in the horizontal redistribution of fiscal resources among the townships.

The primary concern of counties has traditionally been agricultural production and rural livelihood. In the planned economy, their responsibilities included coordinating and financing investments in rural infrastructure such as water conservation, land improvement, and road-building projects. Counties also invested directly in state-owned enterprises, especially those engaged in activities in support of agriculture, such as the production of farm machinery, chemical fertilizers, cement, and energy.[1] They managed the allocation of key supplies under planned distribution, such as coal, cement, machinery, and chemical fertilizers, and provided agricultural extension services and administrative support for industry and commerce. In addition to these production management and support responsibilities, the counties performed government functions such as administration, law enforcement, disaster relief, welfare assistance, and the provision of education and health-care services.

In the transition period, counties, like other levels of government, have shed much of their direct role in economic management—mainly their responsibilities related to direct investment in SOEs, material allocation, and price control. At the same time, they have gained new responsibilities. The growth of county towns has led to many counties acquiring "city" status in recent years (including two of the four in our sample). Even those without such status often have growing county

---

[1] See Wong (1982) for a history of the "five small industries."

towns and share some of the concerns of urban administrative units, such as housing and road construction, and supply urban services such as water and sewerage. Moreover, with the extremely rapid growth of township and village enterprises through the reform period, manufacturing has come to dominate the rural economy in many counties (and townships as well). The expanded role imposed by these recent developments on counties and townships significantly blurs the traditional divide between urban and rural government, thus bringing urban-rural and agricultural-industrial tensions within the same unit of government. In this sense, county administration has become far more complex. The breakdown of budget expenditures in the five counties in our fieldwork sample show that budgetary outlays are roughly divided into social services (40-45 percent of the total), administration (20-30 percent), and capital expenditures (10-15 percent) (Table 5.1). Agriculture, which takes up a significant share of both capital and administrative expenditures, has had a declining share in county budgets, while the portion allotted for urban maintenance has grown.

TOWNSHIP

The abolition of people's communes in 1983 reinstated the township as a level of rural government. Nationwide there are 46,500 townships and towns, down from the nearly 56,000 reported by the State Statistical Bureau in 1991, as a result of mergers. The 1991 total included 43,660 townships and 11,882 towns. Before 1992, Guizhou had districts (*qu*), an administrative level intermediate between counties and townships/towns. Zunyi County, for example, had 18 districts with 141 townships and towns under them; in 1992 districts were eliminated, and the 141 townships and towns were merged into 41.

Whereas the commune, at the apex of the three-level collective agricultural system, had direct oversight and management responsibilities over its subordinate brigades and teams, the township has no direct control over agricultural production in its subordinate villages. Table 5.2 shows that the expenditure responsibilities of townships primarily pertain to providing social services (principally education and health and welfare) and government services (administration of law and order and disaster relief). Infrastructure support to the economy—agricultural extension,

Table 5.1: Breakdown of Expenditures in County Budgets
(Y million)

	Shandong		Guizhou		Hebei
	Qufu	*Penglai*	*Zunyi*	*Puding*	*Xinji*
Capital expenditures	19.62	13.90	14.03	0.69	10.06
Capital construction	2.64	4.09	3.26	0.03	3.26
Agriculture	9.62	6.12	6.94	0.57	3.36
Urban maintenance and construction	7.36	3.69	3.83	0.09	3.44
Economic services	5.45	4.56	7.27	1.84	2.13
Social expenditures	57.40	42.52	52.97	11.56	24.41
Culture, education, science, and health	52.68	33.82	44.33	9.60	21.14
Education	...	...	34.19	6.88	12.52
Health	...	...	...	...	...
Welfare and disaster relief	4.31	8.39	3.89	1.15	3.27
Disaster relief	...	...	1.54	...	...
Aid to poor regions	...	...	4.68	0.72	...
Administration	42.92	18.87	30.92	6.67	15.48
Government	24.40	12.70	25.08	4.82	12.80
Subsidies	10.29	7.17	5.69	0.02	1.82
Price subsidies	7.47	4.24	3.75	0.02	1.82
Enterprise loss subsidies	2.82	2.93	1.94	...	...
Earmarked expenditures	1.20	1.97	1.42	0.04	1.53
Others	2.67	7.64	9.68	4.18	6.54
Total	139.55	96.63	121.98	25.00	61.97

(cont'd)

Table 5.1: Breakdown of Expenditures in County Budgets (cont'd)
(Percent)

	Shandong		Guizhou		Hebei
	Qufu	Penglai	Zunyi	Puding	Xinji
% of total:					
Capital expenditures	14.06	14.38	11.50	2.76	16.23
Economic services	3.91	4.72	5.96	7.36	3.44
Social expenditures	41.13	44.00	43.43	46.23	39.39
Culture, education, science, and health	37.75	35.00	36.34	38.41	34.11
Education	...	...	28.03	27.52	20.20
Administration	30.76	19.53	25.35	26.68	24.98
Subsidies	7.37	7.42	4.66	0.09	2.94
Earmarked expenditures	0.86	2.04	1.16	0.16	2.47
Others	1.91	7.91	7.94	16.72	10.55
Total	100.00	100.00	100.00	100.00	100.00

... Not available.

Notes: Expenditure categories are regrouped from Chinese data.

"Capital expenditures" includes capital construction, technical renovation, simple construction, science and technology, aid to agriculture, and urban maintenance.

"Economic services" includes operating expenses for production departments (*shiyefei*): agriculture, animal husbandry, forestry, water conservation, industry, transport, and others.

"Social expenditures" includes education, culture, health, science, welfare and disaster relief, and aid to underdeveloped regions.

"Administration" is government administration (*xingzheng guenlifei*) and operating expenses of other departments including law and order.

"Earmarked expenditures" comprises primarily expenditures of education surcharge and pollution fees.

"Others" sometimes includes aid to poor regions.

Data are for 1993 except for Hebei which are for 1992.

Source: Fieldwork data.

Table 5.2: Breakdown of Expenditures for Two Townships, 1993

	Daxindian Town [a]	Maguan Town [b]
Budgetary (Y)	1,725,861	1,901,069
% of total:		
Agriculture and water conservation	3.90	6.07
Culture, education, and health	42.82	57.43
Economic services	0.74	2.86
Welfare assistance	27.60	-
Government administration	22.79	17.83
Public security	1.35	-
Price subsidies	0.73	-
Others	0.06	15.80
Extrabudgetary (Y)	473,000	172,015
% of total:		
Above-plan childbirth	...	77.62
Land management	...	15.41
Local government administration	...	6.98
Self-raised funds (Y)	273,000	143,140
% of total:		
Education surcharge	...	23.75
Local training	...	6.41
Subsidy for demobilized soldiers	...	8.55
Subsidy for village cadres	...	57.01
Hospital registration assistance	...	4.28

... Not available.
[a] In Penglai City, Shandong Province.
[b] In Puding County, Guizhou Province.
Source: Finance departments of Daxindian and Maguan towns.

water conservation, farm mechanization, and other capital investments in the rural sector—is a county responsibility.

Because of the newness of township-level finance, townships are far less autonomous in fiscal matters than other levels of local government, as shown later in this chapter by the very high proportion of revenues they remit, as well as by the large subsidies returned to them. Moreover, the division of labor between counties and townships is in a state of flux. For example, nationwide rural education is a county-level expenditure in about 50 percent of the counties, but a township-level expenditure in the others. Zunyi County in Guizhou Province has devolved rural education to township management, but Puding County in the same province, after assigning the responsibility to the townships, shifted the responsibility back to the county level in 1994. More than 50 percent of the financing of rural education in Guizhou now comes from county budgets, since township budgets are often too small to cover even the salaries of teachers.

VILLAGE

After the agricultural collectives were disbanded, the traditional name of "village" (*cun*) was once more applied to the production brigades and production teams. In this section, however, the term refers to the former production brigades, rather than to the smaller units that replaced the production teams (usually called "small villages," or *xiaocun*).

Villages are not a formal level of government but have inherited a framework of governance from the collectives, including a residents' committee and a Party branch which share in village decisions. Particularly relevant to this study are the significant expenditure responsibilities of villages despite their having no independent fiscal powers. These responsibilities, such as salary or subsidy payments to village cadres, social welfare for the aged and infirm, and sometimes supplementary educational or health-care expenditures, are a legacy of the collective economy. All these were considered obligations of the collective which it had to finance from its proceeds. Since many villages still perform these functions, they must find new financing mechanisms, usually nontax levies on rural incomes and production. The level and incidence of these levies are all aspects of rural public finance.

STATUS OF BUDGETS IN FIELDWORK COUNTIES

As noted in Chapter 1, there were 2,166 county-level administrative units, including 371 county-level cities, at the end of 1993. Each county had a population of nearly 400,000 on the average, distributed among 21.5 townships or towns.

In fiscal terms, the rural sector is the opposite of the urban sector. Cities are "cash cows" of the fiscal system, while rural administrative units are revenue-poor, mainly because of the industry-centered tax structure. Per capita revenues are low; the average county budget is in deficit and depends on transfers from higher-level governments. According to data given in Chapter 1, revenues per county averaged Y57 million in 1993 as against Y74 million in expenditures, for a shortfall of nearly Y17 million that was financed by transfers.[2]

This revenue shortfall was pervasive at the county level, as confirmed by data on both Shandong and Guizhou. In Shandong data, 63 of the 99 counties (including 25 county-level cities) spent more than they collected in 1991—Y57.3 million in average expenditures (Y81 per capita) versus Y53.3 million in average revenues (Y75.4 per capita). As expected, the revenue-expenditure pattern was significantly different between county-level cities and nonurban counties. The former had average revenues of Y93.52 million and average expenditures of Y83.55 million; in the latter, revenues averaged Y40 million and expenditures Y48.7 million. Altogether, the nonurban counties spent Y635 million more than they collected, offsetting the Y243 million surplus of the county level-cities and producing a net deficit of Y392 million for the county level (*Shandong Statistical Yearbook* 1992). The narrower difference between county-level cities and nonurban counties in 1993 resulted in average revenues per county of Y71.7 million (Y100.4 per capita) and average expenditures of Y72.7 million (Y101.8 per capita), for a cumulative deficit of Y100 million.[3] In Guizhou, the average nonurban county had revenues of only Y24.1 million in 1993, or Y67.4 per capita. The direction of financial flows to the county level cannot, however, be determined for lack of expenditure data.

---

[2] These calculations are based on unadjusted total revenues of Y508.9 billion and expenditures of Y528.7 billion for the country (SSB 1994a).
[3] These calculations assume a total of 99 county-level units, with 82 percent of the total population of the PRC, the same as in 1991.

Three of the four county-level units in our sample are *"yiyuan* counties," with revenues exceeding Y100 million in 1993 (Table 1.7). This unfortunately makes our sample somewhat unrepresentative, since the PRC in 1993 had only a few hundred *yiyuan* counties. However, Zunyi is significantly different from the two Shandong counties. Its collected revenues of Y134 per capita in 1993 were twice as high as the average for Guizhou but still far behind Qufu's Y235 and Penglai's Y214. Puding, with its collected revenues of only Y38 per capita in 1993, faces a fiscal environment that is far different from that of the other counties, as befits its designation as a poor county.

COMPOSITION OF REVENUES

Tables 5.3-5.6 showing the composition of revenues for each of the four counties have two noteworthy features. First, the layout differs

Table 5.3: Qufu City - Budgetary Revenue, by Source, 1986-1993 (Percent)

	1986	1988	1990	1992	1993
Industrial and commercial taxes	76.63	72.40	84.05	86.73	92.62
Turnover taxes	64.59	61.09	71.95	78.03	86.32
Direct taxes on nonstate enterprises	6.03	4.53	1.68	1.68	0.56
Urban construction	3.26	3.75	4.43	3.02	1.88
Resource	-	-	0.06	0.62	0.53
Urban land use	-	-	0.92	0.45	0.26
Stamp	-	-	0.40	0.18	0.16
Investment adjustment fund	-	-	-	1.04	0.06
Construction	1.94	0.83	2.36	-	-
Others	0.81	2.20	2.25	1.71	2.85
Agricultural taxes	10.36	16.22	9.18	8.05	4.85
Direct taxes on SOEs	12.78	9.18	3.43	1.70	0.61
Earmarked grants	0.23	1.03	1.07	1.31	0.84
Others	-	1.16	2.26	2.21	1.09
Total (Y million)	20.89	33.99	43.87	84.52	143.58

"-" Not applicable.

Note: Data have been adjusted by accounting for SOE losses in both revenues and expenditures.

Source: Qufu Department of Finance.

Table 5.4: Penglai City - Budgetary Revenue, by Source, 1986-1993
(Percent)

	1986	1988	1990	1992	1993
Industrial and commercial taxes	80.05	82.22	79.36	79.44	85.37
Turnover taxes	57.87	66.00	55.41	63.56	71.58
Direct taxes on nonstate enterprises	16.14	9.40	6.62	8.44	6.09
Urban construction	2.57	2.69	2.80	0.01	2.55
Urban land use	-	-	0.53	0.46	0.20
Stamp	-	0.01	0.25	0.17	0.08
Investment adjustment fund	-	-	-	0.92	1.09
Construction	2.39	1.69	2.85	0.52	-
Others	1.08	2.43	10.90	5.36	3.78
Agricultural taxes	5.60	6.34	10.76	10.32	7.85
Direct taxes on SOEs	12.03	7.94	5.69	5.60	3.74
Earmarked grants	1.64	2.29	2.28	2.80	2.05
Others	0.68	1.21	1.90	1.83	1.00
Total (Y million)	38.31	45.70	60.62	77.49	104.52

"-" Not applicable.
Note: Data have been adjusted by accounting for SOE losses in both revenues and expenditures.
Source: Penglai Department of Finance.

Table 5.5: Zunyi County - Budgetary Revenue, by Source, 1980-1993
(Percent)

	1980	1984	1988	1990	1992	1993
Industrial and commercial taxes	80.98	76.97	82.06	81.34	82.51	82.61
Agriculture, animal husbandry, and farmland utilization	18.31	16.58	10.13	9.58	9.76	10.35
SOE income and profit remittance	0.20	4.68	6.21	3.49	2.84	2.01
Others	0.50	1.77	1.41	4.29	3.19	3.33
Education surcharge fees	-	-	0.19	1.30	1.70	1.71
Total (Y million)	19.93	28.83	69.68	81.61	117.24	142.41

"-" Not applicable.
Note: Data have been adjusted by accounting for SOE losses in both revenues and expenditures.
Source: Zunyi Department of Finance.

Table 5.6: Puding County - Budgetary Revenue, by Source, 1980-1993
(Percent)

	1980	*1984*	*1988*	*1990*	*1992*	*1993*
Collected revenues	20.60	26.06	37.52	51.23	52.05	59.10
Industrial and commercial taxes	12.84	15.29	24.27	37.91	33.41	40.50
Quota subsidies	39.32	41.66	30.01	21.50	17.70	19.11
Earmarked grants	39.88	32.28	27.27	25.09	27.38	21.04
Other subsidies	0.19	0.00	5.20	2.18	2.87	0.76
Total (Y million)	7.22	9.16	14.84	20.71	25.17	23.31

Note: Data have been adjusted by accounting for SOE losses in both revenues and expenditures.
Source: Puding Department of Finance.

between the two provinces but is similar for counties within each province, indicating that provinces set their own reporting formats and requirements for their subordinate counties. Second, the share of revenues from agricultural taxation is tiny in all four counties, despite the vastly different levels of revenue collection. Even in Puding, industrial and commercial taxes accounted for a steadily increasing share of revenues throughout the transition period, and made up 80 percent of collected revenues in 1993.

REVENUE TRENDS

The importance of industry and the industrial-commercial tax (ICT) to revenue growth is exemplified by Qufu. Table 5.3 shows the composition of its revenues for selected years during the period 1986-1993. Contrary to the national trend, Qufu's budgetary revenues have grown rapidly, at an annual rate of 31.4 percent since 1980 (unadjusted revenues), outstripping the GDP growth of 18.6 percent over the same period. Moreover, the growth in revenue has been accelerating. Revenue grew by an average rate of 31.7 percent during 1986-1993, and, since 1990, has grown at an average of about 50 percent yearly. In 1991 the city ranked only 18th among the 25 county-level cities in Shandong with a per capita collection of Y90, compared with the group mean of Y118 and Penglai's Y136. In the pooled sample including all 99 county-level units in Shandong Province, Qufu ranked 35th in per capita revenues. Yet by 1993 Qufu had become a *yiyuan* county with a revenue collection that was 70 percent higher than that in 1992, and 135 percent higher than its 1991 revenues. Figure 5.1 plots the impressive growth of Qufu's total revenues.

This remarkable growth in revenue collection is driven by the rapid increase in industrial-commercial taxes, by 27 percent in 1991, 56.4 percent in 1992, and 81.4 percent in 1993. A surge in the production of liquor, with local producers proclaiming winemaking to be a family tradition from Confucian times, is largely responsible. Much of the increase in taxes is, in fact, contributed by the phenomenally successful Confucius Family Winery (the owners are not descended from the sage) in Qufu City, reportedly the fastest-growing "name-brand" winery in the PRC. The winery has made significant inroads on the mass market; it sells well even in Guizhou, home of the famous mao-tai. This winery alone generated profits and taxes of Y110 million in 1993 (compared with budgetary revenues of Y143 million for the city during the year), more than double the Y50 million in 1992. Given the contribution made by the liquor industry to city revenues, it is not surprising to hear the mayor of Qufu declare repeatedly that "To be a good mayor means you have to run a good winery."

Revenues also grew rapidly in the other three counties during the late 1980s to the early 1990s, albeit somewhat more slowly than in Qufu. Revenues grew 15.4 percent per year in Penglai from 1986 to 1993. From 1984 to 1993, revenue growth averaged 19.4 percent per year in Zunyi and 10.9 percent in Puding. In all four counties, growth in industrial-commercial taxes, mainly turnover taxes, was responsible for the rising revenues. From 1986 to 1993, turnover taxes grew by 37.3 percent yearly in Qufu and by 19 percent yearly in Penglai; from 1984 to 1993, they grew by 20.4 percent yearly in Zunyi and by 23.6 percent yearly in Puding. The share of ICT and turnover taxes in total revenues is rising in all four counties, while that of agricultural taxes is flat or declining, direct taxes from SOEs have a rapidly dwindling share, and, somewhat surprisingly, direct taxes from nonstate enterprises in Qufu and Penglai are of progressively less importance in total revenues. However, counties experiencing slow growth in ICT revenues would also face slow growth in total revenues.

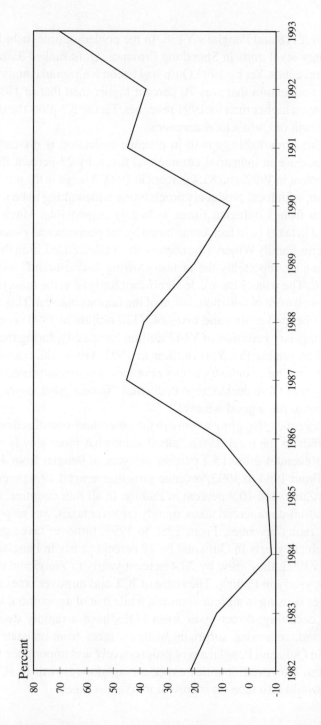

Figure 5.1: Growth Rate of Revenue in Qufu, 1982-1993

Source: Qufu Department of Finance.

REVENUE SHARING WITH HIGHER LEVELS

In 1994, of the four counties, only Puding received quota subsidies from higher levels; the others were under fiscal contracts stipulating fixed remittances which increased with revenue growth. Qufu's contract began in 1987 with a base remittance of Y3.03 million (Table 5.7). This amount was to grow by 8 percent if the county's revenues grew by up to 8 percent. If revenues grew by more than 8 percent but less than 15 percent, the remittance would grow by 8 percent plus 5 percent of the incremental revenue over 8 percent. In 1989 the county's expenditure base was adjusted upward, and the remittance base was reset at Y3.49 million. In addition, the county made annual special remittances to the province of 40 percent of the growth in liquor taxes. The county also remitted to the central government (bypassing the province) 5 percent of the urban land occupation tax revenues and the

**Table 5.7: Qufu City - Fiscal Interaction
with Higher Levels, 1980-1993
(Y million)**

Year	Total Revenue	Total Expen- diture	Total Remit- tances	Quota Remit- tances	Other Remit- tances	Total Subsi- dies [a]	Net Flows to County
1980	4.84	11.63	0.00	0.00	0.00	0.00	0.00
1981	12.46	10.02	0.00	0.00	0.00	2.54	2.54
1982	15.12	12.48	0.00	0.00	0.00	3.70	3.70
1983	16.92	14.85	0.00	0.00	0.00	4.82	4.82
1984	15.49	15.48	0.00	0.00	0.00	5.15	5.15
1985	14.44	24.16	0.00	0.00	0.00	12.04	12.04
1986	15.97	33.16	5.27	0.00	5.27	17.30	12.03
1987	23.17	33.14	3.39	3.03	0.36	11.54	8.15
1988	32.09	43.36	3.52	3.28	0.24	10.63	7.11
1989	38.58	49.43	3.73	3.49	0.24	10.17	6.44
1990	41.34	62.78	4.59	3.85	0.74	19.40	14.81
1991	59.91	72.83	7.59	4.27	3.32	17.99	10.40
1992	82.65	101.06	11.44	4.75	6.69	14.63	3.19
1993	140.76	136.73	18.61	5.13	13.48	11.05	-7.56

[a] Composed entirely of earmarked subsidies.

Source: Qufu Department of Finance.

county's share of periodic "loans" and "contributions." By 1993, because of the rapid growth of liquor taxes, these "other remittances" had grown to Y13.5 million, surpassing the quota remittance of Y5.13 million. The multistranded fiscal interaction of the county with higher levels is shown in Table 5.7.

Penglai's fiscal contract began in 1988, with a remittance base of Y16.25 million and an incremental growth of 8 percent. Table 5.8 shows that by 1993 this remittance had grown to Y24 million. "Other remittances" amounted to Y3.9 million, and total remittances were Y27.8 million, from total revenues of Y101.6 million.

In Guizhou Province, Zunyi County has been on a fiscal contract since 1986, when its remittance base was set at Y12.66 million and a subsidy growth rate of 5 percent yearly was stipulated. In 1993 the county remitted Y48.8 million under the contract, and 3.23 million in other remittances (Table 5.9). Because of its extremely low revenue

**Table 5.8: Penglai City - Fiscal Interaction
with Higher Levels, 1980-1993
(Y million)**

Year	Total Revenue	Total Expenditure	Total Remittances	Quota Remittances	Other Remittances	Total Subsidies a	Net Flows to County
1980	6.67	10.35	1.75	1.70	0.05	3.01	1.26
1981	16.82	10.69	10.50	10.50	0.00	2.87	-7.62
1982	18.17	15.48	10.28	10.28	0.00	6.40	-3.88
1983	21.74	17.02	12.35	12.35	0.00	5.09	-7.26
1984	24.17	20.64	13.80	13.80	0.00	5.54	-8.26
1985	34.07	21.53	18.17	18.17	0.00	4.50	-13.67
1986	35.30	28.91	18.36	18.36	0.00	8.05	-10.31
1987	37.29	31.72	14.89	14.89	0.00	11.12	-3.77
1988	43.77	45.20	16.25	16.25	0.00	15.40	-0.85
1989	49.74	45.73	18.31	17.55	0.76	12.48	-5.83
1990	56.07	57.83	19.91	18.95	0.95	19.72	-0.19
1991	66.96	60.76	22.80	20.54	2.26	16.19	-6.61
1992	73.17	68.46	24.62	22.18	2.44	16.74	-7.88
1993	101.59	93.70	27.83	23.95	3.88	17.43	-10.40

a Composed entirely of earmarked subsidies.
Source: Penglai Department of Finance.

Table 5.9: Zunyi County - Fiscal Interaction with Higher Levels, 1980-1993
(Y million)

Year	Total Revenue	Total Expenditure	Total Remittances	Quota Remittances	Other Remittances	Total Subsidies	Quota Subsidies	Earmarked Subsidies	Other Subsidies	Net Flows to County
1980	19.93	19.33	7.06	3.18	3.88	6.18	0.00	6.18	0.00	-0.88
1984	28.83	34.12	7.58	0.00	7.58	9.72	0.00	7.37	2.35	2.14
1988	69.68	53.52	25.13	24.10	1.03	15.48	0.00	17.86	-2.38	-9.65
1990	81.30	83.01	32.41	27.41	5.00	30.86	5.78	20.28	4.80	-1.55
1992	115.35	100.46	50.08	39.59	10.49	35.19	8.80	18.81	7.58	-14.89
1993	140.47	120.04	52.00	48.77	3.23	30.97	17.16	13.05	0.76	-21.03

Source: Zunyi Department of Finance.

capacity, Puding County has always received quota subsidies from higher levels to help cover its fiscal expenditures. A subsidy growth rate of 10 percent per year during the period 1980-1985 was stipulated, although the growth was actually lower, as shown by data in Table 5.10. Since 1988, this fixed subsidy has been frozen at Y4.45 million.

EARMARKED AND OTHER SUBSIDIES

While three of the four counties remit surplus revenues to higher levels, all four receive earmarked subsidies. In 1993, these subsidies amounted to Y11.05 million (Y18.1 per capita) for Qufu, Y17.4 million (Y35.6) for Penglai, Y13.05 million (Y10) for Zunyi, and Y4.9 million (Y13.6) for Puding. These financed 13 percent of Qufu's expenditures, 36 percent of Penglai's, 8 percent of Zunyi's, and 56 percent of Puding's.

Table 5.10: Puding City - Fiscal Interaction
with Higher Levels, 1980-1993
(Y million)

Year	Total Revenue	Total Expenditure	Total Remittances	Total Subsidies	Quota Subsidies	Earmarked Subsidies	Other Subsidies	Net Flows to County
1980	1.49	6.67	0.00	5.73	2.84	2.88	0.01	5.73
1981	1.78	6.36	0.64	5.22	3.13	1.75	0.35	4.58
1982	2.23	6.77	1.06	5.54	3.38	2.07	0.09	4.48
1983	2.45	8.38	1.00	6.59	3.50	3.08	0.00	5.59
1984	2.39	10.19	0.97	6.78	3.82	2.96	0.00	5.81
1985	3.11	10.25	0.14	7.98	2.63	5.35	0.00	7.84
1986	2.47	10.43	0.16	9.09	3.13	4.52	1.44	8.93
1987	4.44	13.25	0.44	9.30	3.28	5.21	0.80	8.86
1988	5.57	14.16	1.10	9.27	4.45	4.05	0.77	8.18
1989	7.68	16.50	1.24	9.62	4.45	5.06	0.10	8.38
1990	10.61	19.43	1.77	10.10	4.45	5.20	0.45	8.33
1991	11.30	23.41	0.93	11.52	4.45	6.31	0.76	10.59
1992	13.10	23.57	0.88	12.07	4.45	6.89	0.72	11.19
1993	13.78	25.00	0.86	9.54	4.45	4.90	0.18	8.67

Source: Puding Department of Finance.

Tables 5.11 and 5.12 show the various uses of these earmarked funds in Qufu and Penglai, respectively. Price subsidies are the largest component in both cities—these are mainly disbursed from the central budget to cover some of the costs of maintaining the low retail price of grain and oil in cities. Even though urban retail prices for grain and oil were freed to market determination in mid-1992, these subsidy payments have continued, partly to build up grain reserves for price stabilization, but also partly to repay the huge accumulated debt in the grain system (discussed in Chapter 8). Other main uses of earmarked funds are agricultural support, investment in agricultural infrastructure (including TVEs), welfare assistance and disaster relief, and urban maintenance. All but the last item (urban maintenance) are pass-throughs from central and provincial grants. The higher levels of earmarked subsidies for Qufu and Penglai in per capita terms, compared with those for Zunyi and Puding, are probably due to their larger grain subsidy and urban maintenance allocations.

Table 5.11: Qufu City - Distribution of Earmarked Grants, by Use, 1993

	Amount (Y thousand)	% of Total
Enterprise renovation	150	1.4
Agricultural support	2,070	18.7
Agriculture, forestry, and fisheries administration	810	7.3
Urban youth job placement	20	0.2
Culture, education, health	1,240	11.2
Education	260	2.4
Health	310	2.8
Other administration	750	6.8
Welfare assistance	1,280	11.6
Administration	100	0.9
Law administration	90	0.8
Price subsidies	3,100	28.1
Others	1,440	13.0
Total	11,050	100.0

Source: Qufu City Finance Bureau.

**Table 5.12: Penglai City - Distribution of Earmarked
Grants, by Use, 1993**

	Amount (Y thousand)	% of Total
Three science and technology fees	80	0.5
Enterprise renovation	110	0.6
Agricultural support	2,720	15.6
Agriculture, forestry, and fisheries administration	610	3.5
Industry and transport administration	120	0.7
Urban maintenance	1,350	7.7
Urban youth job placement	10	0.1
Culture, education, health	610	3.5
Education	200	1.1
Health	180	1.0
Other administration	800	4.6
Welfare assistance	3,010	17.3
Administration	530	3.0
Law administration	220	1.3
Price subsidies	3,740	21.5
Others	3,520	20.2
Total	17,430	100.0

Source: Penglai City Finance Bureau.

ASSESSMENT

In three of the four counties, transfers have declined as a proportion of total revenues, as shown in Figure 5.2. (The share of transfers in provincial revenues was shown in *Fiscal Management and Economic Reform in the People's Republic of China*, and in Tables 4.3, 4.5, and 4.11 for Guizhou and Shandong provinces). In Qufu the ratio of total remittance to total revenues fell from 33 percent in 1986 to 13 percent in 1993. In Penglai it fell from over 60 percent in the early 1980s to 27 percent in 1993. In Puding, subsidies financed about 80 percent of the county's budget through the mid-1980s, but fell to just 40 percent in 1993. These declining shares are consistent with the national trend toward self-financing in every administrative unit (see Wong, Heady,

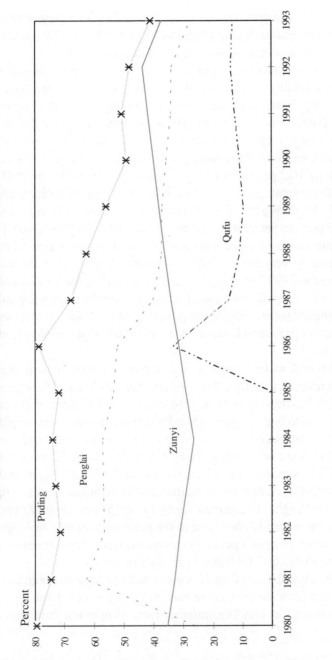

Figure 5.2: Transfers as a Proportion of Revenues, 1980-1993

Note: Data for Qufu, Penglai, and Zunyi refer to remittances as a percent of revenues; for Puding data refer to subsidies as a percent of the sum of subsidies and revenues.

and Woo 1995). The conspicuous exception is Zunyi County, whose remittance rates gradually rose from 1984 to 1992, to over 40 percent of revenues, before declining to about 37 percent in 1993.

While it is obviously imprudent to generalize from this small sample, three findings merit special attention. The first is the fiscal state of Puding County. On the face of it, the county's rising rate of revenue self-sufficiency is a positive development, indicating that incentives may be working to stimulate tax effort in the county. Indeed, in recent years the county has made good progress in raising revenues, which grew by 10.2 percent per year in real terms from 1988 to 1993, faster than the revenue growth in other fieldwork counties except Qufu (Table 5.13). Yet during the same period the county's expenditures grew by only 2.9 percent per year in real terms because of declining subsidies. This situation is of concern because per capita fiscal expenditures in Puding remain very low. At Y69 it was only 37 percent of the national average in 1993,[4] and very low compared with Qufu's Y224 and Penglai's Y192. At such low expenditures, pushing the county toward self-financing means prolonging the government's inability to meet its responsibility of providing basic services, a problem that is highlighted in Chapter 6.

The second salient point is the apparent counterequalizing direction of revenue transfers. When all components of fiscal flows are considered, it can be seen in Table 5.14 that Penglai, Qufu, and Zunyi are net remitters to higher levels, while Puding is a net recipient. (Qufu was actually a net recipient every year from 1980 to 1992. Only in 1993 did it become a net remitter.) In 1993 Penglai remitted 2.4 percent of its collected revenues under its fiscal contract, Qufu 3.6 percent, and Zunyi 34 percent. Including other remittances, the remittance rates were 2.7 percent for Penglai, 13.2 percent for Qufu, and 37 percent for Zunyi. These rates are inversely correlated to the per capita income rankings of the three units. Penglai's per capita income is nearly three times that of Qufu, and Zunyi lags far behind the other two.

The situation of Zunyi County is noteworthy because its remittance rate seems too high for its income and budgetary status. Even more noteworthy is the fact that its remittance rates were rising throughout

---

[4] The national average was Y185, derived as an unweighted average of total expenditures of Y74 million for an average county, divided by an average population of 400,000.

Table 5.13: Real Revenue and Expenditure Trends in Four Counties, 1980-1993
(Y million)

Year	Price Level (1950=100)	Qufu Total Revenue	Qufu Total Expenditure	Penglai Total Revenue	Penglai Total Expenditure	Zunyi Total Revenue	Zunyi Total Expenditure	Puding Total Revenue	Puding Total Expenditure
1980	146.9	3.29	7.92	4.54	7.05	13.57	13.16	1.01	4.54
1981	150.4	8.28	6.66	11.18	7.11	...	...	1.18	4.23
1982	153.3	9.86	8.14	11.85	10.10	...	...	1.45	4.41
1983	155.6	10.87	9.54	13.97	10.94	...	...	1.57	5.38
1984	160.0	9.68	9.68	15.11	12.90	18.02	21.33	1.49	6.37
1985	174.1	8.29	13.88	19.57	12.37	...	...	1.79	5.89
1986	184.5	8.66	17.97	19.13	15.67	...	...	1.34	5.66
1987	198.0	11.70	16.74	18.83	16.02	...	...	2.24	6.69
1988	234.6	13.68	18.48	18.66	19.27	29.70	22.81	2.37	6.04
1989	276.4	13.96	17.88	18.00	16.54	...	...	2.78	5.97
1990	282.2	14.65	22.25	19.87	20.49	28.81	29.42	3.76	6.88
1991	290.4	20.63	25.08	23.06	20.92	...	...	3.89	8.06
1992	311.9	26.50	32.40	23.46	21.95	36.98	32.21	4.20	7.56
1993	358.0	39.32	38.19	28.38	26.17	39.24	33.53	3.85	6.98
Annual growth rates, 1988-1993 (%)		23.50	15.60	8.70	6.30	5.70	8.00	10.20	2.90

... Not available.

Sources: SSB (1994a): Finance departments of Qufu, Penglai, Zunyi, and Puding counties.

**Table 5.14:   Comparison of Remittance Rates
Across Counties, 1993**

Per Capita Figures (Y)	Qufu	Penglai	Zunyi	Puding
GDP	2,717	7,248	1,298	438
Contracted remittance	8.4	48.9	37.5	-12.4
Total remittance	30.5	56.9	40.0	-10.0
Net transfer	-12.4	-21.3	-16.7	24.1
Revenue	230.0	207.6	134.0	38.0
Expenditure	223.8	191.5	94.0	69.0
Total remittance as % of revenue	13.3	27.4	29.8	-26.3
Collected revenue as % of GDP	8.5	2.9	10.3	8.7

Sources: Tables 5.7-5.10; provincial statistical yearbooks.

the late 1980s and early 1990s, contrary to the national trend. This finding, together with the one mentioned above, gives rise to the hypothesis that provincial location is the most important determinant of a county's fiscal status. Rich counties in poor provinces like Guizhou have to bear a greater part of the burden of financing intraprovincial redistribution than similar counties in a richer province. The rising remittance rates for Zunyi may have resulted from the declining resource transfers from the central government to Guizhou Province, and the cost of self-financing at the provincial level. This interpretation seems to be supported by the higher ratio of collected revenue to GDP in the two Guizhou counties, despite their much lower incomes compared with the Shandong counties (Table 5.14). It is also consistent with Susan Whiting's analysis of township finance in Shanghai, Jiangsu, and Zhejiang provinces (Whiting 1993).

TOWNSHIP FINANCE

The township was created as an administrative unit in October 1983, following a State Council ruling that townships should replace peoples' communes. At that time, township budgets were part of county budgets—all revenues were collected by the counties and all expenditures at the township level were disbursed from county budgets. Since the late 1980s, all provinces except Tibet have set up fiscal departments at the township level, with 253,000 personnel in more than 46,000 bureaus (each one with an average of five staff members). However, this process of separating township from county finance has proceeded at different rates across provinces. Some townships acquired independent budgets beginning in 1986; other townships in provinces like Shandong and Guizhou still have budgets that are very much incomplete, and many of their expenditures continue to be allocated directly from the county budget. Since February 1993, townships have also set up 126,000 treasuries to handle tax receipts, with accounts at branches of the Agricultural Bank and the Industrial Commercial Bank.

Budgetary resources available to townships vary widely. Among the 46,500 townships nationwide, six had annual revenues exceeding Y100 million in 1993; these are called *"yiyuan xiang"* and are all located in Guangdong Province. Another 936 townships had revenues of Y10-Y100 million, and 2,430 had revenues of Y5-Y10 million, while more than 30,000 had revenues of less than Y1 million. The average township had revenues of Y1.4 million and expenditures of Y1 million. In per capita terms, these translated into Y70 in budgetary revenues, and Y50 in expenditures.[5] At the aggregate level, townships had a total surplus of revenues over expenditures of Y18.7 billion in 1993.[6]

Given the limited buoyancy of agricultural taxation, townships also depend on industries for revenue growth. The growth of TVEs in recent years has enlarged the share of townships in the nation's consolidated revenues. However, since TVEs are distributed unequally over the countryside, revenue capacity is just as uneven. Our fieldwork showed a very high correlation between the share of revenues from ICT and the level of per capita revenues in each township.[7]

COMPOSITION OF REVENUES

Budgetary revenues at the township level consist of minor local taxes paid by local taxpayers, including the agricultural tax, the agricultural

---

[5] Based on an estimated average population of 20,000 per township.
[6] Calculated as the gap between the share of townships in aggregate total revenues and total expenditures (Ministry of Finance).
[7] This finding is supported by other studies, such as Sun Tanzhen (1994) and Oi (1992).

special products tax, the farmland utilization tax, the animal slaughter tax, and the title tax. Tax revenues of SOEs—even those in the rural areas—do not accrue to townships.

Budgetary accounts for four townships are presented in Tables 5.15-5.18. Several points are noteworthy. First, the accounts are simple, and reporting categories are coarse. Relatively few taxes are collected: industrial-commercial taxes, agricultural taxes, and, since 1991, the new special agricultural products tax. Third, there is a high correlation between the share of revenues from ICT and the level of per capita revenue in each township, with the richer townships collecting the bulk of their revenues from industry and commerce. Profits remitted by township enterprises and management fees paid by TVEs do not appear in budgetary accounts. Instead, these funds are kept in a different account, as "self-raised funds."

REVENUE SHARING WITH COUNTIES

Four types of revenue-sharing arrangements are in use at the township level. The most common form is the fixed-rate remittance of incremental revenues (type 1). "Sharing total revenues" (type 2) is the form most

**Table 5.15: Maguan Town (Puding County, Guizhou)
Budgetary Revenue, 1992 and 1993**

	1992	1993
Collected revenue (Y)	626,159	1,323,547
Per capita revenue (Y)	8	16
% Shares of total revenue:		
Industrial and commercial taxes	37.78	54.70
Agriculture, animal husbandry, and	43.17	22.28
farmland utilization		
Agriculture and animal husbandry tax	40.77	21.00
Special product tax	0.95	1.01
Title	1.45	0.27
Others	19.05	23.02

Source: Maguan Town Finance Bureau.

Table 5.16: Shiban Town (Zunyi County, Guizhou) Budgetary Revenue, 1993

Collected revenue (Y million)	1.27
Per capita revenue (Y)	40.00
% Shares of total revenue:	
Industrial and commercial tax	4.34
Tobacco product tax	35.34
Agriculture and animal husbandry tax	12.24

Source: Shiban Town Finance Bureau.

Table 5.17: Daxindian Town (Penglai City, Shandong) Budgetary Revenue, 1993

Collected revenue (Y million)	3.13
Per capita revenue (Y)	136.00
% Shares of total revenue:	
Industrial and commercial tax	92.97
Product	8.02
Value-added	40.89
Business	6.77
Collectively owned enterprise income	2.08
Individually owned enterprise income	0.00
Urban construction	2.24
Consolidated industrial and commercial	23.19
Vehicle utilization	0.45
Urban land use	0.99
Housing	1.53
Investment adjustment fund	1.41
Others	5.40
Agriculture, animal husbandry, and farmland utilization	7.03

Source: Daxindian Town Finance Bureau.

**Table 5.18: Nanzhiqiu Township (Xinji City, Hebei)
Budgetary Revenue, 1986-1993**

			Percent Share		
Year	Per Capita Revenue (Y)	Total Revenue (Y thousand)	Industrial and Commercial Taxes	Agricultural Taxes	Special Agricultural Tax
1986	...	656.6	85	14.9	0.0
1987	...	786.5	86	13.2	0.0
1988	...	939.0	88	11.2	0.0
1989	...	924.0	87	12.1	0.0
1990	...	1,005.0	88	11.1	0.0
1991	...	1,489.0	73	7.5	18.6
1992	117	1,867.0	77	7.4	14.6
1993[a]	...	2,125.0	85	7.0	14.3

... Not available.

[a] Planned.

Source: Nanzhiqiu Township Finance Bureau (1986-1992).

often applied to prosperous townships, and the sharing rate is set annually. The third form (type 3) is the fixed-term contract that stipulates a lump-sum remittance (or subsidy). Finally, those townships whose finances are still embedded in those of the county remit all revenues, and all their expenditures are disbursed from the county budget (type 4).

The 13 townships and towns under Qufu County are on type 1 and type 3 contracts. For townships in surplus the remittance rate increases by 8 percent per year. In 1993 four townships remitted to the county a total of Y4 million, of which 3.6 million came from a single town, Qufu Zhen. The nine others received a total of Y2.4 million in quota subsidies, which were to be reduced by 4 percent each year. After all transfers (including earmarked and other subsidies), the 13 townships and towns accounted for 24.2 percent of the county's consolidated revenues but spent 27.5 percent of consolidated expenditures. On the average, each township or town collected revenues of Y2.84 million and spent Y2.95 million. The township level received a net transfer of about Y2.1 million.

All of the 20 townships and towns in Penglai are on type 2 contracts. In 1993 they collected Y39.8 million in revenues (for an average of Y2.2 million per township), accounting for 39.2 percent of the total revenues of the county. They remitted Y19.7 million to the county, or 49.5 percent of collected revenues. However, the county returned Y7.95 million in quota subsidies to the townships in deficit, along with 2.5 million in other subsidies and 1.5 million in earmarked subsidies. Unlike Qufu, the net transfer was from the townships and towns to the county, totaling Y7.7 million, or 19.4 percent of revenues collected at the township level in 1993.

Zunyi's 41 townships and towns are divided into three categories according to their fiscal status and placed under type 1, 2, or 3 contracts. Altogether the townships and towns collected Y65.5 million in revenues in 1993, equal to 46.6 percent of consolidated revenues for the county. They spent Y66.2 million, or 55.8 percent of the consolidated total. Townships in surplus remitted a total of Y27 million to the county, but this was offset by quota subsidies and earmarked subsidies to produce a rough balance in the two-way flow. Each township had an average of Y1.6 million in revenues and Y1.61 million in expenditures.

In Puding all seven townships and four towns received quota subsidies from the county through 1993. In 1994, with the transfer of educational expenditures from township budgets to the county, all but one township shifted to remitting some revenues to the county.

ROLE AND COMPOSITION OF SUBSIDIES

The importance of subsidies as a source of finance at the township level appears to vary significantly across counties even within the same province. The breakdown of earmarked subsidies by use for townships in Qufu and Penglai is shown in Tables 5.19 and 5.20. In Penglai the Y7.45 million in earmarked subsidies financed 23 percent of the Y32 million in aggregate expenditures for the 20 townships and towns. These subsidies included nearly Y3.5 million in funds allocated from higher administrative levels, plus another Y1.5 million in earmarked subsidies and Y2.5 million in other subsidies financed from the county budget. In contrast, in Qufu the Y1.065 million in total subsidies financed only 3

**Table 5.19: Allocation of Earmarked Grants
to Townships in Qufu, 1993**

	Total (Y thousand)	Share of Total (%)
Support for agricultural production	139	13.1
Administration costs	186	17.5
Agriculture, forestry	130	12.2
Other departments	56	5.3
Welfare and disaster relief	650	61.0
Others	90	8.5
Total	1,065	100.0

Source: Fieldwork data.

**Table 5.20: Allocation of Earmarked Grants
to Townships in Penglai, 1993**

	Total (Y thousand)	Share of Total (%)
Support for agricultural production	280	3.8
Administration costs	1,720	23.1
Agriculture, forestry	1,450	19.5
Other departments	270	3.6
Welfare and disaster relief	5,380	72.2
Others	70	0.9
Total	7,450	100.0

Source: Fieldwork data.

percent of the Y38.4 million in expenditures of the 13 townships and
towns. A comparison of Tables 5.17 and 5.18 with Tables 5.9 and 5.10
shows other differences between these two counties. The Y7.45 million
in total subsidies granted by Penglai represented a high proportion of

the Y17.43 million in incoming subsidies to the county, whereas in Qufu only 10 percent of the Y11.05 million in incoming subsidies was turned over to townships and towns. However, this difference may have been due mainly to the unusually large expenditure on subsidies for disaster relief (Y5.4 million), which are primarily granted by the central and provincial governments and are merely passed through the city level. In both counties, support for agriculture was a significant component of incoming subsidies, which were largely retained at the county level for centralized allocation, as is the practice for other capital expenditures. On the other hand, in Penglai agricultural administration appears to be a township-level expenditure that is subsidized by the county—the county provided Y1.45 million in grants for administrative costs for agriculture and forestry, exceeding its own receipts of Y610,000 in that category. In contrast, in that category Qufu received Y810,000 from above but transferred only Y130,000 to lower levels.

ASSESSMENT

The budgetary status of an "average" township in four counties (including Xinji County in Hebei) in the fieldwork sample is given in Table 5.21. The table shows that townships are net recipients of transfers in Zunyi and Qufu counties after revenue sharing and subsidies. However, behind these averages are widely divergent revenue capacities among the townships and towns within each county. In Penglai, for example, only four of the 20 townships remitted surpluses to the

**Table 5.21: Per Capita Budgetary Status
for an Average Township, 1993
(Y)**

Location	Revenue	Expenditure	Surplus
Qufu	67	71	-4
Penglai	73	68	5
Zunyi	52	53	-1
Xinji (1992)	51	19	32

Source: Fieldwork data.

county, but these remittances were greater than the sum of quota subsidies from the county to the other 16 subordinate townships which on the average equaled 42 percent of their available revenues. Similarly, in Qufu 90 percent of all remittances from the township level came from a single unit, Qufu Town, while another three townships made small remittances, and nine townships are recipients of transfers from the city. In Zunyi, 15 townships remitted surpluses that financed subsidies to the other 33 townships equal, on the average, to more than 20 percent of available revenues there.

These sizeable transfers across townships indicate that the county level plays an important redistributive role. In fact, rich townships are subject to surprisingly high revenue-sharing burdens under fiscal contracts with their counties. In Hebei Province, the 31 townships in Xinji County had remittance rates that ranged from 19 percent of collected revenues to 87 percent, with an unweighted average of 55 percent. In one township (Nanzhiqiu), budgetary expenditures were only 18.4 percent of collected revenues in 1992, implying a remittance rate of 82 percent, a figure that is higher than the remittance rates for the largest metropolises. In per capita terms, Nanzhiqiu collected revenues of Y117 and spent only Y21.6, remitting Y75 to higher levels. However, Hebei Province seems out of line with other provinces, where township expenditures are more restricted, reflecting a higher degree of concentration at the county level.

VILLAGE FINANCE

The village was originally not included as a unit of analysis in this study because it does not have independent budgetary status. However, five villages—two in Shandong and three in Guizhou—were visited by the team in the course of visits to townships. From these brief visits, a number of general observations can be made.

There appear to be significant differences in the provision of public goods and services across villages. In the two Shandong villages, the village/town paid for significant shares of educational and health expenditures to supplement provisions by the township level. For example, in 1992 Hanjia Village spent Y30,000 to build a primary school (jointly financed with two neighboring villages), so that its children would not have to commute to the school provided by the township. In addition, the village itself pays the full salary of one of the four teachers in the school, to improve the quality of schooling available to village children. Similarly, Qufu Village subsidizes the town health clinics and covers the out-of-pocket medical expenses of town residents. In contrast, two of the three Guizhou villages spend nothing for education and health; their public expenditures are confined to paying nominal salaries (a "subsidy") to village officials and these are financed by a levy on each villager.

The differences are largely due to variations in the extent of village control over resources, which in turn seems to depend on two factors: whether production continues to be collective or cooperative in nature, and whether the village owns a significant amount of collective assets that are revenue-producing. The two villages in Shandong Province covered by our study, one in Qufu County and the other in Penglai County, appear to be more "collectively" oriented than those in Guizhou. In Qufu Village, on the outskirts of Qufu County, many enterprises are collectively owned by the village, and they remitted more than Y1 million of profits to the village, enabling the government to finance some Y400,000 of public expenditures aside from reinvesting in TVEs. Hanjia Village collects 50 percent of all income from fruit growing, and has thus been able to finance a variety of public goods and to invest in a collectively owned fruit-canning factory a few years ago.

These supplementary funds at the village level help to explain some of the disparities in service provision across regions that are discussed in the next chapter. The fact that these expenditures at the village level, albeit public, are neither reported upward nor captured by aggregate national statistics has two implications for this study. The first is that total government expenditures are underestimated. The second is that the extent of regional disparities in service provision in rural PRC is probably underestimated as well. The greater ability of village governments in Shandong to spend on public goods and services implies not only that wealthier provinces have greater budgetary resources, but that village governments also have resources to supplement service provision. If this is also true in other parts of the PRC, then the extent of regional disparities may be even greater than can be measured.

"OFF-BUDGET" REVENUES

COMPOSITION

While all levels of government depend to a varying extent on users' fees, asset sales, and other nonbudgetary resources, at the township level there is explicit official recognition of nonbudgetary sources for financing government. Since 1986, townships have been required to report receipts and expenditures of "three types of funds" to the county level: budgetary, extrabudgetary, and self-raised funds. The national totals for the three funds for 1986-1993 are shown in Table 5.22. In the 1990s, nonbudgetary resources account for more than one-fourth of revenues and about one-third of expenditures at the township level. For some of the fieldwork sites, the proportions are even higher.

At the township level there are few extrabudgetary revenues, and these primarily comprise surcharges. Nationwide surcharges in 1993 totaled Y3.6 billion, of a total EBF of Y5.67 billion. The largest is the rural education surcharge, which is levied on sales incomes of enterprises and sometimes farm households, generating revenues of Y2.9 billion in 1993. A 15 percent surcharge on the agricultural tax produced revenues of Y0.5 billion. A salt tax retention of 1 percent, a

Table 5.22: Township Finance, 1986-1993
(Percent)

	1986	1987	1988	1989	1990	1991	1992	1993
Total revenue	100.0	100.0	100.0	100.0	100.0	100.0	100.0	100.0
Budgetary revenue	83.3	82.7	80.0	75.9	74.6	72.0	71.5	73.8
Extrabudgetary revenue	5.0	4.7	5.6	6.0	6.4	6.9	7.1	6.5
Self-raised funds	11.7	12.6	14.4	18.1	19.0	21.1	21.5	19.8
Total expenditure	100.0	100.0	100.0	100.0	100.0	100.0	100.0	100.0
Budgetary expenditure	77.5	76.6	74.3	69.4	69.0	66.3	65.9	67.6
Extrabudgetary expenditure	6.4	6.1	7.0	7.2	7.4	7.7	7.6	7.0
Self-raised funds	16.2	17.3	18.7	23.4	23.6	25.9	26.5	25.4

Source: Ministry of Finance.

surcharge for fishery investments of 3-8 percent of income derived from fishing, and surcharges on public services round out the list.

Self-raised funds come from fees, rental income from collective assets, profits and other remittances from TVEs, and, in some provinces, the "unified levy" *(tongchou)* on villages. The common sources of SRF are also listed in Table 5.23. While most of the fees are levied on enterprises, many also fall on rural households. For example, townships in Shandong impose a "unified levy" to finance five services— rural education, militia training, cadre subsidies, and old-age and welfare support. These are collected from households by village officials and turned over to the township for unified allocation.

Of the two types of off-budget funds, EBF is the more clearly defined, with its origins in the Soviet-type system that was adopted in the 1950s (Wong, Heady, and Woo 1995). Until rules were changed in 1993 to exclude SOE funds, national statistics on EBF were reported in three portions. The smallest was that controlled directly by local governments, which composed 2.4 percent of total EBF in 1992. It comes from surcharges on taxes and public utilities, and from the income of extrabudgetary enterprises owned by local governments. The portion of EBF under administrative agencies composed 23 percent of the total in 1992. The sources for this portion are the myriad fees and charges, including road maintenance fees, educational surcharges, surcharges on agricultural taxes, rental incomes from public housing, market management fees, and management fees collected from individual and private enterprises (see Table 5.23). In addition, this category includes the income of enterprises run by administrative agencies, such as workshops and factories owned by schools, and hotels and restaurants run by industries. In the 1980s this was the fastest-growing component of EBF, growing at a rate of 20.7 percent per annum from 1978 to 1992. In Shandong, administrative units collected 39 percent of EBF in 1993, while local governments collected only 5 percent.

By far the largest portion of EBF was made up of funds of SOEs (retained profits, depreciation, and funds for major repairs), which composed about three-quarters of total EBF until they were excluded in 1993. These SOE funds are theoretically not subject to local-government allocation, since they are meant to give SOEs more autonomy and better incentives for maximizing profits. Nevertheless, cash-starved local governments have often found it difficult to resist

Table 5.23: Sources of Extrabudgetary and Self-Raised Funds

EXTRABUDGETARY FUNDS

I. *Under Local Governments*
   Industrial-commercial tax surcharges
   Agricultural and animal husbandry
      tax surcharges
   Urban public utility surcharges

II. *Under Administrative Agencies*
   Agency development funds
   Staff welfare funds
   Staff bonus funds
   Road maintenance fees
   Surcharges on vehicle purchase
   Transport management fees
   Higher education fund
   Middle and primary school fees
   Incomes of middle and primary
      school enterprises
   Rural education surcharge
   Rental incomes
   Market management fees
   Individual enterprise management
      fees

Until 1992 only:
III. *Under State-Owned Enterprises
   and Supervisory Departments*
   Renovation and reconstruction
      funds
   Retained profits
   Major repairs fund
   Technical development fund
   Oilfield maintenance fees
   Natural gas exploration fund

SELF-RAISED FUNDS

I. *Contract Fees*
   Farmland
   Fishponds
   TVEs
   Others

II. *Collective Incomes*

III. *Fees*
   Land management and town
      construction
   Transport
   Management fees from TVEs
      and commercial enterprises
   Farmland use fees
   Agricultural support
   Water fees
   Electricity
   Unified levy
      Militia training
      Education
      Welfare and old-age support
      Cadre subsidies
      Army family subsidies

IV. *Other Contributions*
   Road building and maintenance
   Farmland improvement
   Others

the temptation to tap this rich resource. In the absence of clear property rights, enterprises have been in a weak position to fend off such predation. While excluding SOE funds was a welcome step that eliminated a longstanding anomaly in budgetary accounting practice in the PRC, it is unlikely, by itself, to alter the relationship between local governments and these funds. At the county and township levels, where SOEs are few or nonexistent, TVEs and their profits play much the same role in financing government, albeit under the category of self-raised funds.

The uses of EBF and SRF are virtually identical to those of budgetary revenues, justifying the popular reference to these funds as "the second budget." They are spent on education, health, farmland investment, road maintenance and construction, family planning services, administration (paying salaries and subsidies for cadres), and the like, in ways that clearly supplement the budget. Sometimes explicit transfers are made from EBF to augment budgetary revenues, as was done in Penglai County, whose budgetary account showed a transfer of Y3 million from EBF to cover budgetary expenditures in 1993.

ASSESSMENT

The growth of EBF and SRF has eased fiscal pressures for many local governments, but has also produced two undesirable side effects. First, it has hastened the decline of the formal fiscal system by providing an alternative outlet for the local-government tax effort. By liberally offering tax expenditures, local governments can shift funds from the sector where they are "taxed" (i.e., subject to revenue sharing with higher levels) to the sector where they are not (i.e., the off-budget sector). Second, it has created a quasi-tax system which is increasingly beyond the central government's control, and whose structure of fees and charges is extremely chaotic, nontransparent, and often inequitable.

Taxlike Characteristics. As noted in Chapter 2, public finance theory distinguishes between user fees and taxes for the financing of public services. User fees are generally recommended when the users of the service are easily identifiable and separable, and where the service produces few or no external benefits. For example, users' fees generally finance public utilities, some parks, and the like. Taxes, on the other hand, are considered the appropriate tool for financing public services that involve significant external benefits or costs (such as basic education and preventive health care) and produce nonexclusionary benefits (such as police and fire protection),[8] or that are recognized and accepted as a general social obligation (such as providing welfare and housing for the indigent).

In the PRC, a number of EBF/SRF are clearly user fees, such as surcharges on public utilities, rental incomes from public housing, and animal slaughter taxes, whose incidence falls on beneficiaries. However, many others are either levies on the general public or are intended to finance general social obligations, and should be considered taxes. Examples of this latter type include one of the newly introduced surcharges for rural education, which is levied on urban building construction, as a flat fee per square meter of constructed space. Similarly, fees are levied in many provinces (including Jiangsu, Guangdong, and Shanghai) on profits of township and village enterprises to finance subsidies for agriculture. In both of these cases, since the levies fall on nonusers, and the funds are used to finance general social obligations (education and rural development, respectively), they are quasi taxes, and not user fees.

Tax Base and Incidence. Most of the fees and quasi taxes have the same tax base and narrow incidence as the formal tax system. This is true of all the surcharges tacked onto existing taxes, which generate the bulk of the EBF accruing to local governments and administrative agencies, as shown in Table 5.23. The industry-dependent characteristic of the formal tax system appears to be true of many local levies as well. For example, Whiting (1993) reports that in suburban Shanghai, the bulk of nonbudgetary revenues come from four fees: an annual levy of Y220 on each worker, "using industry to support agriculture" (*yigong zhinong*); a fee of Y84 per worker to support agricultural sidelines; a rural education fee of 2 percent of gross profits; and a social expenditure fee of 7 percent of taxable profits. All are levied on TVEs.

---

[8] A nonexclusionary good is one whose consumption cannot be restricted, once it is provided, and whose consumption by anyone does not exhaust its supply. Classic examples of public goods with this property include, aside from fire and police protection, national defense and television and radio broadcasts.

Decentralized Control and Ad Hoc Character. In the formal fiscal system, all taxing powers reside in the central government, which levies taxes, sets the rates, and defines the tax base. In contrast, the off-budget system is decentralized, and all levels of government have the power to impose levies and set their rates. Even though each level of government attempts to set guidelines and limits on quasi taxes, there is substantial autonomy at the lower levels. In general, quasi taxes are ad hoc and levied for specific purposes, as illustrated by the four fees cited above. They are often administered by government departments or agencies, rather than the finance departments.

Uncontrollable Proliferation. The ad hoc nature of fees and levies and the decentralized control over them contribute to their pro-liferation, which the government has found impossible to curb despite repeated calls and edicts. For example, one survey in Hunan Province found that TVEs were subjected to more than 100 types of fees, paid to 60 odd administrative units and agencies (cited in Furusawa 1990). These levies can be burdensome. One study by the World Bank found that taxes, profit remittances, and fees and contributions absorbed 65-75 percent of pretax profits of TVEs in Jiangsu Province, 35-45 percent in Guangdong and Shandong, and 53 percent nationwide (Ody 1992).

In spite of the strong preference among rural officials for taxing enterprises rather than households—taxing enterprises is relatively pain-less (since the costs are hidden) and more lucrative (since agricultural incomes are low)—levies on rural households have also grown over time, especially in regions where TVEs are weak or nonexistent.

The dominance of this quasi-tax system in governing the rural economy is illustrated by a study by the Ministry of Agriculture, which surveyed the tax burden on farm households. The study found that in 1988, the large sample of farmers in 27 provinces paid an average of 74 types of fees costing a total of Y39.1, or 8.22 percent of per capita net income, exceeding the State Council guideline calling for holding levies on farm households to no more than 5 percent of rural income. Of the total, only 27 percent (or Y10.4) went to formal taxes—the agricultural and special product taxes. All the rest went to EBF and SRF.[9] The informal system of quasi taxes is clearly used as a substitute

---

[9] *Nongye Jingji Wenti*, translated in JPRS-CAR-90-037, pp. 71-75.

for fiscal revenues at the lower tiers, where the formal fiscal system is at its weakest.

Equity and Efficiency Implications. This system is inefficient. The proliferation of fees and levies cited above points to a system of quasi taxes that is extremely complex, where uncoordinated, multiple fees are imposed on the same taxpayer, using different bases for calculation. For example, the four fees in suburban Shanghai are levied on gross profits, taxable profits, and workers. If these fees are typical, then the system of quasi taxes clearly fails the test for transparency and simplicity. It is also likely to fail the tests for efficiency and equity, since the fees are designed by local officials with little analytical ability, usually to minimize the costs of revenue collection. It is unlikely that any attempt is made to ensure neutrality of the fee, to match charges to beneficiaries, or even to distribute the burden of cost equitably.

The crude methods of assessment and collection used at the lowest tiers of government often result in a more regressive tax structure than intended. At the township and village levels, per capita levies are commonly used to finance public services formerly provided by the collectives, mainly because the governments lack the capability to carry out sophisticated assessments of taxable capacity. These levies per head often result in higher tax rates (as a percentage of income) on poor households/villages. For example, in one township we visited in Shandong, township officials insisted that because they lacked accurate information on household incomes, they had to collect the "unified levy" (*tongchou*) from villages, and the Y27 fee was calibrated to be equal to less than 2 percent of rural incomes. According to data provided, the per capita levy actually ranged from Y13.2 to Y33.4 across villages in 1993, which translated into a tax rate of only 1 percent of income in one of the most prosperous villages, but 5.3 percent in the poorest one (Table 5.24).

Amplifying Regional Disparities. The coincidence of taxes and quasi taxes on the same tax base (industry) means that budgetary and off-budgetary revenues are closely correlated in size: prosperous localities are rich in both, while poor localities facing tight fiscal constraints find little relief from EBF/SRF. At the provincial level, the correlation between budgetary revenues and EBF is extremely high—0.89-0.96 in 1983-1990. Studies of rural finance confirm this coincidence of budgetary and off-budgetary resources (Sun 1994; Oi 1992). The growing

Table 5.24: Tax Rates for Unified Levy
in One Township (Shandong), 1993

Village	Per Capita Income (Y)	Population	Total Payment (Y thousand)	Per Capita Levy (Y)	Tax Rate on Income
1	1,336	1,068	26.0	24.3	1.8
2	1,149	931	26.0	27.9	2.4
3	1,330	976	28.5	29.2	2.2
4	1,269	763	21.0	27.5	2.2
5	1,015	697	17.8	25.5	2.5
6	1,250	212	6.0	28.3	2.3
7	1,200	213	5.0	23.5	2.0
8	1,197	131	3.0	22.9	1.9
9	1,378	503	15.0	29.8	2.2
10	954	261	5.0	19.2	2.0
11	1,217	331	6.7	20.2	1.7
12	1,228	526	14.2	27.0	2.2
13	1,200	268	6.6	24.6	2.1
14	964	170	3.9	22.9	2.4
15	1,200	623	14.8	23.8	2.0
16	1,319	599	17.0	28.4	2.2
17	1,228	341	10.0	29.3	2.4
18	1,000	245	5.0	20.4	2.0
19	1,248	419	11.3	27.0	2.2
20	964	215	6.0	27.9	2.9
21	974	403	11.3	28.0	2.9
22	1,275	959	23.7	24.7	1.9
23	1,213	813	20.0	24.6	2.0

(cont'd)

Table 5.24: Tax Rates for Unified Levy in One Township (Shandong), 1993 (cont'd)

Village	Per Capita Income (Y)	Population	Total Payment (Y thousand)	Per Capita Levy (Y)	Tax Rate on Income
24	1,330	404	10.0	24.8	1.9
25	1,218	445	10.0	22.5	1.8
26	883	178	3.8	21.3	2.4
27	950	213	5.4	25.4	2.7
28	1,200	536	13.2	24.6	2.1
29	1,319	759	10.0	13.2	1.0
30	1,228	867	29.0	33.4	2.7
31	1,214	252	8.0	31.7	2.6
32	1,218	807	20.0	24.8	2.0
33	1,217	639	16.0	25.0	2.1
34	590	264	8.3	31.4	5.3
35	1,015	340	9.0	26.5	2.6
36	1,230	83	2.2	26.5	2.2
37	974	512	12.0	23.4	2.4
38	1,217	1,151	31.0	26.9	2.2
39	913	397	9.2	23.2	2.5
40	1,250	787	21.0	26.7	2.1
41	1,220	270	7.3	27.0	2.2
42	1,248	808	21.1	26.1	2.1
43	1,230	342	9.2	26.9	2.2
Minimum	590.0	83.0	2.2	13.2	1.0
Maximum	1,378.0	1,151.0	31.0	33.4	5.3
Mean	1,157.5	505.1	13.0	25.5	2.3
Standard deviation	157.3	282.6	7.8	3.6	0.6
Coeff. of variation	0.14	0.56	0.60	0.14	0.26

Source: Daxindian Town Finance Bureau.

reliance on off-budget funds to augment the budget has clearly amplified the growing regional disparities in the PRC, as the decentralizing reforms moved the economy toward greater self-financing through the 1980s. With budgetary transfers declining throughout the period, the gap in service provision grew between rich and poor regions. Moreover, we can interpret the rising quasi-tax burden on rural households as an indication that fiscal pressures are growing more intense in the poor regions, forcing local governments to resort to imposing levies directly on households despite the high political costs.

ISSUES

Examining the budgets at the county, township, and village levels in this chapter has allowed us to uncover a number of issues. Most important are the large regional disparities in resources available to local governments, and the growing problem of revenue inadequacy in the poor localities. The continued dependence of the tax system on industry for revenues has made the rural sector relatively revenue-poor. But as transfers have declined across the board during the transition period, for both localities with surplus revenue and those in deficit, fiscal pressures vary greatly across localities. Evidence from the fieldwork sites suggests that in richer provinces counties have lower remittance requirements and more is left for local allocation. The situation of counties in poor provinces is much more dire. In Guizhou, counties in surplus, such as Zunyi, face high remittance rates, while poor counties receive dwindling subsidies as central subsidies to the province have diminished through the reform period. In fact, in 1993 the whole rural sector shifted from net recipient to net remitter status in the province, with counties and townships in Guizhou supporting urban finance (see Table 5.25 and Figure 5.3).

The growing importance of off-budget finance has helped to alleviate fiscal pressures but has at the same time exacerbated regional inequalities, since off-budget funds are highly correlated with budgetary revenues, tending to reinforce rather than offset regional differences in revenue capacity. Moreover, unlike budgetary revenues, off-budget funds are not subject to revenue sharing or redistribution, so that the shift from the budget to a mix of budgetary and off-budgetary resources for financing government in the PRC reduces the overall proportion of redistributed funds.

**Table 5.25: Total Net Budgetary Revenue Transfer
at Each Government Level, Guizhou Province, 1980-1993
(Y million)**

Year	Total	Province	Prefecture	County
1980	641	268	158	215
1984	924	538	103	283
1988	1,240	1,002	20	218
1990	1,273	1,000	(79)	352
1992	1,284	1,297	(107)	94
1993	1,169	1,437	(127)	(141)

Notes: County data include those for townships.
          Negative numbers, in parentheses, represent a net transfer out of level.
          Positive numbers represent a net transfer to level.
Source: Guizhou Provincial Department of Finance.

These findings highlight the urgent need to extend fiscal reform to the lower levels of government. Through September 1994, subprovincial governments had not yet learned how the tax-sharing system would affect their revenue-sharing arrangements with higher levels. The slowness of reform was a reflection of difficulties faced by policymakers in extending the 1994 measures to the countryside. The dependence of rural budgets on turnover taxes means that the TSS reform will reduce rural retained revenues and must be offset by new transfers. In view of the tightness of rural finance, local officials are understandably loath to announce changes until the central government has clarified its own transfer programs.

The loss of indirect tax revenues in the rural sector will severely affect the fiscal status of rural governments and may reverse the recent trend of a rising share of total revenues accruing to the township level. It will also exacerbate the problem of poor incentives for tax collection from TVEs. While shifting consumption tax revenues on liquor and tobacco entirely to the central government will help to eliminate the scramble to build local wineries and cigarette plants, its effect is likely to be even more severe and regionally unbalanced. Its full

**Figure 5.3: Net Flows of Budgetary Resources Between Administrative Levels
in Guizhou Province
(Y million)**

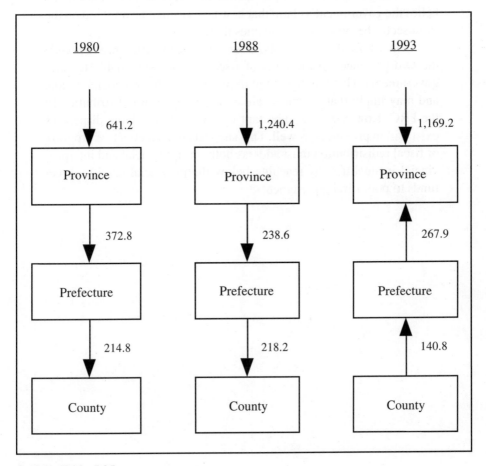

Source: Table 5.25.

implementation will have a devastating impact on localities like Qufu which have grown so dependent on liquor taxes.

Tax reform must also be broadened to incorporate and rationalize the structure of levies and quasi taxes that are applied in the rural sector. In effect, the present system cedes a large share of rural taxation to the off-budget system. The prevalence of levies on farm households belies the government's claim that new taxes cannot be imposed on the farm sector because of low incomes there.

Finally, fieldwork data show very significant differences between the two provinces in the level of fiscal resources available to rural governments. This highlights the importance of the provincial divide, and may imply that provinces are a barrier to fiscal redistribution in the PRC. However, it is important to note that very large disparities exist within provinces as well. This suggests that an effective program of fiscal redistribution must address both intraprovincial and interprovincial inequalities, by reaching below the provincial level to direct funds to poor rural governments.

Chapter 6

PROVISION OF PUBLIC SERVICES IN RURAL PRC

by Loraine A. West

The adequacy of revenues at the county and township levels can be assessed only in relation to expenditure needs. While inadequate investment in public goods generally hinders economic growth and human development, expenditure needs vary with time, place, and constituency. This chapter assesses the delivery of the key services of education, health care, and social welfare in rural PRC, largely based on information gathered in two Shandong counties, Qufu and Penglai, and two Guizhou counties, Zunyi and Puding.[1] Public services in the four counties are compared; where possible, the comparison is made with reference to targets set by the state, which define minimum local expenditure needs. Finally, the efficiency and responsiveness of local governments and agencies in providing the services are also assessed, since these, in addition to revenue adequacy, determine the delivery of public goods and services.

The first section addresses education which typically accounts for the largest share of county and township budgets (Table 6.1). The second section focuses on the delivery of public health services, while the third section deals with the provision of social welfare services. The chapter concludes with an outline of identified issues.

---

[1] See the Annex for a general description of these four counties and Chapter 1 for a discussion of the urban and rural levels of government.

**Table 6.1: Share of County Budget Allocated
to Major Public Services in Selected Counties, 1993
(Percent)**

	Penglai	*Qufu*	*Zunyi*	*Puding*
Culture, education, health	35.00	37.75	36.34	38.42
Education	...	...	28.03	27.53
Agriculture	10.23	10.52	11.43	9.16
Welfare assistance	8.69	3.09	3.19	4.58
Law enforcement	2.96	5.05	...	4.52

... Not available.
Sources: Penglai, Qufu, Zunyi, and Puding County finance bureaus.

RURAL EDUCATION SERVICES

Basic education in the rural areas is the focus of this section. From a summary of the major education goals of the government, it goes on to describe the organization of rural education, then enumerates and discusses the various financing methods and sources used. Finally, the section assesses the level and quality of rural education.

EDUCATION GOALS

The delivery of rural education services is critical in the PRC where over 70 percent of the population is rural. In 1993, 72 percent of all primary students and 60 percent of all junior high school students were enrolled in rural schools. Furthermore, depending on its quality, rural education will either hasten or retard the modernization of agriculture (Lin 1991) and the industrialization of the countryside, and, through the migrant labor force, affect the development of the urban sector.

In recognition of the importance of a higher-quality labor force to the modernization and growth of the country, the Chinese government in 1986 passed a nine-year Compulsory Education Law. The law covers the six years of primary school and three years of junior high school that compose basic education.[2] Although the law was passed at the national level, decentralized financing has left its implementation to the local levels.

Following the passage of the law, each of the lower levels of government drew up plans for the gradual expansion of basic education in their jurisdictions. The plans specified the projected number of students and the number of additional classrooms and teachers that would be needed. Planning by the individual counties also involved calculating the funds required to hire more teachers and to build and equip more classrooms. Province education officials, in consultation with local governments, then prepared a schedule for the achievement of nine years of universal education by each county and city.

For the country as a whole, the target is to provide nine years of education to 85 percent of the population, primarily those living outside the poor areas, by the year 2000. The schedules vary regionally, with more developed areas expected to achieve the target earlier. Guangdong, one of the PRC's wealthiest provinces, expects to implement compulsory education throughout the province by the year 2000. For Shandong the announced target date is 1997. By then, according to Shandong education officials, 90 percent of all children will have completed nine years of education. As of 1994, more than 10 counties and 30 percent of all townships in Shandong had already implemented compulsory education. Poorer provinces, on the other hand, have much more modest targets. Gansu expects to be able to offer nine years of compulsory education to 70 percent of the rural population by the year 2000. Guizhou's goal for the year 2000 is 80 percent of children completing primary school and 60 percent of primary school graduates continuing on to junior high school.

As its second education goal, the government also intends to wipe out illiteracy among the young and the middle-aged (those within the 15-44 age group). The population census in 1990 placed the number of illiterates in this age group at 59 million, or 10 percent. By the year 2000 this rate is to be brought down to less than 5 percent in areas inhabited by 90 percent of the population. By 1996, the government plans to reduce illiteracy to below 5 percent in the 11 most developed

---

[2] Compulsory education does not include kindergarten (*xueqianban*).

provinces and municipalities, including Shandong which had 11 percent illiteracy in 1990. Twelve other provinces are to attain this goal by 1998. Six of the least developed provinces, including Guizhou which had a 29 percent illiteracy rate in 1990, are to reduce illiteracy among the young and middle-aged population to below 15 percent by the end of the century. Xizang (Tibet) is not expected to eradicate illiteracy until after the year 2000.

ORGANIZATION

Preschools in the PRC are concentrated in urban centers; in rural areas, schooling usually begins at the age of six in locales offering kindergarten (*xueqianban*) or at the age of seven if no kindergarten class is available.[3] A primary school education consists of six years of schooling excluding kindergarten.[4] General secondary education is divided into three years of junior high school and three years of senior high school.[5] After primary school or junior high school, students may go into any one of a variety of specialized secondary schools, including vocational and technical. These schools offer two or three-year programs at the lower or upper secondary level.

The introduction of the fiscal responsibility system in the mid-1980s further decentralized both the management and the funding of primary and secondary education in the PRC. The central government provides overall guidance by establishing the basic schooling system, setting standards for school facilities, and prescribing the qualifications of teachers and the basic wage standards for them. The provinces are authorized to determine annual enrolment, examine and select teaching materials, define teaching programs, and set standards for school facilities and teachers' wages for the province. Provinces in turn determine the authority of their subordinate levels of government (county and township).

---

[3] In Guizhou, where more than 70 percent of the preschool age population is rural, only 30 percent of students in preschool reside in rural areas.
[4] A six-year primary school system announced in 1952 was implemented in rural areas only in the 1980s. Now, such a system has replaced the former five-year system in nearly all townships.
[5] A few regions and schools are experimenting with different educational structures. One Penglai township has five years of primary school education followed by four years of junior high school.

Rural schools fall under one of three types of ownership and operation: state-run (*gongban*), community-run (*minban*), or private (*sili*). Senior high schools, most specialized secondary schools, most junior high schools, and all keypoint (*zhongdian*) and central (*zhongxin*) primary schools are state-run.[6] Community-run schools are largely limited to primary schools.[7] Villages, sometimes with the assistance of the township, are mainly responsible for maintaining community-run schools. Private schools, still rare, are mostly found in urban centers and wealthy rural areas. Some private schools have, however, been started by retired teachers in poor areas which otherwise lack educational facilities. In Puding County, two of the 12 junior high schools are located in the homes of retired teachers who established the schools with their savings. One of the four technical schools in Puding is also privately run. It is well-known in the province because the principal invites guest lecturers from colleges in the province to train its students in Chinese traditional medicine.

The county education bureau manages the senior high schools, keypoint primary schools, schools for the handicapped, and teacher training schools. A number of specialized secondary schools are managed by various county-level bureaus. Medical training schools, for example, are managed by county public health bureaus. Lower secondary and primary schools are generally the responsibility of the township education office. In schools managed at the county level, the school party secretary and principal are appointed by the county party and government, and the assistant principal is appointed by the county personnel bureau. In rural primary and lower secondary schools below the county level, village or township officials select the school principal, who then selects the teachers and manages the school.

The number of schools in a region—whether county, township, or village—depends on its population, the level of popularization of

---

[6] A keypoint primary school is run by the county education bureau and is usually located in the county seat. It is the premier primary school in the county. Central primary schools are typically operated by the township education office and are located in the township seat.

[7] With the establishment of townships as the lowest level of government, the terminology for classifying the ownership and operation structure of rural schools changed. Formerly, rural junior high schools were considered to be jointly operated by the state and the community (*lianban*). Now, these same schools are classified as township run (*xiangzhenban*). Central primary schools formerly were classified as community-run. Today these schools, too, are operated by the township and therefore are considered state-run.

education, and the size of individual schools. Urban centers (cities, county seats, and towns) account for only 28 percent of the PRC's population, yet contain 75 percent of all senior high schools (Table 6.2). On the other hand, 84 percent of primary schools are in rural areas to serve the more dispersed population better. Counties typically have three to five senior high schools, at least one of which is in the

Table 6.2: Primary and General Secondary Schools,
by Location, 1993

	Senior high schools	Junior high schools	Primary schools
National	14,380	68,415	696,681
	(100.0)	(100.0)	(100.0)
Urban	4,793	7,384	29,203
	(33.3)	(10.8)	(4.2)
County seats and towns	5,983	11,723	82,998
	(41.6)	(17.1)	(11.9)
Rural	3,604	49,308	584,480
	(25.1)	(72.1)	(83.9)
Shandong	612	5,028	54,009
	(100.0)	(100.0)	(100.0)
Urban	217	525	2,324
	(35.5)	(10.4)	(4.3)
County seats and towns	116	271	2,095
	(19.0)	(5.4)	(3.9)
Rural	279	4,232	49,590
	(45.6)	(84.2)	(91.8)
Guizhou	359	1,360	20,249
	(100.0)	(100.0)	(100.0)
Urban	89	133	503
	(24.8)	(9.8)	(2.5)
County seats and towns	152	176	1,394
	(42.3)	(12.9)	(6.9)
Rural	118	1,051	18,352
	(32.9)	(77.3)	(90.6)

Note: Figures in parentheses are shares of totals.
Source: SSB (1994a), pp. 580, 586.

county seat while the others are in county towns. A junior high school is often attached to the senior high school to form a complete secondary school. Townships average one to three junior high schools with at least one in the township seat. Smaller townships have about 15 primary schools while larger ones have about 30. Keypoint primary schools are in the county seat, but each township has at least one central primary school. Other primary schools are scattered among the villages, although not all villages have a primary school. Throughout the country, there is one primary school for every 1.4 villages.

Primary schools are of two types: complete primary schools (with classes, *ban,* from grades 1 to 6 and possibly kindergarten) and external teaching sites (with classes for the lower grades only or small classes for a mixture of grades). External teaching sites (also referred to as teaching points) are most common in mountainous and poor areas where the population is scattered. These schools can have fewer than 10 students or more than 100.

Over the past decade, the government has undertaken to develop a more suitable labor force through education and training. To this end, it steered an increasing share of students wishing to continue studies beyond the lower secondary level into a growing number of specialized secondary schools. The number of technical secondary schools increased by 37 percent from 1983 to 1993 and the number of students enrolled in them grew threefold (Figure 6.1). While compulsory education has increased the demand for teachers, the 1990s have seen a decline in the number of teacher training schools. The current trend is toward consolidation and larger, more economically efficient, teacher training schools.

FINANCING OF RURAL EDUCATION

In 1993, the government spent a total of Y106 billion on education, 22 percent higher than the previous year. Support for education comes from the following sources: government appropriations from budgets at the central, province, prefecture, county, and township levels; enterprise expenditures for enterprise-run schools; profits from school-run enterprises; donations from the public, including school alumni, overseas Chinese, foreigners, enterprises, and foundations; students' tuition and fees; and self-raised funds of counties, townships, and

Figure 6.1: Specialized Secondary Education, 1983-1993

Number of
Students
(Thousands)

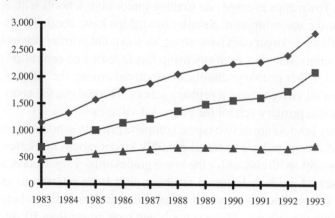

- ◆ Specialized Schools
- ■ Technical Schools
- ▲ Teacher Training Schools

Number of
Schools

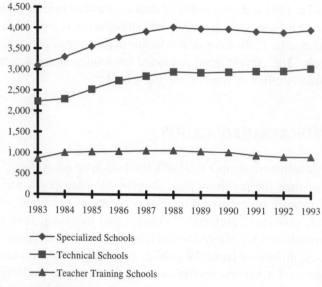

- ◆ Specialized Schools
- ■ Technical Schools
- ▲ Teacher Training Schools

Source: SSB (1994a).

villages. The first source comprises budgetary appropriations and education surcharges which are actually classified as extrabudgetary funds (Table 5.21). At the national level, government budgetary grants account for the majority of education funds, 62 percent in 1992 (Table 6.3). Including education surcharges, the government provides 72 percent of the total funding for education. The combined share is very similar in Shandong (71 percent) but much higher in Guizhou (87 percent). In recent years, however, government budgetary appropriations have decreased in significance, while donations, students' tuition and fees, and self-raised funds have become more important.

The level of support a rural school receives from each of the sources depends in part on whether it is state-run or community-run and whether it is a primary or a secondary school. Location is, however, the overriding determinant of the level and sources of support. The sources of education funds for Penglai, Qufu, Zunyi, and Puding are shown in Tables 6.4, 6.5, 6.6, and 6.7, respectively. Each of the various sources of funds for education is discussed below.

Government Appropriations. The 1993 State Council circular on education reform and development calls for the government to appropriate funds as the main support for education (Xinhua 1993). Officials have set a target allocation of 4 percent of GNP by the year

**Table 6.3: National Expenditures on Education,
by Source, 1992
(Percent)**

	National	*Shandong*	*Guizhou*
Total expenditures (Y billion)	87.00	5.81	1.26
Government budgetary grants	62.13	52.69	79.53
School-run enterprise profits	5.39	4.82	1.57
Tuition and fees	5.07	5.30	3.98
Self-raised funds and donations	8.03	13.79	1.89
Education surcharges	10.13	18.08	7.60
Enterprise-run schools	5.59	2.27	3.90

Sources: State Education Commission (1993), pp. 12-13; fieldwork data.

Table 6.4: Penglai Education Funds, by Source, 1993

Source	Y million	Percent
County budget	23.6	43.5
Township budget	4.0	7.4
Urban education surcharge	1.0	1.8
Rural education surcharge	14.0	25.8
Self-raised funds	4.0	7.4
Tuition and fees	2.0	3.7
School-run enterprise profits	5.6	10.3
Total	54.2	100.0

Source: Penglai Education Bureau.

Table 6.5: Qufu Education Funds, by Source, 1993

Source	Y million	Percent
Grants from above county level	0.4	1.4
County and township budget	20.0	62.6
County and township extrabudgetary funds	6.3	19.7
Tuition and fees	1.5	4.7
School-run enterprise profits	3.7	11.6
Total	32.0	100.0

Source: Qufu Education Bureau.

Table 6.6: Zunyi Education Funds, by Source, 1987-1993
(Y thousand)

Source	1987	1990	1991	1992	1993	1993 % of Total
Grants from above county level	950	722	762	500	700	1.6
County budget	3,791	4,991	5,230	6,601	8,500	19.6
Township budget	9,677	15,995	17,764	22,467	25,500	58.8
Urban education surcharge	300	430	924	1,616	2,800	6.5
Rural education surcharge	a	a	a	1,664	3,700	8.5
Self-raised funds	1,060	2,201	1,428	2,774	b	b
Tuition and fees	705	2,013	2,038	2,107	2,100	4.8
School-run enterprise profits	27	51	63	75	50	0.1
Total	16,510	26,403	28,209	37,804	43,350	100.0

^a Not collected (levied).
^b Self-raised funds are included in the township budget figure for 1993.
Source: Zunyi County Education Bureau.

2000, up from 2.66 percent in 1994.[8] To reach this target, the government will have to spend an average of nearly 18 percent more each year in real terms, assuming that GNP grows in real terms by 8 percent yearly.

Furthermore, the eighth five-year plan (1991-1995) calls for a minimum average of 15 percent in government budgetary appropriations for education during the period. Meeting this target already appears impossible. In the first two years of the plan, budgetary appropriations for education nationwide were only 12 percent of the total. After the major wage adjustment of 1993, the State Education Commission concluded that not even 15 percent of the budget will be enough to meet education needs. Guizhou spent 17 percent of its consolidated budget on education in 1993 and Shandong, 19 percent.

[8] Government allocations include direct appropriations for education, funds used by state enterprises to run their primary and secondary schools, and tax reductions and exemptions for school-run businesses. In India, Indonesia, and Thailand government spending on education represented 3.0, 3.7 and 3.6 per cent of GNP, respectively (Tan and Mingat 1992).

Table 6.7: Puding Education Funds, by Source, 1980-1993
(Y thousand)

Source	1980	1984	1988	1990	1992	1993	1993 % of Total
Grants from above county level	330	283	872	341	1,011	1,557	14.7
County and township budget	1,331	2,316	3,297	4,155	6,548	6,881	64.9
Urban education surcharge	a	a	a	a	60	90	0.8
Rural education surcharge	a	a	a	a	200	530	5.0
County self-raised	103	210	100	323	0	0	0.0
Other self-raised funds	127	1,030	598	354	1,357	943	8.9
Tuition and fees	...	...	...	...	585	600	5.7
School-run enterprise profits	0	0	0	0	0	0	0.0
Total	1,891[b]	3,839[b]	4,867[b]	5,173[b]	9,761	10,601	100.0

... Not available.
[a] Not collected (levied).
[b] Excludes students' tuition and fees.
Source: Puding Education Bureau.

All levels of government have been urged to increase their funding for education at a faster rate than the growth in financial revenue. The urging has often gone unheeded, however, because of competing demands. In 1993 total government revenue grew by 22.5 percent, but education expenditures from the budget increased by only 20.9 percent, to Y65 billion. Indeed, data in Table 6.8 show that the share of education in total expenditures fell from 13.6 percent in 1989 to 12.3 percent in 1993. As a percentage of GDP, education expenditures have long been on the decline.

Government expenditures on education are primarily funded from budgetary appropriations (Table 6.8). Total government expenditures on education are distributed as follows: 21 percent for tertiary education, 36 percent for secondary education, 36 percent for primary edu-

Table 6.8: Government Expenditures on Education
in the PRC, 1989-1993

	1989	*1990*	*1991*	*1992*	*1993*
Total expenditures on education (Y billion)	50.39	54.87	59.95	70.54	79.00
Budgetary expenditures (Y billion)	39.77	42.61	45.97	53.87	65.11
Education expenditures as share of GNP (%)	3.15	3.10	3.02	2.94	2.52
Budgetary expenditures on education as share of total budgetary expenditures (%)	13.59	12.34	12.12	12.17	12.31

Sources: State Education Commission (1993), p. 10; SSB (1994a), pp. 32, 218, 220.

cation, and 7 percent for other types of education (State Education Commission 1993). Government expenditures per student are highest at the tertiary level. In 1992 the government spent Y28.7 at the tertiary level and Y2.2 at the secondary level for every Y1 spent at the primary level. The low budgetary appropriations for the basic levels of education are absorbed by personnel costs. In 1992 these costs made up 88 percent of government budgetary expenditures for primary schools and 81 percent of expenditures for general secondary schools. In 1993 salaries rose faster than government budget appropriations for education. Consequently, personnel costs rose to 90 percent of primary school operating expenses and to 83 percent of the operating expenses of general secondary schools.

Although tertiary educational institutions take up 97 percent of central-government budgetary expenditures on education, the central government nonetheless provides capital outlay subsidies for rural primary and secondary education through targeted grant programs (Table 6.9). All of these programs, however, require matching funds by local governments. The central government provides Y100 million in annual subsidies to normal schools (teacher training schools). Funds in one program are being used to establish a teaching school in each of

**Table 6.9: Central-Government Grants
to Rural Education in the PRC, 1993**

Use of Grant	*Funding (Y million)*
Teacher training schools	100
Compulsory education in poor areas	50
Vocational schools	50
Minority education	20

Source: Poverty Alleviation Committee.

200 poor counties. The central government also allocates funds each year (Y50 million in 1993) to assist poor areas in implementing compulsory education. Central-government grants for vocational schools (Y50 million in 1993) and minority education (Y20 million in 1993) are also available. Funds for minority education go to 143 poor minority counties by rotation.

Central-government and matching funds for capital outlays are distributed and used in ways that vary over time and between counties. A major use is the construction or repair of school buildings. Dilapidated (*weifang*) classrooms and dormitories were repaired or torn down and rebuilt in a nationwide drive in the early 1980s. As a result, the dilapidated school space in rural PRC dropped from 13 percent of classroom area to only 2.2 percent in 1992. In Shandong dilapidated schools are now virtually nonexistent. From 1981 to 1992 Guizhou reduced the amount of dilapidated school space in primary and secondary schools from 30.5 percent of total area to only 6.4 percent. Nevertheless, the slight increase in the percentage of dilapidated rural school area to 2.3 percent in 1993 reported by the State Education Commission indicates the continuous need for funds for reconstructing dilapidated school buildings in poor regions. Another major use of central-government capital outlays in more recent years has been the building of new classrooms and schools to accommodate the growth in student enrolment under compulsory education. A third use of investment funds is the improvement of rural school facilities and environment.[9]

Provinces allocate central-government grants for compulsory education in different ways. Shandong distributes central and provincial funds for compulsory education only to the 54 poorest counties (out of a total of 98 counties) to be used for facilities and equipment. In 1993 these funds totaled Y9 million. In Guizhou central-government funds for compulsory education (Y20 million in 1993) are primarily used for the repair of dilapidated schools, dormitories, and teachers' housing; the construction of more teachers' training schools; and the improvement of school facilities and equipment. Central-government subsidies have figured importantly in improving the education infrastructure in Guizhou. Of the Y420 million invested in primary and junior high school education, special education, and teacher training schools in Guizhou from 1986 to 1993, 46 percent, or Y195 million, came from the central government.

Simple formulas are often used in allocating province and prefecture-level funds for recurrent education expenditures to counties. Prefectures in Guizhou, for example, transfer budgetary funds for education to counties on the basis of total population.

Education Surcharges. In 1986 the State Council approved the levying of an education surcharge (*jiaoyu fujiafei*) on several existing taxes. The surcharge was first levied on state, collective, and private enterprises, at 1 percent of their total tax liability (comprising product, value-added, and business taxes). The State Council approved an increase in the surcharge rate to 2 percent in August 1990 and a further increase to 3 percent was allowed in 1994 (Pepper 1995). The surcharge, collected at the same time as the three enterprise taxes, accrues to the level of government responsible for the enterprise (based on the subordination relations of the enterprise). Even though education surcharges are considered budgetary revenue, they are distinguished from regular revenues by earmarking and also by the fact that appropriation

---

[9] Throughout the 1980s and into the 1990s a series of programs to improve education facilities were undertaken, including the *liang you* (every class having a classroom and every student having a desk and stool), the *ba peitao* (outfitting every primary and secondary school with a gate, garden, toilets, drainage, cultural room, laboratory, library, and sportsyard), and the *san tong* (providing water, electricity, and road linkups to every school) (Sun 1994).

is tied to the level of collection. This treatment makes the surcharge more akin to extrabudgetary revenues. The revenue from the education surcharge can generally be used to improve education conditions, to increase teachers' benefits, and to supplement education operating funds. A distinction is made between the urban education surcharge (*chengshi jiaoyu fujiafei*) and the education surcharge being levied in rural areas. The revenue from the urban education surcharge is to be used primarily for primary and secondary schools, including secondary vocational schools, run by counties, cities, and higher-level governments.

The revenue from the education surcharge on enterprises that run their own schools is returned to those enterprises by the central government, effectively exempting them from the surcharge. In 1993 state enterprises owned by the central government which ran their own schools received back from the government the Y60 million in education surcharges that they had paid. Units involved in the purchase of tobacco leaves and the production of cigarettes can, moreover, avail themselves of reductions of up to 50 percent in the education surcharge. Imported products are exempt from the surcharge but exported products are not, and the surcharge on the latter is not rebated.

The central government accounts for a tiny portion of the revenues from the education surcharge. In 1992 the central government collected only Y83.5 million from the urban education surcharge while local governments collected Y8.7 billion. Shandong has had a dramatic increase in revenues from the urban education surcharge, from Y16.9 million in 1986 to Y185 million in 1992. In Guizhou the surcharge has yielded more modest revenues although they have risen rapidly as well, from Y25 million in 1990 to Y51 million in 1992 (Table 6.10).

Most counties derive limited revenue from the urban education surcharge because the tax base for the surcharge is concentrated in cities. Furthermore, the total budgetary revenue of counties has not been growing fast enough to meet their anticipated education expenses plus other expenditures. Local-government officials have therefore increasingly turned to extrabudgetary revenue sources to fund compulsory education. Rural education surcharges (*nongcun jiaoyu fujiafei*) were first levied on rural residents and rural enterprises in the late 1980s. These surcharges are treated as extrabudgetary revenue. They are typically levied at 1 to 2 percent of the per capita income of rural residents

Table 6.10: National and Selected Provincial
Education Surcharge and Tax Revenue, 1991 and 1992
(Y thousand)

	1991	*1992*
Total	7,515,830	8,780,610
Central	1,300	83,500
Local	7,514,530	8,697,110
Shandong	950,010	1,050,490
Urban	147,020	185,250
Rural	758,900	806,420
Guizhou	57,810	95,440
Urban	29,120	50,970
Rural	22,860	34,990

Note: The total education surcharge and tax revenue consists of revenue from the urban education surcharge (*chengshi jiaoyu fujiafei*), the rural education surcharge (*nongcun jiaoyu fujiafei*),
and other miscellaneous surcharges and taxes earmarked for education.
Source: State Education Commission (1993), pp. 77-87.

and 1 percent of the taxes paid by township, village, and private enterprises. Township governments collect the revenue from the surcharge
and then hand the funds up to the county. The county education bureau
manages these funds and decides how they should be allocated back to
the townships for the support of education. Typical of poorer areas,
Zunyi County uses the revenue from the rural education surcharge primarily to pay the salaries of community teachers, to rebuild dilapidated school buildings, and to cover the tuition of poor students. Better-off areas, such as Shandong, use the funds to improve school facilities (add more laboratories, expand the library, etc.) and upgrade teachers' training. County officials may not divert funds from the rural education surcharge to other expenditure uses.

Local governments needing more resources to finance rural
education have recently begun levying additional education surcharges
and earmarking fees and taxes already collected for education. Starting
in 1990, for example, local governments were authorized to levy a fee
on the construction of residential and commercial buildings to earn

revenues for education. The fee varies by location. Yicheng County in Hubei charges Y2.5 per square meter for new private structures and Y5 per square meter for new state and collective structures (Sun 1994). Qingxin County in Guangdong collects Y10 per square meter for all new residential and commercial structures (West 1994). The use of residential and commercial water and electricity and the sale of pork and coal are subject to surcharges in some areas. In many counties a portion (up to 2 percent) of the salaries of party, government, and state and collective enterprise workers and staff are being garnished for education. Education officials in Qufu report raising education funds through ten different means (Table 6.11). All of these revenues are considered extrabudgetary funds. While not all counties collect all of these miscellaneous taxes and fees for education, nearly all counties collect some.

Started under local initiative, the levying of these miscellaneous fees and taxes for education is now sanctioned by the central government. Oversight responsibility for these fees and taxes has been delegated to the province to ensure that local governments are making an

Table 6.11: Channels for Collecting Funds to Support Education in Qufu County, 1993/94

- Surcharge on electricity of Y0.01/kilowatt-hour
- 30 percent of fines collected for violating family planning rules
- 100 percent of fines collected for illegal use of land (e.g., squatting, illegal conversion from agricultural to residential or commercial use)
- 100 percent of fines collected for unauthorized purchase of goods by organizations and enterprises
- 15 percent of increase in fiscal revenue
- 2 percent of basic wage of workers with fixed wages (including permanent, contract, and temporary workers)
- 15 percent of investment expenditure on urban development (*kaifa feiyong*)
- 10 percent of urban construction allocation from the budget
- Surcharge on coal of Y1/ton
- 30 percent of ticket revenue from tourist attractions

Source: Qufu Education Bureau.

effort to raise funds for education and at the same time that the local burden does not become too onerous. County and township governments decide which taxes and fees to levy and at what rates, based on the strength of the local economy and subject to higher-level approval.

In 1992, the urban, rural, and miscellaneous education surcharges and taxes yielded a total of Y8.8 billion in revenues for education nationwide (Table 6.10), with Shandong collecting the largest share, 12 percent. The surcharges and taxes accounted for 18 percent of total expenditures on education in Shandong and 8 percent in Guizhou. In 1993, Penglai's revenues of Y14 million from the rural education surcharge and Y1 million from the urban education surcharge represented 28 percent of total education funds (Table 6.4). Zunyi collected Y6.5 million from the rural and urban education surcharges—15 percent of total education funds (Table 6.6). Puding began levying the urban education surcharge only in 1992 and derived minimal revenue from it. Its revenue from the rural education surcharge was more than half a million yuan in 1993, but this, together with the urban education surcharge, accounted for less than 6 percent of total education funds (Table 6.7).

Division of Responsibility Between Levels of Government. In general, the lowest levels of government, the county and the township, are responsible for allocating funds to support the recurrent operating costs of rural basic education. Among our study sites, Penglai received no funds for education from higher levels in 1993 and Qufu received only Y450,000. The central government has already put local governments on notice that they will have to supply more of the funds they need to educate the present student population and to provide for the future expansion of education services under the Compulsory Education Law. These levels of government appropriate funds to pay the salaries of state (*gongban*) teachers and a subsidy to community (*minban*) and substitute (*daike*) teachers in the county's rural primary and secondary schools (see Box 6.1 for the classification of teachers). Salaries are the largest component of the recurrent costs of rural basic education, at about 85 percent of the total. The rest of the community teachers' salaries must then be paid by the villages. The counties vary in the specific assignment of expenditure responsibility to the county and the township.

Box 6.1: Classification of Rural Teachers

State (*gongban*) teachers are considered government (state) employees and as such are paid out of the government budget and are entitled to retirement benefits. State teachers are usually paid a premium of approximately 10 percent over the salaries of comparably educated local cadres to attract teachers to the profession in rural areas.

Over the years, community (*minban*) teachers have been hired when the number of state teachers assigned to local schools was insufficient to meet enrolment needs. The government is responsible for paying a subsidy to community teachers, and the local community (township and village) pays the remainder of the salary. Community teachers are also entitled to a retirement pension, although it is less generous than the pension received by state teachers. At various times since the 1950s, there have been efforts to convert community teachers to state teacher status. These efforts have succeeded in a few townships. Starting in 1986, the central government decreed that no more community teachers would be hired. One reason given for the hiring ban was that the government wanted to ensure that all teachers would be rewarded equally and that some of them would not have to depend on village resources for their livelihood. A more frequently cited reason for the ban was the government's desire to halt the rise in the number of out-of-plan teachers who were entitled to government-sponsored retirement benefits.

The ban on the hiring of community teachers and the inadequate increase in the number of state teachers have led to a rise in the number of a third category of teachers called substitute (*daike*) teachers. These do not play the same role as substitute teachers in the United States who fill in for absent regular teachers for a day or more. *Daike* teachers (also translated as supplementary or temporary teachers) play much the same role as community teachers used to, filling in the shortage in state teachers. Substitute teachers are paid a salary by the government; however, the salary is very low and the teachers are not entitled to a pension. Villages are not required to supplement the teachers' pay and most villages do not. Because these teachers are viewed as temporary, they are not included in official statistics on teachers and staff. These teachers receive relatively low education and training.

All three types of teachers can be found in both state-run and community-run schools at the primary and lower secondary level. Community and supplementary teachers, however, constitute a larger share of teachers in primary schools than in junior high schools. Virtually all senior high school teachers are state teachers.

Counties follow one of three general models in dividing expenditure responsibility. Under the first model, the county government assumes primary responsibility for educational expenditures, and the county budget finances all the salaries of state teachers and the subsidy for community and substitute teachers. The county finance office either pays teachers directly or transfers funds to the township finance office for disbursement. Villages, sometimes with the help of the township government, pay the rest of the salaries of community teachers. This model imposes uniformity in state teachers' salaries across townships. It is common in poor townships and villages where the tax base is weak and financial revenue is insufficient to support the schools, and so expenditure responsibility falls on the county.[10] In Puding, which follows this model, the county education bureau has decided to stop transferring funds for teachers' salaries to the township office because some townships occasionally divert these funds to other uses and teachers are not paid on time. The county now pays teachers directly and in the process has done away with the variation in teacher salary arrears across townships. Officials in Qufu also said they are considering switching from this model to one of increased expenditure responsibility for the township.

A second model divides the responsibility for paying state teachers between the county and the township. The county government appropriates funds to pay the basic wages (*jiben gongzi*) of state teachers and a subsidy to community and substitute teachers, while the township pays state teachers' subsidies and benefits (*buzhu* and *fuli*) and villages pay the rest of the community teachers' salaries. Common in middle-income counties in Guangdong Province and in most townships in Zunyi, this model introduces a variation in state teachers' salaries between townships in the same county. Penglai, which practices a variant of this model, continues to fund all the salaries of state teachers out of the county budget; however, it has passed on to the townships and villages nearly all of the burden of subsidy to community teachers. Penglai County allocates an amount in its budget for an average of 9 percent of the annual salary (Y360) of each community teacher; townships and villages provide the remaining 91 percent (Y3,640).

---

[10] If the county government receives net transfers from higher levels of government, then support for rural basic education actually comes not only from the county but also from those higher levels of government.

Finally, local governments may also divide expenditure responsibility by transferring all the salaries of state teachers and the subsidies to community and substitute teachers out of the county budget to township budgets. This model offers townships even more flexibility in competing for the services of state teachers and is practiced in the wealthiest areas of the PRC, such as the Pearl River Delta. Zunyi, by no means a wealthy county (per capita rural net income in 1993 was Y770, below the national average of Y922), has adopted this model in a few of the county's wealthiest townships. In other townships the county shares the expenditure burden. Townships in Zunyi have long played a dominant role in financing education. In 1987 they supplied 72 percent of the combined budgetary appropriations of the county and townships for education (Table 6.6).

Because they are paid partly by villages, community teachers within the same township or county can have widely divergent salaries, depending on the ability of the villages to provide supplementary pay. Community teachers in some rich villages earn more than state teachers. In contrast, community teachers in poor villages are often paid a fraction of what state teachers in the same school are paid. Community teachers in Guizhou are among the lowest paid in the country. In Puding, for example, the county paid state teachers an average of Y234 a month and community teachers only Y44 a month in 1993, and the supplementary pay to community teachers from locally raised funds ranged from zero in the poorest villages to Y50/month in better-off villages. Schools in middle and upper income counties in the PRC, on the other hand, are typically able to double or triple the subsidy paid by the local government to community teachers. These differences are illustrated in Table 6.12, which shows that in Penglai, community teachers' salaries average 71 percent of state teachers' salaries, while in Puding they average only 27 percent. The practice of teachers receiving widely divergent salaries and from several sources is highly unusual in other countries.

The pay of state and community teachers and that of teachers and personnel with comparable credentials in local state-owned enterprises are to be gradually equalized, according to a State Council ruling (Xinhua 1993). But in some places where wages in state enterprises have stagnated, the prospect of equal pay may not be so attractive to teachers. If the major wage adjustment of 1993 were to be implemented

**Table 6.12: Average Monthly Salary of Teachers,
by Type, in Selected Counties, 1993
(Y)**

	Penglai	*Puding*
State teachers	467	234
Community teachers	333	64
Substitute teachers	95	40

Source: Education officials in Penglai and Puding counties.

fully, teachers would receive 25-50 percent more in salaries. In Qufu, education officials said community teachers should be paid 1.8 times the average local salary. Based on per capita rural net income (*nongmin cun shouru*), which the officials use to measure this average, community teachers were paid 2.7 times the average local salary in 1993 (per capita rural net income was Y940). This measure is not appropriate, however, because it is total income divided by the total population, including those working and their dependents, and does not represent the average salary of the labor force.

Enterprise-Run Schools. Expenditures of enterprises on their own schools account for 5.6 percent of all funds spent on education throughout the country. In Shandong the share was 2.3 percent of the total and in Guizhou, 3.9 percent. Enterprise-run schools are largely an urban phenomenon and are rare in rural areas. Enterprises and government units that employ and house thousands of workers and staff at one site frequently set up and run their own schools. Depending on the number and ages of the children of staff and workers, the work unit may establish on its property a primary school and in a few cases a junior high school. Some of the work units that commonly run their own primary school are universities and large-scale centrally run state enterprises. As mentioned above, the urban education surcharge levied on these enterprises is rebated to them.

School-Run Enterprise Profits. Another extrabudgetary source of funds for education is the profits of school-run enterprises. Schools establish enterprises to provide students with work opportunities and to generate funds for their own use. In reality, students seldom participate in the activities of school-run enterprises. Instead, the management is contracted out by the school which assigns a teacher or a member of the school staff to coordinate with the enterprise. The contractor then hires workers from the community. Schools generally lack the management expertise, technology, and capital to manage an enterprise successfully. This is particularly true in poor areas, where rural enterprises are few or nonexistent. The jobs that these enterprises open up for the rural underemployed may, however, still interest local officials in establishing a school-run enterprise. Furthermore, the tax-exempt status of these enterprises can give them a competitive advantage over other enterprises. In rural areas, school-run enterprises are usually attached to a secondary school. Among the four sites visited, Penglai derived the most funds for education from school-run enterprises (Y5.6 million), followed by Qufu (Y3.7 million) and Zunyi (Y50,000). Puding had no profitable school-run enterprises.

Voluntary Donations. Donations from the public, including overseas Chinese and foreigners, were identified in the 1993 State Council circular on education reform and development as a source of additional funds for education that should be exploited (Xinhua 1993). Donations are classified as self-raised funds. In recent years, a number of philanthropic foundations with an educational focus have been established in the PRC. Some of these were established and are being run by local governments. An annual fund-raising campaign for education by the Guangzhou city government, for example, brought in over Y60 million in contributions in 1993. Several educational foundations based in Hong Kong also support education in the PRC.

The best-known national foundation, Project Hope (*Xiwang Gongcheng*), was begun by the central committee of the Communist Youth League in the late 1980s. The League established a nongovernmental organization, the PRC Youth Development Fund, to support schools in the poor areas of the PRC and to help poor schoolchildren. As of 1994, Y201 million had been collected in support of 549,000 children and 204 primary schools nationwide. Overseas contributions compose more than half of all donations, and the central government has donated about Y5 million. Many Chinese are sympathetic to the objectives of the campaign, and enterprises as well as individuals have given generously.

Among the four counties in the field study, only Puding receives support from Project Hope. Information on that county illustrates the low level of support provided by the program. Students in Puding County began receiving support from Project Hope in 1990, and 953 students now receive assistance. These students are guaranteed support, first at Y20 a semester and since September 1993 at Y30 a semester, for six years. Of the Y53,500 spent so far, Y40,000 came from the provincial branch of Project Hope, Y8,500 from the county and townships, and Y5,000 from donations of individuals and work units in the county. To qualify for assistance from Project Hope, a child must be 7 to 12 years of age and live in a household with a per capita income of less than Y150. Limited funds prompted a decision to concentrate resources on those students who had already attended school and showed promise but were hindered by financial difficulties from enrolling. But although more than 7,000 students in Puding meet these criteria, only a fraction receive assistance. Of the students receiving support, 250, or 19 percent, belong to minority nationalities.

Another way of raising funds is through organized donations by students in urban and better-off rural areas to support students in poorer counties. Schools also benefit from contributions made by alumni and former residents of the locality. It is not unusual for township education officials to contact former students for contributions when a new school or dormitory needs to be built. Contributions in cash or in kind likewise come from current residents and enterprises.

Student Fees. The State Council has decreed that students in the compulsory education program are to pay only a miscellaneous fee (*zafei*). Many schools, however, charge other fees as well including a community education (*minban jiaoyu*) fee to support community-sponsored teachers and schools, a class association (*banhui*) fee to support teachers, and a capital construction (*jijian*) fee. The last-named fee is usually charged only when the schools plan to repair dilapidated school buildings or to build new classrooms, dormitories, or housing for teachers. Students have also reportedly been charged fees for recreation, law and order, cafeterias, tree planting, locks, and broomsticks (Deng 1993).

School fees and tuition are treated as extrabudgetary funds and are managed by the education bureau. The miscellaneous fee paid by students stays with the school that collected the fee. A portion of the capital construction fee may be handed up to the county for redistribution to other schools as needed. The miscellaneous and other fees may be adjusted each year by the province (or the county, if price control authority has devolved to it).

The term "commissioned" (*daishou*) fees is often used by education officials to refer to another group of student fees. The school collecting these fees is deemed to be acting on behalf of another unit, and so does not keep the funds but rather passes them on to that unit. The collection of such fees as the physical exam fee and insurance policy fee by schools has aroused controversy. The value and necessity of having students purchase insurance, for example, has been questioned by parents. Also at issue is whether or not schools or teachers are receiving some benefit in exchange from the providers of these services. Otherwise, as long as the teachers or schools earn no commission from the book distribution company, for example, parents find it acceptable for schools to arrange for the purchase of textbooks by students.

Several of the so-called commissioned fees, such as water, electricity, and fuel fees are clearly meant to reimburse school expenditures. Some schools charge a fee for teaching instruments (*jiaoyu yiqi*) and pass the collections up to the township or county government. The local education bureau then periodically allocates teaching equipment, such as laboratory instruments, to the school at no cost. A school desk (*kezhou*) fee collected in many schools pays for a desk and stool for each student. Education officials in Qufu explained that the families of first-time enrollees pay Y80 for a stool and desk. Students use these until graduation after which they may resell or keep them.

In the 1993 academic year, an average of Y21.55 per student was collected from rural primary school students and Y44.03 from rural junior high school students in miscellaneous fees (Table 6.13). Students in rural schools generally pay lower fees than urban students but, because of lower total expenditures for rural schools, end up paying a slightly higher share of total costs. In Shandong, urban primary and secondary schools charge a miscellaneous fee that is 50 percent higher than that charged by rural counterpart schools. Penglai County raised the ceiling on the miscellaneous fee in 1994 in an effort to keep up with inflation. Rural primary schools in Penglai are now allowed to charge up to Y20 per semester (versus the former Y8) and rural junior high schools may charge up to Y30 (versus Y16).

Schools, except those at the compulsory education level, are allowed to charge tuition aside from the miscellaneous fee. General se-

**Table 6.13: Tuition and Fees Collected,
by Level of Education, 1993**

Level of Education	Tuition and Fees per Student (Y)	Total Cost per Student (Y)	Tuition and Fee Share of Total Cost (%)
General senior high school	118.00	917	12.87
General junior high school	47.00	477	9.90
Rural general junior high school	44.03	413	10.66
Primary school	22.84	247	9.25
Rural primary school	21.55	225	9.58
Rural vocational school	181.52	993	18.28

Source: State Education Commission.

nior high schools typically charge at least the same amount as the miscellaneous fee. Vocational schools are more expensive than general academic schools, in part, because of a low student-to-teacher ratio. The total cost per student in a rural vocational school averages Y993, as compared with Y413 for a rural junior high school and Y917 for a senior high school (Table 6.13). Students in rural vocational schools bear a greater burden of the total cost through higher fees and tuition (Y181.52 in 1993).

The contrast with the situation in the early 1980s when students paid less than Y10 to attend primary school (Zhang 1993) is striking. As government funding lags behind the rise in education costs, students are forced to help meet the shortfall. Tuition and fees accounted for only 4.4 percent of total funds for education in 1991; in 1993 the share had increased to 8.2 percent (State Education Commission 1993). Poorer counties tend to be more dependent on tuition and fees than better-off areas. Among the four counties surveyed, the reliance on tuition and fees to fund education was found to be inversely related to degree of wealth.[11]

[11] Tuition and fees made up 3.7 percent of education funds in Penglai, 4.7 percent in Qufu, 4.8 percent in Zunyi, and 5.7 percent in Puding.

The Minister for State Education recently threatened to punish schools that overcharge their students, as part of the ongoing anticorruption campaign. But whether fees are excessive or not is difficult to determine without considering incomes. School fees that may be considered excessive in Guizhou would be perfectly acceptable in coastal Shandong. Qufu education officials estimate that to put a student through primary school, the family must spend Y200 per year, or 21 percent of rural per capita income in 1993. On the other hand, students in Puding pay some of the lowest school fees in the country—only about Y90 per school year for fees, books, and supplies—yet school expenses take up 26 percent of rural per capita income. Moreover, the Y200 paid by Qufu students buys art materials and music lessons, while Puding students receive only the most basic of educational supplies. Local education officials are authorized to exempt a limited number of poor students from paying school fees or to lower the fees for them. In Zunyi, the miscellaneous fee is not imposed on a maximum of 5 percent of primary school students.

Other Self-Raised Funds. Self-raised funds are another important source of supplementary funds for education. In 1992 self-raised funds, including donations, made up 8 percent of funds spent by the government on education that year. By 1993 the share had risen to 10 percent. Except for village *tongchou* funds, which are raised to supplement the salaries of community teachers, self-raised funds are primarily used by schools to fund their investments in fixed assets. The funds fill the gap left by government appropriations which mostly go to recurrent costs or salaries, leaving little for school improvements. Loans for such expenditures and investments are also not available to schools and local governments. Local governments and communities need to raise funds to match the limited available grants from upper levels and to repair dilapidated classrooms or dormitories or to build new ones, and to purchase school equipment. The value of donated community labor (usually required of each household or laborer) for school maintenance and construction is considered part of self-raised funds. The financial burden on rural residents has become onerous in many areas, and farmers now refer to the demand for self-raised funds as the education tax. In Hainan one county required each resident to contribute Y55 for the construction of a school; one village charged each resident Y75 and required households to contribute rocks and stones.

Even though poorer areas receive more generous grants from upper levels of government for the expansion of the education infrastructure, the investment burden on the local government and the community is still very heavy. From 1987 to 1993, Zunyi County spent over Y39 million to rebuild 295 schools. Self-raised funds from the township composed 63 percent, while appropriations from the county and higher levels of government accounted for only 37 percent. Wealthy rural areas similarly rely on locally raised funds for education infrastructure. In 1993, capital construction for education in Penglai was funded with Y500,000 from the county budget, Y500,000 from the urban education surcharge, Y4 million from township budgets, and Y4 million in self-raised funds. Furthermore, local governments and communities must provide for the operation and maintenance of the new structures. To the extent that funds appropriated for recurrent expenditures are taken up by salaries, local governments often rely in part on self-raised funds to cover operation and maintenance expenses.

IMPLICATIONS FOR THE QUALITY OF EDUCATION

The Compulsory Education Law is intended not only to increase the number of children completing nine years of education but also to improve the quality of their education. This section examines current levels of educational attainment and indicators of the quality of education in rural areas, particularly in the fieldwork sites. The indicators comprise measures of the human as well as the physical resources of rural schools.

Attendance at School. A wide gap in educational attainment exists across the PRC. Shandong, for one, is well on the way to achieving its target of nine years of universal education in 1997. In 1993, 83 percent of primary school graduates continued on to junior high school. Qufu, with 85 percent of primary school graduates entering junior high school in 1993, is slightly ahead of the average for the province. Qufu plans to improve this share to 100 percent in 1996. On the other hand, only 42 percent of primary school graduates in Guizhou (72 percent in urban areas and 36 percent in rural areas) continue on to junior high school. In fact, one-third of Guizhou's counties still have not attained universal primary school. Zunyi is one of the few rural areas in Guizhou that are likely to achieve nine years of compulsory education before the year 2000. Since 1985 virtually all children in Zunyi complete six years of education, and in 1993, 82 percent of primary school graduates entered junior high school. Puding education officials also plan to achieve nine years of compulsory education by the year 2000. But with only 42 percent of primary school graduates entering junior high school, Puding has much further to go than Zunyi.

A survey conducted by the State Statistical Bureau revealed that 30 million children aged 6-14 have never been to school or have dropped out (Hou 1994). Moreover, about 4 million schoolchildren are forced to interrupt their studies every year, mostly because their families are too poor. Among all rural children in the age group 6-14, 20 percent were not enrolled in school in 1989/90 (Table 6.14). In Shandong the share was lower at 15 percent, and in Guizhou the share was much higher at 36 percent. The gender gap was also more pronounced in Guizhou. In 1992, females made up only 43 percent of primary school students in Guizhou and only 35 percent of junior high school students in the province.

Only 64 percent of students throughout the PRC, and an even lower 42 percent in Guizhou, complete primary school in their first six years at school. This low rate is attributable to high failure and dropout rates. Each year over 8 percent of primary school students in Guizhou fail, as compared with only 2.5 percent in Shandong (Table 6.15). The failure rate is significantly lower among junior high school students, who must pass required tests before being admitted to that level. How-

**Table 6.14: Proportion of Children Aged 6-14
Not Enrolled in School, 1989/90 Academic Year
(Percent)**

	Both Sexes	Male	Female
PRC	19.13	16.10	22.38
Rural	20.29	16.62	24.24
Shandong	14.47	11.76	17.38
Rural	15.33	11.90	19.02
Guizhou	34.04	25.06	43.82
Rural	35.89	26.10	46.55

Source: Yang (1994), p. 59.

Table 6.15: School Attendance Indicators
for Shandong and Guizhou, 1992
(Percent)

	Shandong	*Guizhou*
Junior middle school students passing standards for all subjects	75.9	21.8
Primary school students passing standards for all subjects	89.0	38.3
Primary school dropout rate	1.3	7.1
Primary school student failure rate	2.5	8.0
Junior middle school dropout rate	2.1	3.6
Junior middle school student failure rate	0.4	2.9

Notes: The dropout rate is based on the number of students who dropped out and did not return to school within the same school year.
          The failure rate is based on the number of students who were not promoted to the next higher grade at the end of the school year.
Source: State Education Commission (1993), pp. 72-73.

ever, the dropout rate among junior high school students is still higher in Guizhou than in Shandong. Education officials in Guizhou report dropout rates approaching 30 percent in the poorest areas. Students in rich and poor areas alike drop out of school, but for different reasons. Students in rich areas often drop out of school to go to work, while those in poor areas are kept out of school by lack of funds for school fees. According to the Guizhou Education Department, females constitute the vast majority of dropouts. Of 2,400 children aged 7-14 surveyed in three poor minority counties in Guizhou, 268 were not in school. In all three counties economic difficulties were the overwhelming reason. Other reasons given were the need for children to help out at home, poor conditions at school, family preference for investing in the education of male children, and learning difficulties (Wang 1994).

As compared with Shandong, where 76 percent of junior high school students passed subject standards in 1992, Guizhou, with only a 22 percent rate, provides education of much lower quality (Table 6.15). The gap between the two provinces is similarly wide for primary school students: 89 percent in Shandong but only 38 percent in Guizhou passed subject standards in 1992.

Another indicator of the quality of education is the percentage of the graduating class that passes the exam for the next higher level of schooling. This indicator has some drawbacks, however. There appears to be a strong correlation between the number of students passing the exam and the number of seats open at the next higher level. For example, if only 50 percent of those graduating from sixth grade can be accommodated in junior high schools, then no matter how smart a sixth grade class is, not all can enrol in junior high school, and the number of students passing the entrance exam reflects this limitation. In Longkeng Township in Zunyi, which is implementing compulsory education, 583 of the 591 students graduating from primary school who sat for the junior high school entrance exam passed, for a pass ratio of 98 percent. In contrast, Maguan Township in Puding, where compulsory education has not yet been implemented, only 280 out of 890 students passed.

Teachers' Academic Credentials. Another important measure of the quality of education is the academic credentials of teachers. According to present standards, qualified primary school teachers must have graduated from senior high school or a secondary teacher-training school; qualified junior high school teachers should have two to three years of postsecondary training equivalent to a *dazhuan* degree; and senior high school teachers should have a college degree (Paine 1992). Data from the four field sites indicate that more developed areas tend to have a higher proportion of qualified teachers. All teachers at one primary school visited in Penglai, including the one substitute teacher and the nine community teachers, were qualified. Throughout Penglai, 90 percent of all primary school teachers are qualified, but only 47 percent of junior high school teachers and 44 percent of senior high school teachers meet the standards (Table 6.16). In contrast, only 69 percent of all primary school teachers in Guizhou are qualified. In Puding primary schools, 74 percent of the state teachers and only 35 percent of the community and substitute teachers are qualified, for an overall qualification rate of 59 percent. One-third of all teachers in Zunyi do not even meet the standards for primary school teachers.

The various levels of government share the responsibility for training teachers and upgrading the skills of the teaching staff. In most

**Table 6.16: Qualified Teachers, by Level of School
in Guizhou, Puding, and Penglai, 1993
(Percent)**

	Guizhou	*Puding*	*Penglai*
Primary school	69	59	90
Junior high school	56	63	47
Senior high school	...	37	44
Vocational school	63	...	...

... Not available.
Note: Qualified teachers meet the minimal education standards for each level of school. See text
for details.
Sources: Guizhou Department of Education; Puding Education Bureau; Penglai Education
Bureau.

provinces, the province is responsible for training senior high school teachers, the prefecture for training primary and junior high school teachers,
and the county for conducting refresher training for teachers. To raise
teaching standards, both Qufu and Penglai send unqualified teachers back
to school for several months to several years. Poor counties, such as Puding,
must direct their limited resources to upgrading the physical infrastructure
and have few resources left for such supplementary training.

School Facilities and Equipment. The quality of education depends partly on school facilities and equipment. The aforementioned campaigns to improve the physical infrastructure of education have eliminated dilapidated school facilities in most areas. Dilapidated schools no
longer exist in Qufu and Penglai, according to reports from those counties. Now only smaller areas throughout the PRC still have the problem.
In Guizhou, dilapidated school space accounts for 9.5 percent of the total
area of primary and junior high schools but remains a serious problem in
28 out of the 75 counties (including county-level cities) of the province.
One of these counties is Puding where 26 percent of the school space is
still classified as dilapidated and dangerous. Visits to several schools with
no electricity, open windows, and holes in the floor, walls, and ceiling
confirmed the extent of the problem. Such conditions cannot help but
have a negative effect on the quality of education.

Despite national and provincial standards for school facilities and equipment, the PRC has a tremendously wide range of school conditions. At one extreme are the teaching points (*jiaoxuedian*), one-room schoolhouses where all children from within walking distance are taught by a single teacher, usually a substitute teacher with no more than a junior high school education. There are no teaching materials, except perhaps for a chalkboard in a few schools. At the other extreme are the school systems in the PRC's wealthiest rural areas, such as the Pearl River Delta. Primary and secondary schools in these areas exceed the highest standards of the country and, in some cases, even the standards of Hong Kong. Some schools are already better equipped than most Chinese schools in Hong Kong.

Most schools fall between these two extremes. None of the four junior high schools and 16 primary schools in Shiban Township, Zunyi, has a separate room for a library, laboratory experiments, or music, but the schools do have a separate classroom for each grade. The primary school visited in Penglai had separate library, laboratory, and music rooms and seven projectors.

The counties, townships, and schools visited in Guizhou reported poorer physical conditions than those found in Shandong. In Guizhou, 47 percent of primary schools do not meet the standards of the area for compulsory education schools, and 80 percent of complete (*wanquan*) primary schools do not have the required laboratory equipment. Only 9 percent of junior high schools have the required scientific teaching equipment. A mere 1.4 percent of junior high schools have adequate music equipment and 3.9 percent have libraries that meet standards. Not all students in Guizhou have even a desk and stool. By the end of the century Guizhou plans to have enough desks and stools for 80 percent of primary school students and 70 percent of junior high school students. In addition, 80 percent of primary schools and 50 percent of secondary schools are to have the teaching equipment necessary to satisfy national third-class standards.

RURAL PUBLIC HEALTH CARE

This section examines public health services provided by rural governments. The section first addresses the organizational delivery of these services and then evaluates the quality of health-care services in the field sites. Finally, it assesses the role of the various sources of financing for rural public health.

ORGANIZATION

Health-care services are provided to the rural population of the PRC through a three-tier system at the county, township, and village levels. This system has existed since the late 1960s, when a health-care unit was established at the then brigade level, joining existing county and commune facilities.[12] This same system continues to the present with some modifications in management and financing as described below (Figure 6.2).

The upper level of health care at the county level is provided by at least one county general hospital, a maternal and child health (MCH) station, and an epidemic prevention station, all managed by the Public Health Bureau of the county.[13] Some counties also run a separate hospital that specializes in Chinese traditional medicine. The county hospitals typically have outpatient clinics. If the county seat is large, additional medical clinics serve the urban population. Aside from serving the residents of the county seat and attending to referrals from lower levels, the medical personnel of county hospitals are expected to supervise and train medical personnel at the lower levels.

The epidemic prevention station is responsible for controlling the spread of infectious diseases and for ensuring general environmental sanitation throughout the county. To this end, the station organizes and supervises inoculation campaigns, checks water quality, and controls waterborne parasites. Epidemic prevention station personnel assisted by lower-level health aides also carry out inspections to maintain good hygiene in eating places, public toilets, schools, and industry.

The MCH station provides family planning services and prenatal and obstetrical care, and monitors the development of infants and

---

[12] A 1965 State Council directive calling for health reform and more emphasis on rural services led to the training of barefoot doctors and the extension of health care to the village level (Chen, P., 1976, p. 31).

[13] The MCH and epidemic prevention stations were mostly established in the 1950s.

Figure 6.2: Rural Health-Care Organizational Structure

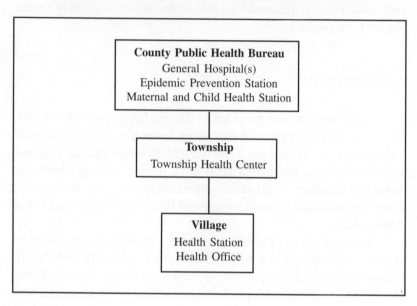

children. MCH personnel also oversee the training of rural birth attendants.

At the township level, a township health center (*weishengyuan*) is the middle tier in the rural health care system.[14] While separate units provide curative, preventive, and MCH care at the county level, at the township level, the township health center provides all three services. The township health center typically houses a small hospital, an outpatient clinic, and offices for preventive and MCH care. The center and all health activities in the township are overseen by the township vice-head who holds the public health portfolio.[15] The operations of the township health center are supported and supervised by the three health-care units at the county level (general hospital, epidemic prevention station, and MCH station).

---

[14] Many of these health centers date from the time of collectivization. In 1986, the commune health center became officially known as the township hospital or township health center.
[15] Before township governments were established, the commune health center was supervised by the local commune management committee and the Party committee.

The lowest tier and often the first line of rural health-care delivery is the village health station (*weishengsuo*) or health office (*weishengshi*). A health office tends to be smaller than a health station and serves as a medical outpost. Medical personnel at the village health stations and offices are responsible for basic curative, preventive, and MCH care. Rural doctors and health aides at the village level diagnose and treat only common medical problems and refer more serious illnesses to the township health center. They provide family planning services, such as fitting IUDs. In addition, village doctors and health aides give immunization treatment, attend to uncomplicated deliveries, and provide health education under the guidance of health personnel from the township and county levels.

Ideally, patients who come to the village health facility are subjected by medical personnel to the first level of screening. Village health personnel are trained to deal with the most common and basic illnesses and, more importantly, to diagnose the seriousness of illnesses and injuries. Serious cases are referred to the next higher level and the referral can continue up the line, with township hospitals referring more complicated cases to the county hospital and the latter referring cases beyond its capabilities to the province-level hospital. Patients themselves can choose to go directly to township and county clinics and hospitals, instead of their village health station.[16]

QUALITY OF HEALTH CARE

The central government, through the Ministry of Public Health, initiates programs and sets targets for rural health care. Current programs and targets for health-care facilities, personnel, and public health emphasize basic and preventive health care. For the upper tier of the rural health-care system, the priorities of the ministry are the reconstruction of county general hospitals (particularly those built before 1960), the upgrading of the medical equipment at county facilities, and the establishment of a Chinese traditional medicine hospital in

---

[16] Bypassing the village health station can, however, render the patient ineligible for reimbursement of expenses under an insurance program.

those counties that do not yet have one.[17] At the township level, a priority is the reconstruction and upgrading of equipment at township health centers.

In 1990, the Ministry of Public Health with several other government agencies proclaimed a set of rural health-care objectives (Chen, M., 1994). Among the objectives for the year 2000 is the allocation of 8 percent of county and township annual budgets to health care. Also by the year 2000, 90 percent of all villages in poor counties and all villages in wealthy counties are to have a health station. Within five years, infant mortality was to be decreased by 20 percent in poor counties and by 5 percent in wealthy counties, and maternal mortality was to be reduced by 30 percent in poor counties and by 15 percent in wealthy counties. The resurgence of contagious diseases brought under control in the 1960s and 1970s caused the Ministry of Public Health to include child inoculation targets in the program. Poor counties are to provide immunization coverage of four vaccines for childhood illnesses to a minimum of 85 percent of their population, while wealthy counties are to cover 95 percent of their population.

With hospitals increasingly dependent on revenue generation for their operating expenses, local public health authorities sometimes have priorities that differ from those at the national level. Hospitals want to offer high-technology medical care because some patients are willing to pay for it and the hospital thereby earns a profit. Local officials accordingly focus on upgrading county and higher-level hospitals which serve those who can afford better medical care. But such medical care is seldom preventive or affordable to rural patients. A case in point is the new wing that the Qufu Public Health Bureau plans to add to the county's general hospital to serve high-level officials and foreigners. Rooms are to be air-conditioned and equipped with color television sets. Although the Ministry of Public Health will not support this project, it cannot prevent local governments from investing public funds in it.

National statistics and information gathered in Shandong and Guizhou indicate uneven achievement of the ministry's targets and, consequently, uneven quality of rural health-care services throughout the PRC.

---

[17] The World Bank study on the health sector (1990b) questioned the efficiency of maintaining separate Western and Chinese traditional medicine systems with their duplicate facilities.

Facilities. All four counties visited are served by at least one general hospital, a Chinese traditional medicine hospital, an epidemic prevention station, a skin disease station, and an MCH station. The counties also have various other units under the Public Health Bureau. The Qufu Public Health Bureau runs a school of traditional Chinese medicine, and the Penglai Public Health Bureau oversees a tuberculosis sanatorium and a health inspection station for seamen.

By the early 1990s, nearly all townships in the PRC (93 percent) had a health center (Table 6.17). The centers were mostly built in the late 1950s when communes were established, but they vary in size and state of repair within and across regions. A number of centers in better-off areas, such as Shandong, were remodeled and rebuilt in the past decade. A new hospital with several multistory buildings was being built in one township visited in Penglai. Township health centers in Shandong typically have several examining rooms, a room for gynecological examinations and obstetrical deliveries, a room for minor surgery, an inoculation room, and a pharmacy-dispensary.

On the other hand, 15 percent of Guizhou's townships still have no township health center and the health centers in some townships do not have their own building. Health centers occupy rented space in 18 of the 38 townships in Zunyi and in four of the 11 townships in Puding; often, as in Puding, the center is housed in a single room. Furthermore, one-third of the space occupied by township health centers in Guizhou are considered dilapidated (*weifang*) and dangerous. The estimated dilapidated area was over 10 percent in Zunyi and 50 percent in Puding.

Limited building space translates into fewer beds, an average of only 10, in Guizhou township hospitals. In contrast, township hospitals in Qufu have from 20 to 50 beds each, and the typical township hospital has 31 beds. The key township health centers in Penglai, at about 80 beds each, are even larger. Including beds in county hospitals, Penglai has twice as many beds per capita as Zunyi and Puding (Table 6.17). The bed-to-population ratio is more favorable at the provincial level because of the inclusion of major provincial hospitals located in urban areas. Guizhou as a whole has 1.56 beds per 1,000 population but only 1.12 beds in the rural areas. Shandong residents have better access to health care with 2.27 beds per 1,000 population. Nationwide, there are 2.61 beds per 1,000 population; however, these beds are concentrated

Table 6.17: Public Health-Care Facilities, 1992/93

	National	Shandong	Qufu	Penglai	Guizhou	Zunyi	Puding
% of townships with health centers[a]	93.00	...	100.00	100.00	85.00	100.00	100.00
No. of health stations and offices per village[b]	...	...	1.10	1.20	0.43	0.79	0.09
% of villages with no health station or office	10.90	3.20	0.00	0.00	40.30	...	81.00
No. of beds/1,000 population	2.61	2.27	1.60	2.02	1.56 / 1.12[c]	0.92	0.84
% of beds in rural areas[d]	35.00	...	45.00	41.00	28.00	...	51.00

... Not available.

[a]Included in this statistic are townships with no health center but located in the county seat and having access to county-level health facilities.

[b]This statistic is per administrative village. In some cases the village establishes its health facility in conjunction with the nearby township health center.

[c]In rural areas.

[d]Number of beds below county level as a percentage of the total.

Sources: SSB(1994b), p.19; Ministry of Public Health (1994), pp. 1-3,32,33; Guizhou Statistical Bureau (1994), p.280; public health officials in the areas visited.

in urban centers such as Beijing and Shanghai.[18] In principle, rural residents have access to medical facilities in urban centers through referrals; in practice, access is limited. From 1988 to 1994, only 15 percent of the inpatients at a major Shanghai hospital were from outside Shanghai and some of these were likely to be residents of other cities (Hu, T., 1992).

Eighty-nine percent of all villages nationwide have achieved the goal announced in the mid-1960s of establishing a health-care unit with part-time trained medical personnel in every village (former brigade). However, villages without a health-care facility are concentrated in some provinces such as Guizhou (Table 6.17) where only 43 percent of the villages have a health facility. A health facility is found in 79 percent of the villages in Zunyi, Guizhou's wealthiest county, but in only 9 percent of the villages in Puding. Most villages in Puding have at best privately run medicine shops. Both Zunyi and Puding fall well short of the objective set by the Ministry of Public Health for the year 2000. On the other hand, every administrative village in Qufu and Penglai is served by its own health station or is adjacent to the township center and can use township facilities.

Throughout the PRC, medical equipment exhibit both vertical and horizontal variation: they increase in sophistication as one goes up the administrative hierarchy and vary in quality across townships and counties. Qufu, which has benefited over the years from a number of international and national projects designed to improve health care, has relatively advanced medical equipment. Qufu was one of 20 key counties that received over Y95,000 worth of medical equipment from the Shandong Public Health Department in 1978. In the mid-1980s, the county was able to purchase $346,000 worth of medical equipment under a World Bank project and Y105,000 worth of equipment under a Ministry of Public Health project. Most of this equipment is found in the county general hospital and the epidemic prevention station, although some township hospitals have ultrasound machines purchased with part of the funds. The county's most advanced medical facility, the People's Hospital, has two CAT scan machines and other computerized medical equipment imported from the United States and France.

---

[18] The number of beds per 1,000 population is 5.50 for Shanghai and 6.24 for Beijing.

With this modern equipment the hospital can perform heart operations and neurosurgery. In contrast, the county general hospital in Puding only has three x-ray, two electrocardiograph, and two ultrasound machines, and six operating tables.

Ultrasound machines, a general diagnostic and monitoring tool, are commonplace in township health centers in coastal provinces. In Shandong 90 percent of all townships have one. Even some village health stations in coastal provinces have ultrasound and x-ray machines. Key township hospitals in Penglai are comparable to county hospitals in counties such as Puding.

Township hospitals in Guizhou have received minimal new equipment in the past ten years. Most township hospitals provide medical care with only a stethoscope, a blood-pressure cuff, and a thermometer. In Puding, none of the township hospitals are equipped to perform even the simplest of operations. None have an ultrasound machine and only one township has an x-ray machine. Longkeng, one of the better-off townships in Zunyi, has one x-ray machine, two microscopes, and a sterilizer, aside from a simple operating table and a delivery table. Doctors said they could deal with cuts, hepatitis, and typhoid.

Health-care facilities at the township and village level in Penglai were observed to use disposable needles, a practice absent in similar facilities in Zunyi and Puding. Township health centers in Shandong are more likely to offer orthodontic care than are centers in Guizhou. The public health system in Qufu County has 13 vehicles for its use, while Puding County has only one ambulance.

Personnel. The PRC has 3.47 health-care professionals per 1,000 population, concentrated in densely populated urban areas, as is the case with hospital beds. At the province level, Shandong has 2.99 medical personnel (*weisheng jishuyuan*) per 1,000 population versus Guizhou's 2.69. Consistent with the concentration of medical facilities and personnel in urban areas, the number of medical personnel per capita in the two Shandong counties is lower than the average for the province, but higher than the number of medical personnel per capita in Zunyi and Puding (Table 6.18).

Everywhere, county-level facilities have more highly skilled medical personnel than townships and villages. But again, the quality of the medical staff varies across regions. Qufu has 31 doctors at the associate professor level working at county facilities. Puding has 20

Table 6.18: Health-Care Personnel, 1993

	National	Shandong	Qufu	Penglai	Guizhou	Zunyi	Puding
No. of medical personnel/1,000 population	3.47	2.99	2.08	2.48	2.69 1.67[a]	1.37	1.44
Average no. of health workers per village	1.81	1.73	...	1.53	1.08	1.47	0.15

... Not available.

[a]In rural areas.

Sources: SSB (1994a), p.59; Ministry of Public Health (1994), pp. 2, 32-33; public health officials in areas visited.

college graduates among its county-level staff, but only two are at the associate professor level. At the lower levels, in particular the village level, health-care practitioners without specialized degrees predominate. Many are barefoot doctors from the 1970s and have long experience. In Penglai and Qufu, the younger staff (recent hires) are probably graduates of a secondary medical school. In Guizhou, 98 percent of village-level public health professionals have no specialized secondary or tertiary education degree.

The educational attainment of township-level staff spans a wider range. About 10 percent of township-level health practitioners in Qufu are graduates of tertiary medical technical schools (*dazhuan*) and 3 percent are college graduates (*benke*). Doctors at township hospitals in Zunyi graduated from college in the 1960s, completed secondary and tertiary medical school (*zhongzhuan* and *dazhuan*), or, in the case of 20-30 percent, had no formal medical education. In Shiban, one of the poorest townships in Zunyi County, the highest level of education among medical personnel is secondary medical school. The hospital in Longkeng, one of the wealthiest townships in Zunyi, has two tertiary medical school graduates (*dazhuan*) on the staff. One-third of all rural public health professionals in Guizhou have at least a specialized secondary education degree; two-thirds have no specialized degree.

Both national and local public health officials do not give high priority to training, yet the four counties, to differing degrees, provide continuing education and training to their health-care workers. In Penglai, health-care workers at the village level receive 15 or more days of training annually. Penglai staff at township and county facilities receive training when new equipment is acquired or new medical procedures, such as cataract surgery, are introduced. Lack of new equipment and inadequate facilities for new procedures contribute to the low perception of the need for training in places like Guizhou.

Health Status of Population. To reduce infant and maternal mortality, the Ministry of Public Health has established MCH stations and in the 1950s began a campaign to popularize modern delivery methods. Banister (1987, p. 58) noted: "The 'old method of delivery' included the midwife biting the umbilical cord or cutting it with a nonsterile instrument, then placing dung or a piece of cloth over the cut. Unsanitary techniques caused tetanus in newborns and puerperal fever in mothers." Because the majority of births in the 1950s occurred at home with midwives in attendance, training programs were directed at rural midwives (birth attendants). In Qufu rural midwives were trained in new, more sanitary delivery methods, and by 1959, 73 percent of all births in the county used the modern methods. The rate went up to 99.4 percent in 1982 and to 99.7 percent in the 1990s. The statistics for Penglai are similarly high, with 89 percent of all babies being delivered at a county-level hospital or at one of the five key township hospitals. Such practices have enabled Penglai to reduce infant mortality to 13.7 per 1,000 and maternal mortality to 2 per 10,000. Both of these statistics are well below the national average for counties (Table 6.19).

In remote and poor areas, the use of modern birth methods is not as widespread. In 1990, only 65.3 percent of deliveries in rural areas of Guizhou used such methods. In Zunyi, less than half of all births take place in a township or county hospital. Most births in Puding occur at home, because township hospitals are so poorly equipped and the county hospital is too distant and costly. Not all villages in Puding have a midwife; therefore, only about half of all births use modern methods. For this reason, infant mortality rates in Guizhou are more than three times the national average for rural areas and are more similar to infant mortality rates for low-income countries (Table 6.19). A survey of 300 poor counties in the PRC, funded by UNICEF and UNFPA, revealed

Table 6.19: Health Status Indicators, 1992/93

	National[a]	Shandong	Qufu	Penglai	Guizhou	Zunyi	Puding
Infant mortality rate (no./1,000)	... (21.50)	17.9	30.0	13.7	73.20[b]	34.40	90.90
Maternal mortality rate (no./10,000)	9.5 (11.49)	...	...	2.0	24.62[b]	13.79	...
% of births using new methods	93.7 (93.20)	...	99.7	...	80.80	...	51.05
% of births in hospital	50.6 (45.50)	...	90.0	89.0	65.30[b]	<50.00	...
Child immunization rate (4 vaccines)	95.0	...	100.0	94.5	90.00	90.00	85.40

... Not available.

Note: These statistics are based on incomplete reporting and may contain biases. The infant mortality rate, for one, is underreported in the PRC.

[a] Figures in parentheses pertain to counties only.

[b] In rural areas.

Sources: Ministry of Public Health (1994), pp. 70, 81, 96-97; public health officials in areas visited.

an infant mortality rate of 68 per 1,000 in 1989 (Table 6.20). Among the counties were 20 from Guizhou whose average infant mortality rate was even higher, at 108. Infants in the Guizhou counties were more likely to die at home or on the way to a hospital than infants in the other poor counties. Maternal mortality rates in the 20 Guizhou counties were also higher than the average for the sample as a whole. The extremely limited access to medical facilities means that women in the poorest regions of Guizhou are more likely to die in childbirth at home than are women in other poor regions of the PRC.

The PRC began to vaccinate high-risk populations against infectious diseases as early as the 1950s. At first, the effort was hindered by the need for a cold train to preserve the effectiveness of the vaccines when distributed to rural areas. This problem was largely solved in the 1960s and 1970s. Decentralization of the funding and management of health care contributed to the recent reemergence of childhood diseases that were formerly thought to be under control. A nationwide program calls for all young children to be inoculated against tuberculosis (BCG vaccine), against diphtheria, whooping cough, and tetanus

**Table 6.20: Infant and Maternal Mortality in Poor Counties
in the PRC and Guizhou, 1989**

	300 Counties in the PRC	*20 Counties in Guizhou*
Infant mortality rate (no./1,000)	68.0	108.0
Place of infant death (percent)		
county hospital	10.5	4.8
township health center	8.5	4.4
home/on the way to hospital	81.0	90.8
Maternal mortality rate (no./10,000)	20.2	47.1
Place of death of mother (percent)		
county hospital	19.3	11.5
township health center	14.0	9.6
village health station	0.8	0.3
home	52.7	71.6
on the way to hospital	13.2	6.9

Source: Baseline survey in 1989 for the 300-county project entitled "Strengthening MCH/FP Services at the Grassroots." The projects was funded jointly by UNICEF and UNFPA.

(DPT vaccine), and against poliomyelitis and measles. Qufu has achieved a 100 percent immunization rate for these diseases and Penglai, 94.5 percent. Guizhou reports that vaccines for these diseases were given to 90 percent of children in the province in 1990. Recently, however, measles has broken out in some prefectures and the incidence of polio is increasing. The target for 1995 was for every township in Guizhou to inoculate 85 percent of the children against these diseases. Health officials of the province, however, believe that this target will be difficult to meet. Among the counties in Guizhou, Zunyi had a 90 percent inoculation rate in 1993 and Puding, 85.4 percent.

FINANCING OF RURAL PUBLIC HEALTH CARE

Operating expenses and capital outlays for rural public health care are covered by government budget appropriations, several medical insurance programs, personal payment for medical care, private and self-raised funds, and foreign and domestic loans. Funds came from basically the same sources in pre-reform days, but the degree of reliance on the various sources has shifted over time. The mandate issued to hospitals and other health institutions in the 1980s to become more self-financing by earning more from services reduced the importance of government budget appropriations. These declined from 37 percent of total health-care expenditures in 1980 to only 23 percent in 1988 (World Bank 1990).[19]

Government Budget Appropriations. All levels of government, from the township to the central government, appropriate funds for health care.[20] In the absence of special or earmarked taxes for public health care, funds are allocated out of general revenue. The health-care budget of each level of government is intended for health-care units at that level and has separate allocations for recurrent operating expenditures and any capital investment expenditures.

---

[19] These percentages exclude government expenditures on medical insurance for government employees.

[20] Prior to reforms, communes relied on counties to include part of commune-level public health expenditures in the county budget and otherwise depended on the commune welfare and accumulation funds to support health-care work. With the establishment of township fiscal authority, local public health expenditures are now to be included in the township budget.

In view of the continued emphasis of the government on preventive health care, units such as the epidemic prevention station and MCH station tend to be fully funded out of government budgets. Now, user fees are charged for some activities of these stations such as immunizations. The fees, however, go only to the rural doctor or health aide who administers the shot and do not cover the cost of the vaccine. The emphasis on preventive medicine makes for more efficient use of limited resources. According to the Ministry of Public Health, this is an especially important consideration in a country which uses only 1 percent of the world's health resources (as measured by expenditures on health care) to assist 21 percent of the world's population.

In the case of hospitals and clinics, which provide curative health care, budgetary funds only partially subsidize operations. Fees for services and revenue from the sale of medicine are additional sources of funds for these units. While hospitals and clinics clearly earn revenue, they are considered nonprofit service organizations and exempt from taxes.

To bridge the gap between what a hospital or clinic earns and its actual operating costs, the government provides a subsidy which usually covers staff salaries (in full or in part) but can also take another form such as a fixed amount per bed. Salaries take up more than 90 percent of government budget expenditures for recurrent operating costs. Before 1980, the budget covered 103 percent of the staff salaries of government-run hospitals and medical facilities and 60 percent of the staff salaries of hospitals and clinics run by collectives. Now most government-run hospitals and clinics are allocated only enough funds to cover basic wages. In Shandong, the basic wage paid by the government represents about 45 percent of the total salary of public health workers. The rest of the salary comes from the revenue earned by the hospital or clinic. In 1992 and 1993, hospitals throughout the country derived 10 percent of their operating funds from the government budget, 30 percent from fees for services, and 60 percent from sales of medicine. The share of the government budget subsidy has declined since the onset of reforms, from the previous 20-30 percent. One consequence of the increased reliance on hospital revenues is a rise in the prescription of medicine which earns a profit for the hospital or clinic.

Similarly, the salaries of medical personnel at the township and village levels are covered in part by the surplus revenue earned by the health centers and stations and in part by government appropriations. The level of government subsidy is higher for staff at the township health center (*weishengyuan*) than for staff at the village level. For example, in Zunyi County, the government pays 60 percent of the salaries of township health center staff, 30 percent of the salaries of health station (*weishengsuo*) staff, and 10 percent of the salaries of health office (*weishengshi*) staff. Staff must rely on fees to make up for the unsubsidized portion of their salaries. Rural midwives typically receive a subsidy of Y10-Y20 a month from the government.

Government budgets can also include earmarked funds for public health fixed assets (medical equipment) and capital construction costs. In addition to funding the operating expenses of province-level facilities, the Shandong Department of Public Health spends Y6 million to Y8 million annually on imported medical equipment for the facilities of the province. It has also spent an average of over Y13 million annually in the 1990s on the construction of such facilities.

In 1992, the government set aside Y10.4 billion, or 2.4 percent of its total expenditure budget, for recurrent expenditures on public health nationwide (Ministry of Public Health 1994). An additional Y3.6 billion from the government budget, or 1.2 percent of the government's total capital construction budget, funded capital construction in the public health sector. The level of funding varies across provinces, counties, and townships. In 1992, the government spent one-third more for recurrent costs of public health in Shandong (Y8.17 per capita) than in Guizhou (Y6.14 per capita) even though both provinces allocated nearly the same proportion of their total budget to health care (4.8 percent in Shandong and 4.9 percent in Guizhou). Zunyi County spent Y3.20 per capita, or 3.5 percent of its total expenditure budget, on public health care in 1993. Puding spent Y3.45 per capita, or 3.7 percent of its total expenditure budget.

Government Transfers. While each level of government is generally responsible for facilities it directly runs, provincial and lower levels of government can receive support for health-care services from a higher level of government. In general, this support takes one of the following three forms:

- Grants for capital construction and purchase of major equipment.

- Part or all of the salaries of health personnel.
- Free or subsidized training for health-care workers.

Aside from supporting the operation of national hospitals, medical colleges, and research institutes, the Ministry of Public Health also transfers grants out of its budget to fund specific capital projects and preventive care activities at the lower levels. For example, central-government funds were used to establish 18 key city hospitals during the sixth five-year plan period (1981-1985). As mentioned earlier, Qufu purchased medical equipment in the mid-1980s with grants from the Ministry of Public Health.

In the eighth five-year plan period (1991-1995), such transfers of investment funds from the central government were directed mostly to rural areas and went down to the county and township levels. This emphasis is expected to continue to the end of this century. Minister of Public Health Chen Minzhang recently announced that the central government will spend Y75 million annually over the next six years to improve rural sanitation and health in the PRC. Various current programs make funds available to lower levels to pay for the construction, equipment, personnel, and training costs related to the repair of dilapidated health-care facilities, the control and eradication of contagious diseases, and the establishment of epidemic prevention and MCH stations in every county and a township health center in every township. The Ministry of Public Health selects the specific projects to be funded after reviewing the proposals from the provinces. The Ministry says that equalization is an important consideration in allocating the funds among the various areas. There is evidence that funds are being directed to poorer areas. In 1993, Shandong received only Y50,000 from the central government for investment in county-level health stations and township health centers while Guizhou received Y3.3 million.

With few exceptions, access to higher-level funds is contingent upon the ability of the lower-level government to raise matching funds. In the case of funds coming through a disaster relief program, for such projects as the repair of a health clinic damaged by floods, there are no matching requirements. Matching ratios are not fixed, although the matching rates are generally less for the poorest areas. Lower governments must often raise several times more than the amount they receive from the higher level. The deputy director of the Public Health

Department in Taian Prefecture cited the example of local governments having to put up Y1 million to get Y100,000 from the central government. Present programs of the Ministry of Public Health tend to support this claim. For the Y200 million contributed by the central government in the first three years of these programs (1991 to 1993), local governments had to raise Y3.8 billion in matching local-government funds (including extrabudgetary and self-raised funds). The contributions of the central government in 1993 made up only 4 percent of total investment in county epidemic prevention stations, MCH stations, and township health centers (Table 6.21).

Both provinces visited are participating in the rural program of the Ministry of Public Health to strengthen township health centers and county epidemic prevention and MCH stations. Shandong, on the strength of its local financial resources, is investing more than twice the per capita investment of Guizhou (Y1.63 versus Y0.69). By the end of 1993, 341 township health centers in Shandong had benefited from this program. Shandong has chosen to invest mainly in equipment (60 percent) and training (24 percent) for these facilities because

**Table 6.21: Investment in Township Health Centers,
County Epidemic Prevention Stations, and Maternal
and Child Health Stations, by Source, 1993
(Percent)**

Source of Funds	National Average	Shandong	Guizhou
Central government	3.77	0.04	14.43
Provincial government	10.56	1.08	28.20
Prefectural/municipal government	5.52	2.39	6.17
County government	21.98	14.73	21.21
Township government	21.28	39.81	29.47
Self-raised	26.97	31.18	0.52
Others	9.92	10.78	0.00
Total investment (Y million)	...	141.10	22.87
Per capita investment	...	1.63	0.69

... Not available.
Source: Ministry of Public Health data.

virtually all its townships and counties already have adequate structures (Table 6.22). The majority of the investment in Shandong is coming from the lowest levels; self-raised funds and township budgets accounted for 71 percent of total investment in 1993 (Table 6.21).

In the first two years of the program (1991 and 1992), Guizhou received Y6.7 million from the central government, Y3.3 million in matching funds from the province planning commission (*jihui*), and Y18.9 million from the prefectures and counties, for a total of Y28.9 million. In 1993, central and provincial-level budgets continued to fund a significant share of this program (43 percent) and the lowest level (townships) supplied only 29 percent (Table 6.21). The funds have been used to renovate 20 county epidemic prevention stations, 19 MCH stations, and 84 township hospitals. While rural public health facilities in Guizhou have certainly improved under this program, officials in Guizhou's Department of Public Health claim these funds solve only a small part of the problem. They estimate a shortage of at least Y70 million worth of equipment and facilities in township hospitals, county epidemic prevention stations, and MCH stations.

Shandong and Guizhou also receive funds from the central government for the prevention and control of contagious diseases. Shandong distributes to the county level the Y2 million it receives per year. Puding County in Guizhou received Y60,000 for inoculations from higher levels of government.

Provincial and county-level governments can also initiate programs to make funds available to lower levels for the provision of health care. These programs, like their national counterparts, specify

**Table 6.22: Uses of Investment Funds for Township
and County-Level Public Health Facilities, 1993
(Percent)**

	National Average	Shandong	Guizhou
Equipment	6.78	59.90	17.31
Training	0.65	24.37	1.13
Structures	92.57	15.73	81.56

Source: Ministry of Public Health data.

the uses of the funds and eligibility criteria. Shandong has allocated about Y2 million annually since the early 1980s for the construction of epidemic prevention and MCH stations in counties. In 1988, the province started funding the construction of county Chinese traditional medicine hospitals (the current level of funding is Y4 million annually). Over the past 13 years, Shandong Province and its prefectures and counties have spent a total of Y726 million out of their budgets to build and equip 130 county hospitals in the province.

Townships in poorer areas often do not have enough funds to pay the basic wages of public health-care workers and therefore require supplemental appropriations from higher levels of government. The government subsidy provides a minimum wage for health-care workers; in poor areas, the subsidy often turns out to be the full wage. According to government salary schedules, a township health center doctor in Maguan Township, Puding County, should earn a total monthly salary of Y210, of which the government pays about 70 percent, or Y146. For the rest of the salary, the doctor depends on revenue earned by the health center. But because local residents cannot afford high fees and do not purchase much medicine, the revenue is minimal. The doctor therefore earns nothing extra and the Y146 from the government constitutes his full salary. In wealthier areas, such as Penglai and Qufu, the township budget provides for the basic wages of township health personnel and village funds usually support village health offices and personnel. Health-care workers in these areas supplement their basic wages with the fees they earn for their services. Medical personnel at village health stations in better-off areas can reasonably expect to earn a total of Y250 per month while those at township health centers typically earn Y350-Y400 per month.

Medical Insurance Programs. Rural residents with medical insurance are covered by one of three major programs: government (state cadres) health insurance (*gongfei yiliao*), labor health insurance (*laodong baoxian*), or cooperative health insurance (*hezuo yiliao*). All three programs began in the 1950s. Comprehensive statistics on the number of rural residents covered by each program are not available. But estimates indicate that the proportion of the rural population covered by medical insurance has fluctuated over the years. It reached a peak in the mid-1970s when over 90 percent of all villages were offering cooperative medical insurance and then dropped to a low in the mid-1980s when less than 5 percent of villages offered such programs. Now less than 20 percent of the rural population is estimated to be insured under public or private medical programs.

The government health insurance program provides cost reimbursement to county and township government workers and to state teachers in rural schools. Only employees, and not their dependents, are covered. This insurance program is funded out of government budgets. State-owned enterprises and large collectively owned enterprises are required under the law to offer labor health insurance to their workers. Many smaller collectively owned enterprises, including some township and village enterprises, also provide this insurance. To fund this program, each enterprise pays about 11 percent of total wages into the enterprise welfare fund. In many cases, the labor insurance program includes some benefits for dependents.

Rural cooperative medical insurance is set up and managed by villages in conjunction with township health centers. This program is funded from several sources. If offered in a village, it is open to all residents, who must register and pay an annual membership fee. The village supports the insurance program out of its funds (*jizijin* or *tiliu*) and the township also contributes from its public welfare fund.

Medical costs have risen rapidly in recent years, straining government and enterprise budgets and necessitating reforms which are still ongoing. Costs have been pushed up by the increasing number of beneficiaries, the higher-cost treatment for such new medical problems as cancer and heart disease, expensive high-technology equipment for diagnosis and treatment, and costly new Western medicines. The rise in costs has led to the introduction of deductibles and copayments in nearly all insurance programs.

Typically, a member of a rural cooperative health insurance program first receives free care at the village health unit and is reimbursed for medical expenses from referrals according to the economic situation of the village or township. The reimbursement can pay for all medical expenses or only the doctors' services (and the patient pays for medicines and tests). Qufu Village in Qufu Township, which is in the county seat, does not charge for services at the village health office. In case of referrals, it reimburses 20 percent of outpatient service and medicine charges, and 40 percent of inpatient expenses. All other costs are borne by the patient.

The three medical insurance programs provide differing coverage across rural PRC. The government insurance system is the most standardized; it covers all government workers everywhere. But some county governments in financial difficulty have been slow to reimburse government workers for covered medical expenses. Since local governments determine the schedule of deductibles and copayments, these details can vary between regions. Participation in the labor insurance program is more common in prosperous regions where township and village enterprises can afford the benefits. Similarly, the 10-15 percent of villages with rural cooperative medical insurance programs are concentrated in the coastal areas. The most generous programs can be found in regions such as the Pearl River Delta. In Shandong, rural cooperative health insurance is quite common. Nearly all villages in Qufu offer this insurance and 84 percent of Penglai's rural population is covered. In Guizhou, however, only 66 out of 25,397 villages offer cooperative medical insurance, and, according to Public Health Department officials, even in these 66 villages the programs receive no financial support from the government; farmers rely completely on themselves for funding.

A shortage of operational funds for epidemic prevention has caused many regions to introduce specialized immunization insurance for childhood diseases. This insurance typically requires a lumpsum premium (Y16 per child in one village) at birth and covers the cost of vaccination (BCG, DPT, measles, and polio vaccines).

Personal Payment for Medical Care. When the government shifted an increasing portion of the financing burden to hospitals, the latter passed the burden on to patients in the form of higher fees. Patient fee payments represented 34 percent of total expenditures on health care in 1992, up from only 14 percent in 1980 (World Bank 1990b) (Table 6.23).[21] The financing burden on rural patients, who are more likely to be uninsured, has risen dramatically since the onset of reforms.

Government subsidy of their operating costs allows hospitals and clinics to charge less than the actual cost of services.[22] They may,

---

[21] This figure includes some fees paid by patients who do not declare their insurance coverage when they visit clinics and hospitals but are later reimbursed by their insurance program.

[22] An official in the Shandong Finance Department reported that fees can equal 86 percent of cost.

Table 6.23: National Expenditures on Health Care,
by Source, 1992

Fund Source	Percentage of Total
Government budget[a]	23.68
Enterprises[b]	34.69
Patient fee payments	34.36
Social, self-raised funds	1.32
Township and village retained funds	5.18
Loans	0.77
	100.00
Total expenditures (Y billion)	90.80

[a]Includes allocations for public health operating expenses and capital investment, family planning administration, Chinese traditional medicines, and government health insurance.
[b]Includes allocations for operating expenses and capital investment of enterprise-run hospitals and clinics and labor medical insurance.
Source: Ministry of Public Health.

however, earn a profit on the sale of medicine. According to the Ministry of Public Health, the profit margin currently averages 15 percent. Fees for services and medicine are set by a board representing the price, finance, and public health bureaus of the province.[23] Required to draw up and price an extensive list of medical items and procedures, the board finds it difficult to keep pace with new medical technologies. Shandong reported that a schedule with more than 4,000 items and procedures was established in 1984 and was last reviewed and updated in 1989. A lack of information on the projected level of use of new technology frequently leads to the overpricing or underpricing of procedures. This in turn leads to the underuse or overuse of certain procedures by doctors and hospitals seeking to earn profits.

---

[23] In provinces where price control authority has devolved to the county-level price bureau, a county board of representatives sets the fees.

The registration cost for a doctor visit remains very low, usually only Y0.10-Y0.20 (Table 6.24). While this fee is highly visible and politically sensitive, it represents only a small portion of all the fees that patients are charged. In Puding, the average visit to a county-level clinic costs a patient Y12.67, including the office visit, laboratory tests, and medicine.

Out-of-pocket medical expenses have risen faster than the general price index. From 1987 to 1993, the price of medicine and medical products in rural areas rose at an average annual rate of 11 percent as compared with a 9 percent increase in the general price level (State Statistical Bureau 1994a). Hospital administrators report a continuous increase in prices. In 1993, a heart operation at Qufu People's Hospital cost Y70; by 1994 the cost had gone up to Y130.

A number of surveys provide estimates of health-care expenditures by rural residents. A rural health survey in 1992 showed that residents made an average of 1.17 doctor visits that year and spent an average of 0.42 days in the hospital. Most rural residents had to pay for these doctor visits and hospital stays. According to a nationwide survey in 1993, rural households spent Y60.6, or 7.3 percent of total household expenditures, on medical care. The annual rural household survey conducted by the State Statistical Bureau shows a rising trend in expenditures on medicines and health-care articles (Table 6.25) and on medical treatment and health care (Table 6.26).

Table 6.24: Range of Medical Fees in Study Sites, 1994
(Y)

First doctor visit	0.10-0.20
Township hospital bed	1.00-2.50
County hospital bed	3.00
Average outpatient bill	4.64-12.67
Average inpatient bill	19.30-50.00
(per day, excluding food)	

Note: These figures reflect the range of medical fees reported by public health officials and medical personnel in township and county clinics and hospitals visited in Qufu, Penglai, Zunvi, and Puding.
Source: Fieldwork data.

Table 6.25: Rural Household Per Capita Expenditures on Medicines and Health-Care Articles, 1985-1992

Year	Per Capita Expenditures (Y)	Share of Total Living Expenditures (%)	Share of Net Income (%)
1985	5.49	1.73	1.38
1988	9.46	1.98	1.74
1989	11.48	2.14	1.91
1990	13.23	2.26	1.93
1991	14.93	2.41	2.11
1992	16.35	2.48	2.09

Source: SSB (1993), pp. 284, 286.

Table 6.26: Rural Household Per Capita Expenditures on Medical Treatment and Health Care, 1985-1993

Year	Per Capita Expenditures (Y)	Share of Total Living Expenditures (%)	Share of Net Income (%)
1985	7.65	2.41	1.92
1990	19.02	3.25	3.16
1991	22.34	3.60	3.15
1992	24.14	3.66	3.08
1993	27.17	3.53	2.95

Source: SSB (1994a), pp. 278- 280.

Rural residents who are uninsured and cannot afford the costs of treatment have few options. They must turn to friends and relatives for assistance because only those with life-threatening injuries and illnesses can expect to be treated at hospitals with no guarantee of payment. By its own estimate, Qufu People's Hospital offers Y30,000-Y40,000 in free services annually, a fraction of its gross revenue of Y10 million. Such care is more limited in poor areas, where the demand for free health care is generally greater. Zunyi County provided an estimated Y20,000 in free services last year and Puding County, Y10,000.

Loans. Loans finance capital outlays and circulating capital for medicine supplies. One township health center reported needing Y80,000 in circulating capital to buy and maintain an inventory of medicine. Subsidized loans are available on a limited basis from the rural banking system.[24] Otherwise, the circulating capital needed to buy medicines comes from individuals and village funds (*tongchou*).

A number of international loans to the PRC have supported a wide range of rural health-care work, ranging from strengthening MCH services to importing medical equipment and upgrading food and water inspection and safety technology. At less than 1 percent of total public health-care expenditures nationwide in 1992, loans still play a relatively minor role.

RURAL SOCIAL WELFARE SERVICES

The government supports myriad social welfare services in part or in full. This section discusses in detail the major programs for social insurance, poverty alleviation, and natural disaster assistance.

SOCIAL INSURANCE PROGRAMS

Few rural residents benefit from the old-age retirement, unemployment, maternity, medical, and workers' disability programs of the PRC. Government workers and employees of state-owned enterprises, which

---

[24] One township reported paying only 2 percent for a loan.

are concentrated in urban centers, are the primary beneficiaries. Large urban collectives typically also offer retirement and medical benefits to their employees. Therefore, in rural areas, county and township government employees, including state teachers, are the only rural residents eligible for government-sponsored social insurance programs.[25] Some profitable rural collective enterprises offer retirement and medical care benefits to workers. Offering these benefits may reduce the contribution of the enterprise to the village or township government that owns it. If so, the local government in fact subsidizes these benefits. Nevertheless, the vast majority of beneficiaries of government-sponsored social insurance programs are urban residents.

Attempts have been made in recent years to establish separate social insurance programs for rural residents. Thus far, these programs have focused on old-age or retirement pensions. The desire to intro-duce old-age pension schemes in rural areas is closely linked with achieving family planning goals. It is argued that the availability of financial support through old-age insurance programs will reduce the demand for children, a traditional source of support for the elderly. In nearly all cases, however, these programs rely on the contributions of individuals while any government contribution is minimal. The most common scheme, managed by the Ministry of Civil Affairs, is open to rural residents between the ages of 20 and 60 who contribute Y2-Y20 monthly. The funds are deposited in bank accounts under the individual's name and the bank may invest these funds in government treasury bonds. The individual may begin withdrawing funds on reach-ing the age of 60.

Shandong leads in establishing this rural old-age insurance program. Currently, one-third of all participants nationwide live in Shandong. By the end of 1993, 16 million, or nearly 50 percent of Shandong's eligible population, were participating in this rural pension program. Contributions totaled Y600 million, or an average of Y37.50 per beneficiary. Penglai introduced this program in 1992 and in the first year collected Y6.4 million. In 1993, an additional Y5.3 million was contributed. The slowdown in contributions was attributed to rising inflation and the relatively low interest received on the funds, which

---

[25] Some community teachers receive partial retirement and medical benefits.

are usually invested in government bonds. The interest on these bonds was 7.1 percent in 1992 and had risen to only 13 percent by mid-1994 despite a jump in the inflation rate, as measured by the rural consumer price index, from 4.7 percent in 1992 to 13.7 percent in 1993 and to nearly 20 percent in 1994. In Penglai, the village matches 28 percent of the contributions of community teachers, and township and village enterprises match a percentage of employees' contributions. Eighty-five percent of those eligible in Penglai participate in this program and most of the remaining county residents have purchased private pension insurance through the People's Insurance Company of China.

Guizhou also introduced this rural old-age insurance program in 1992, but the program is not nearly as widely accepted as in Shandong. In 1993, the program was being pilot-tested in half of the counties in Guizhou. Program participants numbered 370,000, or less than 3 percent of those eligible, and funds totaled Y3.8 million, or about Y10 per participant. To get the program going, the government is encouraging teachers, township and village enterprise employees, and family planning personnel to participate. Participants contribute between Y1 and Y20 monthly. Local governments and enterprises can choose to match up to 5 percent of the participant's current salary. Puding began experimenting with the system in 1993 but only in four of the better-off townships.

POVERTY ALLEVIATION

A nationwide survey in 1992 revealed that 80 million people were living in poverty, down from 125 million in 1985 and 250 million in 1978. All but one million of these poor people (*pinkun renkou*) reside in rural areas.[26] Of the 80 million poor, 46 percent reside in western PRC, 31 percent in central PRC, and 23 percent in the east. The PRC's poor are concentrated in remote, resource-deficient rural areas, such as rock mountains and karst areas, which are prevalent in Guizhou. Besides

---

[26] Policies that severely restricted migration to urban areas, ensured full employment in urban areas, and subsidized urban consumption led to a sharp reduction in urban poverty by the 1960s and has kept it at a very low level since. See World Bank (1992) for a more detailed discussion of poverty policies.

factors external to the household, some household characteristics, such as ill health, high dependency ratios, and a lack of labor, also contribute to poverty. A goal of the government is to eliminate poverty by the year 2000 by boosting income levels among the remaining 80 million poor to Y500 per capita (in 1990 constant prices).

The Ministry of Civil Affairs oversees several income maintenance programs targeted at the poor. The most well-known is the five guarantees (*wubaohu*) program for individuals lacking a livelihood and financial support. For these individuals—primarily orphans, the disabled, and the elderly—the program provides food, clothing, housing, medical care, and burial services. The elderly made up nearly 80 percent of the program's 2.45 million participants in 1993. Needy rural households that are ineligible for the *wubaohu* program may qualify for the poor households (*kunnan hu*) program, which assisted nearly 29 million people in 1993 (Table 6.27). Funds for family members of martyrs and disabled veterans are also available. For all these programs, the village identifies the qualified individuals, and the village cadre and township government applies on their behalf to the county for government support.

**Table 6.27: Number of Persons Receiving
Relief Funds Nationwide, 1985-1993
(Thousands)**

	1985	*1990*	*1992*	*1993*
Persons in rural poor households receiving relief funds	38,004	26,317	24,327	28,869
Persons in rural households receiving five guarantees (*wubaohu*)	2,747	2,506	2,318	2,447
Supported by government funds	226	218	186	142
Supported by collective funds	1,976	1,733	1,543	2,025

Source: SSB (1994a), p. 653.

Financial support for the above programs comes from both the village collective accumulated fund (*jiti tiliu*) and the government. In 1993, the collective (villages) provided 53 percent of income maintenance relief funds and the government, 47 percent (Table 6.28). Support under the *wubaohu* program comes predominantly from the villages. Of the 2.45 million *wubaohu* participants in 1993, only 142,000 received fixed monthly support from the government (Table 6.27). The vast majority were supported from village collective funds. If the village and local governments lack the financial resources, qualified individuals receive reduced or no support. It is not unusual for villages in poor areas to report more qualified households than are actually being supported.

Table 6.28: Major National Poverty Relief Funds,
by Use and Funding Source, 1985-1993
(Y million)

Use of Relief Funds	1985	1990	1992	1993
Total	2,183.49	4,267.72	4,826.35	5,725.89
Government funds	710.97	2,024.56	2,267.18	2,674.68
Collective funds	1,472.52	2,243.16	2,559.17	3,051.21
Funds for family members of martyrs and disabled veterans	1,069.83	2,427.32	2,704.35	3,017.28
Government funds	353.28	1,411.63	1,538.62	1,701.73
Collective funds	716.55	1,015.69	1,165.73	1,315.55
Funds for poor households	287.16	387.44	383.13	532.22
Government funds	118.53	186.50	189.74	216.16
Collective funds	168.63	200.94	193.39	316.06
Funds for orphans, disabled, and elderly	551.96	850.52	983.82	1,105.87
Government funds	66.93	118.51	143.15	163.34
Collective funds	485.03	732.01	840.67	942.53
Funds for urban and rural welfare homes	274.83	602.45	755.05	1,070.52
Government funds	172.51	307.93	395.67	593.45
Collective funds	102.32	294.52	359.38	477.07

Source: SSB (1994a), p. 653.

Long-term interventions designed to strengthen the rural infrastructure and encourage diversification and commercialization of rural activities compose another set of poverty alleviation programs. These are targeted at identified areas of concentrated poverty, usually counties. In 1992, there were 518 nationally designated poor counties in 22 provinces with a total poor population of 58 million.[27] The central government concentrates its support on these nationally designated counties whose average fiscal revenue in 1992 was only Y60 per capita. Most provinces have their own poverty alleviation programs and, based on their own standards, have identified additional poor counties, including some counties that met national poor county standards but were excluded from the national program because of insufficient funds. Provincially designated poor counties rely more heavily on provincial assistance. The programs are administered and coordinated by poverty alleviation offices (*fupinban*) at the county, prefectural, and provincial level in poor regions.

Central funds, in general, are distributed to provinces, prefectures, and counties based on their share of poor population. Under one program the central government provides grants (Y800 million in 1994) for resource development in underdeveloped areas. Another grant program (Y200 million in 1994) is targeted to *Sanxi* (Gansu and Ningxia) development. A third program (Y60 million funding in 1994) is intended for new towns in 250 minority counties.

Most funds, however, take the form of loans. Subsidized loans (*tiexi daikuan*) are available to county enterprises, township and village enterprises, and individuals. These loans are granted in support of agricultural production—the development of forestry, livestock, orchards, fishponds, and cropping—and rural enterprise activities. Most subsidized loans (Y2.5 billion in central funds in 1994) are channeled through the Agricultural Bank of China.[28] A portion of the subsidized

---

[27] Rural per capita income at the county level, as well as average per capita grain production, is used as a measure of poverty. The income standard has changed over time, largely to compensate for inflation. In 1986, the income standard was 150 yuan per capita (200 yuan per capita for old revolutionary bases, or *laoqu*, and minority areas). The national income standard was raised to 320 yuan in 1992 and to 400 yuan in 1994. The grain standard has remained at 200 kilograms per capita.

[28] Poverty alleviation loans now go through the Agricultural Development Bank, which was established in 1994. This new development bank is, however, managed by the Agricultural Bank of China.

loans (roughly Y2 billion in 1994) is provided directly through the Ministry of Finance which charges an annual processing fee averaging 2.88 percent instead of interest. Twenty-six provinces are eligible for the loans from the Ministry of Finance. However, the quotas of these loans to Guangdong, Fujian, Zhejiang, Shandong, and Liaoning are being cut in half each year in the eighth five-year plan period (1991-1995), with a view to graduating these provinces from the program by the end of 1995.

Food for Work programs, begun in 1984, are managed by the State Planning Commission. The central government contributes grain, edible oil, production inputs, and consumer goods and participating provincial governments provide matching contributions. Food for Work activities are primarily geared toward basic infrastructure improvement (*jibenjianshe gaizao*), including irrigation and drainage works, terracing, the construction of hydroelectric power stations, the provision of drinking water sources, and road building and repair. In 1994, the central government contributed Y1 billion worth of goods for these projects. Food for Work projects draw on the accumulated labor (*jileigong*) that rural laborers are required to volunteer each year. For work that exceeds the required voluntary labor, workers receive wages or coupons that they can exchange for commodities. Provinces can also initiate and fund Food for Work projects.

The strategic use of poverty alleviation funds has changed over time. In the mid-1980s, funds were distributed directly to households. This strategy proved costly to administer despite the high loan repayment rate of poor households, about 80-90 percent in most areas. In the late 1980s and early 1990s the emphasis shifted to supporting township and village enterprises to generate employment in poor rural areas. The poorer repayment record of rural enterprises has resulted in failure rates of 25-40 percent. Guizhou Education Department officials complained that poverty funds continue to be poured into failing township and village enterprises. Some funding is still targeted to basic infrastructure for agriculture to stabilize grain production and incomes.

Even though the central and provincial governments provide loans and grants, the bulk of the funding for poverty alleviation projects must come from local governments and residents. Hejiang County in Guizhou received Y4.95 million in loans from the province for rural enterprises. The county invested Y4.73 million, and townships and residents contributed over Y11 million.

Besides the poverty alleviation loan programs, the central government also ensures the availability of investment capital (Y10 billion in 1994) to the banking system in central and western PRC. These funds have no special restrictions on their use and do not carry explicit subsidized interest rates. However, government intervention in directing the flow of capital leads to an implicit subsidy on the cost of capital.

Guizhou has made progress in reducing the number of people living in poverty. In 1979, 70 percent of Guizhou's population qualified as poor, and by 1993 this proportion had declined to 30 percent of the population. Yet much of the province still has large concentrations of poverty. Guizhou has 48 designated poor counties and 19 of these are nationally designated poor counties. The per capita farmer income in these 48 poor counties was Y335 in 1993 as compared with the province average of Y579 and the national average of Y922. In 1993, the province and local governments in Guizhou appropriated Y148 million in support of the full range of income maintenance and poverty alleviation programs. An additional Y116 million was budgeted for projects in underdeveloped areas. That same year collectives, primarily villages, spent over Y24 million (in kind and in cash) for income maintenance social relief programs.

There are 92,000 people receiving *wubaohu* assistance in Guizhou; of these, fewer than 14,000 get regular government subsidy. Villages provided the equivalent of Y10 million in assistance to the remainder in 1993. Beneficiaries receive a subsidy of Y22-Y28 a month, most of which is in kind and only a small amount in cash. The Ministry of Civil Affairs also provides assistance to retired old leaders. In Guizhou, 6,653 retired old leaders live in state-run old-age homes and the government spends about Y225 per year for the care of each of them. Puding, with 740 old people eligible for *wubaohu* support and 400 orphans, has 11 very simple old people's homes with a total of 140 beds.

From 1986 to 1993, the government spent Y1.877 billion on poverty alleviation in Guizhou. Only 18 percent of these funds were provided as grants; subsidized loans made up the remainder (Table 6.29). The largest share of support went to agriculture, followed by township and village enterprises. From 1986 through 1993, the Agricultural Bank of China loaned out nearly Y308 million for poverty

**Table 6.29: Government Poverty Alleviation
Assistance in Guizhou, 1986-1993
(Y million)**

Total	1,877
Grants	337
Subsidized loans	1,540
Agricultural development	870
Township and village enterprise development	435
Land development (terracing)	237
Basic needs	107
Service sector development	73
Energy sources development	107

Source: National Exhibition on Social Development, Beijing, September 1994.

alleviation projects in Guizhou. Agriculture accounted for slightly more than half of the 623 projects approved and funds loaned out, and the remainder went to township and village enterprises. One-third of the loans for agriculture were for the expansion of more scientific agricultural methods, including the planting of hybrid rice and corn. Every year from 1986 to 1993, Guizhou received Y20 million from the Ministry of Finance for the development of poor areas. All of these funds have gone out as loans to the 48 eligible counties. Townships and counties apply for loans to a provincial committee consisting of representatives from the finance bureau and other relevant government bureaus, such as those for water conservation and agriculture. If the loan is approved, the township or county receives the funds and pays an annual fee to cover administrative costs. The fee is about 3.6 percent for projects involving the establishment of a rural enterprise, and 2.4 percent otherwise.

The central government transferred Y500 million in poverty alleviation funds to Guizhou in 1993 and planned to allocate Y600 million in 1994.[29] In 1993, Guizhou's 19 nationally designated poor

---

[29] Central-government support for poor areas totaled Y9.7 billion in 1994.

counties received 150 million kilograms of grain from the central government for use in water conservation and road projects under the Food for Work program.

NATURAL DISASTER ASSISTANCE

Local officials can request natural disaster relief assistance following agricultural losses exceeding 30 percent caused by a drought, flood, hailstorm, pest infestation, or other natural disaster. Disaster relief assistance is administered by the Ministry of Civil Affairs and is designed to assure subsistence, not compensate for losses.[30] Relief to farmers takes several forms: subsidized grain, clothing, and materials and funds to repair agricultural infrastructure. In the 1980s the government spent an average of Y1 billion annually for disaster relief nationwide (Table 6.30). Every year some parts of Guizhou are beset by natural disasters, mostly floods, hailstorms, and frost. During the period 1989-1993, a natural disaster struck over half of Guizhou's agricultural area, or 155 million mu. Disaster relief during that same period totaled Y264 million, of which Y225 million came from the central government and Y28 million came from the province. In Shandong, the Civil Affairs Bureau spent Y52 million in 1992 and Y94 million in 1993 for natural disaster relief.

The Puding Civil Affairs Bureau provided nearly Y1.5 million in disaster relief in 1993. Two-thirds came from higher levels of government, less than 15 percent from the county budget, and the remainder from local cadres who donated grain and cash.

ISSUES

The issues raised below are based on the assessment of public services in the four counties studied but are nonetheless likely to be relevant to rural areas elsewhere in the PRC.

---

[30] In some rural areas the People's Insurance Company of China will insure crops and livestock against natural disaster perils. The proportion of farmers carrying this type of insurance is very small, however, less than 5 percent.

**Table 6.30: National Government Expenditures on Natural
Disaster Relief and Rural Social Relief, 1978-1990
(Y million)**

Year	Natural Disaster Relief	Rural Social Relief
1978	902	245
1980	703	250
1983	845	261
1984	740	284
1985	1,025	265
1986	1,064	269
1987	991	256
1988	1,064	262
1989	1,288	281
1990	1,333	293

Source: SSB (1994a), p. 219.

Unfunded mandates abound in the delivery of public services in rural areas. Central and provincial governments often set and announce targets, such as a specific reduction in the infant mortality rate or schools equipped to meet certain standards, but do not themselves provide the funds needed to achieve the targets. To meet their mandates, rural areas depend primarily on the financial resources of the county and the township. The ability of local governments to raise revenue through budgetary and extrabudgetary channels determines the quantity and quality of the public services they deliver. As rural areas in the PRC vary tremendously in this ability, large disparities in service provision have been observed. Compounding the problem of unfunded mandates is the fact that local officials are judged and evaluated based on their fulfillment of these mandates. This places pressure on local officials to levy additional fees on an already overburdened community to fund the mandates.

Villages, which are not a formal level of government and have no taxing authority, are being required to provide significant support for primary education, public health, and social welfare. These public services have been identified by central and local governments as basic and important, and the assignment of expenditure responsibility to a nongovernmental unit is contradictory. While a village or other unit smaller than the township may run and manage primary schools more efficiently, public funding for those schools should come from governmental units.

The State Education Commission has been asked to address the question of the appropriate distribution and level of support for education by level of government. An initial proposal, which will form the starting point of discussions, is for the central government to fund 10 percent, the province 20 percent, the county 30 percent, and townships 40 percent of total government expenditure on education. Given the present distribution of fiscal revenue, these proposed expenditure shares will not be suitable for all regions of the PRC. This study has shown that townships in poor areas cannot shoulder a large share of the expenditure responsibility, or if they do, the quality of education provided will be far inferior to that in other areas. On the other hand, more prosperous and economically developed townships and counties can increase their share of expenditure responsibility.

The central government needs to decide on a minimum level of social services it wants to see provided to all rural residents regardless of where they live. Then the government must ensure adequate funding for this level of service through a system of fiscal transfers. As discussed in Chapter 2, local governments are in a better position to determine the needs and desires for public services in their communities. Therefore, local governments should have some discretion in how they provide the minimum level of service. Furthermore, local governments should have the option of offering and funding expanded and higher-quality services beyond the minimum level.

Central-government programs and targets emphasize basic and preventive health care. However, incentives in the health-care system are biased against preventive care and in favor of prescription medicines and high-technology medical care. With a large proportion of the rural population uninsured, the poor are thus often unable to afford health care. Preventive care, which frequently offers the highest social payoff, is also at risk of neglect when funds are tight. One consequence has been the reemergence of some childhood diseases.

Chapter 7

EQUALIZATION ISSUES

by Loraine A. West
and Christine P. W. Wong

In pre-reform Soviet-type economies, fiscal transfers played an important role of regional redistribution, offsetting the income effects of the price system and planned transfers of real goods. Even in market economies, governments commonly use fiscal transfers to redress social inequities.

Expanding on the indications and examples of inequality in Chapters 4, 5, and 6, this chapter examines the vertical and horizontal distribution of fiscal resources and disparities in service provision in the PRC to assess the extent to which the present system equalizes resource distribution between administrative levels and regions. The chapter first goes into the horizontal distribution of budgetary resources and the mechanisms and net effect of intergovernmental transfers. Then it examines the distribution of off-budget revenues and assesses disparities in service provision at various levels. Issues relating to vertical distribution of fiscal resources are left to Chapter 8.

HORIZONTAL DISTRIBUTION OF FISCAL RESOURCES

Previous studies have noted unusually large differences in per capita budgetary revenues between provinces in the PRC (World Bank 1990a; Wong, Heady, and Woo 1995). In 1991, the per capita revenues of the richest city, Shanghai, were 15 times those of the poorest province,

Anhui.[1] Excluding the three municipalities of Beijing, Tianjin, and Shanghai and comparing only provinces, the richest province (Liaoning) still had more than four times the per capita revenues of Anhui. Table 7.1 gives the statistical properties of the distribution of per capita revenues across provincial units.

Below the provinces, revenue differences are also very large. Data in Table 7.1 show the distribution of per capita revenues at the city, county, and township levels based on our fieldwork in Hebei, Shandong, and Guizhou provinces. The range of per capita fiscal revenues appears to be largest at the lowest administrative level, the township. In 1993, the richest township in Penglai had a per capita revenue collection of Y294, 29 times the Y10 collected by the poorest township in Puding. In terms of other statistical measures of dispersion, however, substantial disparities appear at the city and county levels as well.[2]

Between counties, disparities in budgetary income are substantial even within the same province. In 1993, among the 69 nonurban counties in Guizhou, per capita revenues varied from a high of Y286 in Guiding County to a low of Y26 in Nayong County, for a ratio of 11:1 of richest to poorest. The corresponding ratio for the 74 nonurban counties in Shandong Province in 1991 was 16.5:1; Changdao County had the most per capita revenues, Y412, and Guanxia County had the least, Y25. In 1991, the average county-level unit in the PRC (including county-level cities) had revenues of Y34 million, but 161 counties had revenues of over Y100 million. These *yiyuan* counties accounted for Y26.55 billion in total revenues and Y12.2 billion in remittances, for an average of Y165 million in revenues and Y75.8 million in remittances per county (Ministry of Finance 1992a, pp. 152-153). Four of the *yiyuan* counties had revenues of over Y400 million, seven had Y200 million to Y300 million, and eight had Y100 million to Y200 million.

---

[1] Tibet, with per capita revenues only one-third of those of the next lowest province, appears to be a far outlier and is therefore omitted from the analysis. If Tibet were included, the ratio of highest to lowest per capita revenues would increase to over 50.

[2] The standard deviation measures the dispersion of per capita revenues from the mean value. Assuming a normal distribution of per capita revenues, approximately two-thirds of the values fall between +1 and -1 standard deviation from the mean. The coefficient of variation is defined as the standard deviation divided by the mean. This measure allows a meaningful comparison of the dispersion of per capita revenues between samples from different administrative levels whose mean per capita revenues may be greatly dissimilar.

Table 7.1: Variation in Per Capita Revenues
by Administrative Level, Early 1990s

Administrative Level	Maximum (Y)	Minimum (Y)	Mean (Y)	Standard Deviation (Y)	Coefficient of Variation
Province (1991)	1,431.9	28.3	266.3	269.9	1.01
Province (excluding Tibet; 1991)	1,431.9	94.1	274.5	270.8	0.99
Province (excluding Beijing, Tianjin, Shanghai, and Tibet; 1991)	404.9	94.1	194.9	68.9	0.35
City (Hebei; 1991)	1,010.5	177.2	571.3	247.5	0.43
City (Shandong; 1992)	1,096.6	100.6	397.2	271.7	0.68
County (Shandong; 1991)	411.9	25.0	65.8	50.9	0.77
County (Guizhou; 1993)	285.7	25.8	67.4	40.7	0.60
Township (Puding; 1993)	36.6	10.2	16.7	8.2	0.49
Township (Zunyi; 1993)	127.1	20.2	52.4	26.0	0.50
Township (Penglai; 1993)	294.4	23.4	73.2	63.3	0.86
Township (Xinji; 1992)	145.0	24.4	51.2	28.3	0.55

Note: At the city level, only prefecture-level cities are included. Guizhou has only two prefecture-level cities: Guiyang and Liupanshui. In 1992, Guiyang had per capita revenues of Y887.2 and Liupanshui, Y106.3. County-level figures include only nonurban counties and exclude county-level cities.
Sources: SSB(1994a); Shandong Statistical Bureau (1992, 1993); Guizhou Statistical Bureau (1994); finance bureaus in Puding, Zunyi, Penglai, and Xinji; fieldwork data.

At the lower end of the distribution, it is estimated that more than half of the 2,000 counties nationwide cannot meet expenditures with the revenues they collect.

The per capita revenues of prefectural-level cities had a slightly narrower range. In Hebei in 1991, they ranged from Y177 in Langfang to Y1,010 in Zhangjiakou. In 1992, prefectural cities in Shandong had per capita revenues ranging from Y101 to Y1,097, and in Guizhou, Guiyang had per capita revenues of Y887 and Liupanshui, Y106.

REDISTRIBUTION MECHANISMS IN THE FISCAL SYSTEM

The sizeable variation in fiscal revenues at all administrative levels raises the important question of whether there are effective mechanisms in the fiscal system to equalize expenditures, or whether disparities in revenue capacity are directly reflected in expenditures. As described in Chapter 1, the fiscal system in the PRC has several channels for redistributing revenues vertically and horizontally among administrative units: revenue-sharing contracts that "tax" rich regions more and poor regions less (or even negatively by providing quota subsidies); earmarked and other subsidies to lower levels; and budgetary grants such as "aid to poor regions" and "social welfare and relief." Budgetary grants are sometimes referred to in Chinese as *xianshang* ("above the line") expenditures by virtue of their inclusion in budgetary accounts,[3] while quota and earmarked subsidies are referred to as *xianxia* ("below the line").

To illustrate the size of earmarked and other subsidies and budgetary grants, Figure 7.1 shows schematically the resources available to the provincial level. For Guizhou, such resources in 1993 totaled Y3,200 million (net of Y23 million in remittances to the central government), of which Y396 million was raised by the province itself, Y1,193 million was in the form of central-government subsidies, and Y1,611 million was remitted from prefectures and cities. That same year, the province spent only Y1,698 million on its own account, leaving Y1,501 million, or 47 percent of the available revenues. These were spent almost entirely "below the line," on subsidies for prefectures and cities that totaled Y1,343 million–Y216 million in quota sub-

---

[3] To avoid double counting in the consolidated budget, "below the line" expenditures do not appear as an expenditure item in the budget of the subsidizing government, but are included in the expenditure budget of the recipient government. "Above the line" expenditures, on the other hand, appear in the budget of the government providing the grant but not in the budget of the recipient government, which is viewed as a disbursing agent of the higher level of government.

Figure 7.1: Resources Available at the Provincial Level

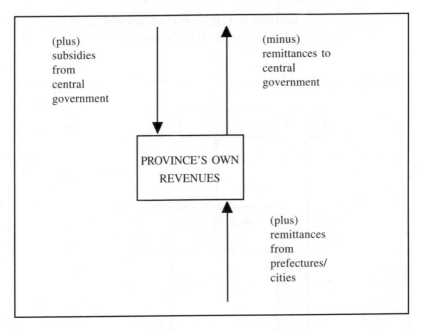

sidies and Y1,127 million in earmarked and other subsidies (see Chapter 4, Tables 4.3, 4.5, and 4.7).

Data for Shandong and Hebei similarly show that "below the line" transfers make up a large proportion—30 percent to 50 percent—of provincial resources. Of the Y5,277 million available to Shandong in 1993, only Y3,127 million was spent at the provincial level, leaving Y2,150 million (or 41 percent) spent "below the line." Hebei spent about two-thirds of its available revenues directly ("above the line").[4] The direction and size of net transfers through the administrative hierarchy in Hebei are shown in Figure 7.2.

The capacity for revenue redistribution at the county level also appears sizeable. Figure 7.2 shows that nearly half of all revenues collected at the township level in Hebei were remitted to the county level,

---

[4] The amount transferred to lower levels is actually somewhat smaller than the difference between the available revenues and own-account expenditures, because part of the unspent funds may be held back at the provincial level as a surplus to be carried over to the next year.

Figure 7.2: Vertical Net Transfers of Total Budgetary Revenue Collected in Hebei Province, 1992[a]

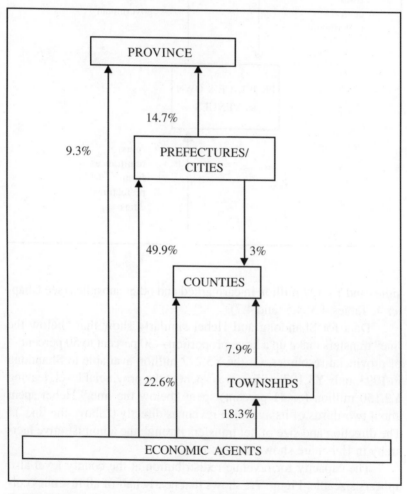

[a]In 1992, Hebei received roughly the same amount in subsidies from the central government as it remitted upward.
Source: Wong (1994).

but this is likely to be an extreme case. Data from a sample of subprovincial units confirm that net remittance rates at the township level are highly variable,[5] as noted earlier in Chapter 5. The disparities in remittance rates among the townships in the counties covered by our fieldwork are summarized in Table 7.2.

Table 7.2: Net Remittance Rates for Townships, 1993
(Percent)

County	Maximum	Minimum	Average	Coefficient of Variation
Penglai	77	-187	-42	-1.77
Qufu	28	-70	-26	-1.13
Zunyi	51	-147	-19	-2.36
Xinji	87	19	55	0.32

Net remittance rate = (total collected revenues - expenditures)/total collected revenues.
Source: Fieldwork data.

NET EFFECT OF INTERGOVERNMENTAL TRANSFERS

If equalization measures work, per capita expenditures should be less widely dispersed than per capita revenues—indeed, per capita expenditures should converge at a single value if equalization is complete.[6] Data in Tables 7.1 and 7.3 show that for our samples at the various administrative levels the coefficient of variation is always lower for per capita expenditures than for per capita revenues, indicating some equalization.

---

[5] The term "net remittances" denotes the surplus of collected revenues over expenditures. This figure is usually smaller than the revenue-sharing remittances because expenditures are enhanced by earmarked and other subsidies from higher levels (i.e., expenditures = collected revenue - remittances + earmarked and other subsidies). A negative remittance rate indicates that expenditures exceeded collected revenues, or a "deficit" unit.

[6] In this extreme case, the standard deviation and coefficient of variation are both equal to zero for the sample of per capita expenditures.

**Table 7.3: Variation in Per Capita Expenditures,
by Administrative Level, Early 1990s**

Administrative Level	Maximum (Y)	Minimum (Y)	Mean (Y)	Standard Deviation (Y)	Coefficient of Variation
Province (1991)	757.6	123.6	297.9	171.76	0.58
Province (excluding Tibet; 1991)	757.6	123.6	284.6	158.26	0.56
Province (excluding Beijing, Tianjin, Shanghai, and Tibet; 1991)	401.5	123.6	239.8	80.86	0.34
City (Hebei; 1991)	422.5	193.1	305.1	81.71	0.27
City (Shandong; 1992)	698.3	104.1	326.0	180.05	0.55
County (Shandong; 1991)	567.1	39.7	84.5	60.11	0.71
Township (Zunyi; 1993)	81.0	34.1	53.4	10.70	0.20
Township (Penglai; 1993)	91.3	42.5	67.8	12.59	0.19
Township (Xinji; 1992)	25.5	8.2	19.0	4.22	0.22

Note: At the city level, only prefecture-level cities are included. Guizhou has only two prefecture-level cities: Guiyang and Liupanshui. In 1992, Guiyang had per capita expenditures of Y427.8 and Liupanshui, Y139.7. County-level figures include only nonurban counties and exclude county-level cities.

Sources: SSB (1994a); Shandong Statistical Bureau (1992, 1993); finance bureaus in Zunyi, Penglai, and Xinji; fieldwork data.

The gap between revenues and expenditures is widest at the township level. The coefficient of variation for townships in Penglai, for example, is 0.86 for revenues but only 0.19 for expenditures, indicating a very strong leveling effect. This reduction in variation is shown in Figure 7.3 which reveals that large transfers from the four richest townships in Penglai County finance extra expenditure in the other 16 townships. In contrast, at the provincial level the coefficients of variation are virtually the same for per capita revenues and expenditures for nonurban provinces excluding Tibet, which seems to imply that there

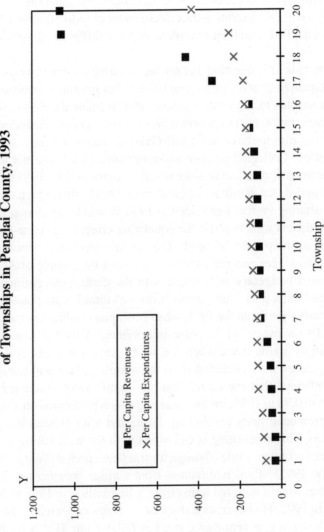

Figure 7.3: Per Capita Revenues and Expenditures of Townships in Penglai County, 1993

Source: Penglai Finance Bureau.

has been little redistribution and equalization among these units. In fact, Figure 7.4 surprisingly shows transfers to favor provinces with mid-high incomes. However, these results must be interpreted with caution since comparing the dispersions of per capita revenues and expenditures provides at best a weak statistical test, and more evidence must be sought to determine the effectiveness of redistributive mechanisms in the PRC and their relative strength at different administrative levels.

There is little question that revenue-sharing contracts were on the whole equalizing: at the provincial level, richer provinces remitted part of their surplus to the central government to finance quota subsidies (negative remittances) to poorer regions. In our sample, Shandong remitted a surplus to the center, while Guizhou received a quota subsidy, as expected. Collected revenue and remittance clearly did not have a linear relationship, however, since revenue contracts from 1988 through 1993 ensured that remittances grew more slowly than revenues. But the tax-sharing system introduced in 1994 should bring changes.

Statistical tests confirm the equalizing effect of revenue-sharing transfers at the provincial level. The partial correlation between per capita remittances and per capita revenues for the sample of 37 units with direct budgetary interaction with the central government (30 provincial units plus 7 line-item cities) was found to be positive and statistically significant for 1991, when per capita remittances increased by Y0.19 for every Y1 increase in revenue.[7] This coefficient was surprisingly stable even when the seven line-item cities and three municipalities were excluded from the sample.[8] Statistical tests have also confirmed that the correlation has significantly weakened over time, from 0.78 in 1985, for the same regression performed on a sample of 28 provincial units (excluding Tibet, and with Hainan not yet a province). This weakening is consistent with the well-known drop in provincial remittance rates through the transition period (Wong, Heady, and Woo 1995). Total remittances from surplus provinces and line-item cities rose in nominal terms from Y40.5 billion in 1986 to Y59.7 billion in 1992. However, as a share of revenues collected at the local level, the aggregate remittance rate has fallen from 31.2 percent to a

---

[7] With a correlation coefficient of 0.19 and T-statistic of 5.34.
[8] The coefficient dropped to only 0.18 (T-statistic of 3.12).

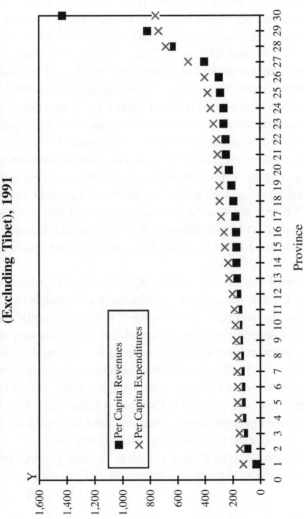

Figure 7.4: Per Capita Revenues and Expenditures of Nonurban Provinces (Excluding Tibet), 1991

■ Per Capita Revenues
✕ Per Capita Expenditures

Province

Source: Fieldwork data.

level of 22-23 percent since 1986 (derived from Table 2.1), and the declining transfer from surplus provinces has rendered the central government less able to finance transfers to poor provinces.

In contrast, the distribution of central earmarked grants exhibits a disequalizing effect. Regressing per capita earmarked subsidy on per capita revenue and per capita income at the provincial level for 1991 produced positive and statistically significant coefficients (0.104, with T-statistic of 5.944, and 0.03, with T-statistic of 6.025, respectively). This indicates that earmarked subsidies were distributed in a way that favored rich provinces. The category "Other subsidies" consists largely of disaster relief which is ad hoc and short-term. Since disasters can strike rich and poor alike, this component can also show a disequalizing effect if regressed on per capita income or revenue.[9]

Data limitations preclude a similar examination of remittance rates and the equalizing effect of revenue-sharing contracts at the subprovincial levels, as well as the distribution of earmarked and other subsidies. Without the needed breakdown, we can measure the gap between revenues and expenditures only as a consolidated transfer (either as a remittance or as a subsidy) to assess the net redistributive effect.

For a small sample of 11 cities—8 line-item cities, plus Anshun, Guiyang, and Taian—a positive correlation was found between per capita remittances and per capita revenues, where the coefficient was 0.64.[10] For this sample, the degree of equalization appears very strong, with remittance rates ranging from 1 percent in Xian to 67 percent in Guiyang (Figure 7.5). Among the four counties surveyed, however, the relationship between remittance rates and per capita revenues runs counter to expectations, as noted in Chapter 5 (Table 5.12): both Zunyi and Penglai have lower per capita revenues than Qufu, yet their remittance rates are more than double Qufu's remittance rate.

However, the overall picture is mixed. A weak positive correlation is found between per capita remittances and per capita revenues

---

[9] However, the level of assistance depends on the ability of the local government to provide supplementary funds. Thus, disaster victims in Guangdong would get much more generous assistance than those in Shanxi.

[10] This sample excludes Shenzhen, an apparent outlier with an extremely low remittance rate. The regression has adjusted R-square of 0.78, and T-statistic of 6.07 on the coefficient.

Figure 7.5: Correlation Between Per Capita Revenues and Remittance Rates in Cities, Early 1990s

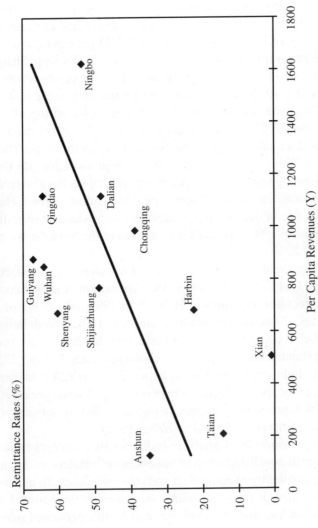

Note: Data are for 1991 except for Guiyang, Anshun and Qingdao which are for 1992 and Taian for 1993.

Sources: Wong, Heady and Woo (1995); Wong (1994); fieldwork data.

for county-level units in Shandong as well as townships in Penglai, Qufu, and Zunyi. However, many exceptions can be found within each subsample. For example, in 1991, Changdao County had per capita revenues of Y412, the highest among 99 counties in Shandong, but still received subsidies (or negative remittances) of Y149 per capita. At the other end of the spectrum, Tancheng County had per capita revenues of only Y47 but spent an even lower Y43 per capita, and so was able to remit a surplus upward. Among the cities, Zibo City in Shandong was required to transfer more than half of its per capita revenues of Y328, leaving only Y152 per capita for expenditures. At the same time, Weihai City, with net transfers of Y203 per capita on top of its per capita revenues of Y495, could afford to spend Y698 per capita. Examples of disequalization are also found in Hebei Province. The bottom half of Table 7.4 shows that Zhangjiakou and Chengde Prefectures had the highest average expenditures per capita, but also received the largest subsidies, about Y40 per capita. At the other extreme, Handan Prefecture, one of the only two prefectures to produce an overall revenue surplus in 1991, achieved it by spending the lowest amount per capita, Y47.8.

The apparently perverse direction of transfers is also reflected in the data in Table 7.5, which shows the distribution of deficit counties across prefectures and cities in Hebei.[11] In 1991, 80 percent of rural counties and 30 percent of urban counties in Hebei ran deficits, but none of the 13 counties in Handan Prefecture did. Indeed, the poorest county in Handan Prefecture had per capita revenues of only Y26.9 yet eked out a slight surplus by holding expenditures to Y24.3. In contrast, a county in Chengde Prefecture had revenues of Y104.8 per capita but spent Y108.1, presumably financed with a net inflow of subsidies (*Economic and Statistical Yearbook of Hebei* 1992).

The province-level analysis indicates that intergovernmental transfers are disequalizing when revenue-sharing transfers are dominated by (or are smaller than) earmarked and other subsidies. To understand the relative size of these subsidies, we return to the national level, where "below the line" expenditures can be disaggregated into four components: quota subsidies (negative remittances); earmarked

---

[11] Deficit counties are defined as those counties whose budgetary expenditures exceed their revenues.

**Table 7.4: Per Capita Revenues and Expenditures
in Prefectures and Cities in Hebei, 1991
(Y)**

	Per Capita Revenues	Per Capita Expenditures
Cities		
Shijiazhuang	768.6	309.5
Tangshan	502.7	258.3
Qinhuangdao	681.0	422.5
Handan	469.9	193.1
Xintai	401.4	229.4
Baoding	830.8	369.0
Zhangjiakou	1,010.5	416.5
Chengde	391.4	277.8
Langfang	177.2	224.3
Changzhou	479.1	350.5
Mean	571.3	305.1
Standard deviation	247.46	81.71
Coefficient of variation	0.4332	0.2678
Prefectures		
Shijiazhuang	71.7	82.2
Handan	52.3	47.8
Xingtai	49.7	71.3
Baoding	58.3	75.6
Zhangjiakou	64.5	104.6
Chengde	64.3	107.3
Changzhou	91.0	90.0
Hengshui	71.6	90.2
Mean	65.4	83.6
Standard deviation	13.10	19.20
Coefficient of variation	0.2005	0.2299

Source: Hebei Statistical Bureau (1992).

subsidies; final-account subsidies made at year-end to help balance provincial budgets; and payments to compensate provinces for reductions in their tax bases caused by enterprise ownership transfers. The third and fourth components can be combined into one since most final-account subsidies are made to compensate provinces for tax-base alterations (see Wong, Heady, and Woo 1995, Ch. 3). Quota subsidies from the central government have stayed at the same nominal level of

**Table 7.5: Distribution of Deficit Counties in Hebei,
by Cities and Prefectures, 1991**

Overall Revenue Status[a]	Cities and Prefectures	Number of Deficit Counties	Total Number of Counties	Share of Deficit Counties (%)
	Cities			
+	Shijiazhuang	1	4	25
+	Tangshan	1	10	10
+	Qinhuangdao	2	4	50
+	Handan	0	1	0
+	Xingtai	1	1	100
+	Baoding	2	2	100
+	Zhangjiakou	1	1	100
+	Chengde	0	1	0
+	Langfang	2	7	29
+	Changzhou	0	2	0
	Subtotal	10	33	30
	Prefectures			
-	Shijiazhuang	9	10	90
+	Handan	0	13	0
-	Xingtai	14	14	100
-	Baoding	14	17	82
-	Zhangjiakou	12	12	100
-	Chengde	7	7	100
+	Changzhou	8	8	100
-	Hengshui	9	10	90
	Subtotal	73	91	80
	Total	83	124	67

[a] Consolidated accounts; "+" refers to a surplus over expenditure, "-" to a deficit.
Source: Hebei Statistical Bureau (1992).

Y8.6 billion since 1988. In the meantime, earmarked subsidies have grown rapidly, from Y7.9 billion in 1980 to Y25.7 billion in 1987 and to Y37.8 billion in 1992. As a result, the share of quota subsidies has fallen steadily. For the three years 1990-1992, quota subsidies accounted for only 14-15 percent of total central subsidies. During this period, the category of earmarked subsidies was dominated by price subsidies for urban grain supply, which took up two-thirds to three-fourths of the total each year. The grain subsidies were obviously disequalizing since the more urbanized provinces received higher subsidies under this category even though they also had higher incomes.

The share of needs-based transfers has declined at the subnational levels as well, also because of the dominance of grain subsidies, which were decentralized to local governments in 1985.[12] In Guizhou, quota subsidies accounted for only 16 percent of total subsidies at the provincial level in 1993, down from over 40 percent in the early 1980s. Although earmarked subsidies are used for other items such as capital construction expenditures in the education and health sectors, it was noted in Chapter 6 that the requirement to provide matching funds often excludes poor localities from participation, reinforcing the disequalizing effect of these subsidies.

Finally, as for the redistributive role of "above the line" expenditures, these expenditures must be quite large to cancel out the disequalizing effect of earmarked subsidies; in reality, they are extremely small. Among the major expenditure components listed in budgetary accounts, only "welfare assistance" and "aid to poor regions" are obviously needs-based. Together these two items compose only 4-5 percent of the consolidated expenditures of both Guizhou and Shandong provinces in the 1990s (Tables 4.6 and 4.13), not enough to make a significant difference in equalizing expenditures across localities.

Among the three methods of intergovernmental transfer, then, only revenue-sharing transfers (quota subsidies) are equalizing, but progressively less so in the transition period. It is no wonder that intragovernmental transfers often have a disequalizing net effect.

HORIZONTAL DISTRIBUTION OF OFF-BUDGET REVENUES

Data on off-budget revenues and expenditures are even more scarce at the subprovincial levels. The reporting system is less detailed and comprehensive, especially because of the weakness of the state statistical

---

[12] In some provinces, these expenditures are a provincial responsibility, but elsewhere, such as in Shandong, they are a city or county responsibility.

system below the county level. Besides, there are incentives for nonreporting.

The analysis in Chapter 5 leads us to expect that off-budget revenue is more unequally distributed. First, per capita extrabudgetary revenue and budgetary revenue are highly correlated since extrabudgetary fees are frequently levied on the same budgetary tax base. Statistically we find the correlation coefficient to be 0.9425 in 1990 for the sample of provincial-level units—the same correlation should hold for lower levels as well. Given that the bulk of self-raised funds are levied on TVEs, the correlation between SRF and budgetary revenues can also be expected to be high. Second, extrabudgetary revenue is not shared with higher levels of government; therefore, extrabudgetary revenue is approximately equal to extrabudgetary expenditure. For the provincial sample, the correlation coefficient was 0.9942 for 1990. In addition, extrabudgetary expenditures are highly correlated with budgetary expenditures (correlation coefficient of 0.9842 in 1990). Thus, areas with high per capita revenues also tend to have high per capita extrabudgetary revenues, which are not subject to redistribution, either vertically or horizontally. One relatively new source of extrabudgetary revenue is the leasing of land. The demand for land and hence revenue capacity varies between regions. Other things being equal, the growing reliance of local governments on off-budget finance is accentuating regional disparities and eroding the equalization achieved by redistributing budgetary revenues.

DISPARITIES IN SERVICE PROVISION

Given their dissimilarities in fiscal resources and the ineffectiveness of redistribution, governments can rightly be expected to provide very different levels of service. Chapter 6 dealt in particular with disparities in the provision of education, public health, and social welfare services in rural areas. This section systematically examines differences in the level of service between regions (across provinces), between urban and rural areas, and within urban and rural areas, to identify the areas of greatest disparity and thus show the way for the reform of the distributional function of the fiscal system.

BETWEEN PROVINCES

Substantial variation exists at the provincial level in a number of education and health indicators, reflecting disparities in the provision of basic services. The 1990 population census in the PRC placed the literacy rate for those aged 15 and above at 76 percent, with a range of 31 percent (Tibet) to 89 percent (Beijing). Shandong has a literacy rate of 77 percent and Guizhou, 63 percent (Table 7.6). Infant mortality and life expectancy indicators for Guizhou are also more unfavorable, being at least one standard deviation away from the national average (Table 7.6). In contrast, infant mortality in Shandong is well below the national average and life expectancy is higher.

The provinces also differ in the distribution of students by level of education. Throughout the country, 1.4 percent of all students at school are at the tertiary level, 29.8 percent are at the secondary level, and 68.8 percent are in primary schools. Shandong has a comparable distribution of 1.2 percent, 34.0 percent, and 64.8 percent, respectively.

Table 7.6: Province-Level Indicators of Education and Health Outcomes

Indicator	Mean	Standard Deviation	Shandong	Guizhou
Literacy rate, ages 15 and above, 1990 (%)	75.90	11.78	76.99	63.27
Infant mortality rate, males, 1990 (per 1,000 births)	34.40	22.40	14.20	60.70
Infant mortality rate, females, 1990 (per 1,000 births)	36.30	20.90	18.00	65.60
Life expectancy at birth, males, 1990 (%)	67.40	3.20	69.50	64.30
Life expectancy at birth, females, 1990 (%)	70.50	3.80	73.00	66.00
Hospital beds per 1,000 population, 1993	2.79	1.08	2.05	1.56
Doctors per 1,000 population, 1993	1.92	0.93	1.28	1.14

Sources: Population Census Office (ed.) (1993), pp. 38-39; Lu, Hao, and Gao (1994); Ministry of Public Health (1994), p.30.

Guizhou, on the other hand, has a much larger share of students at the primary level (79.1 percent) and only 0.5 percent receiving tertiary education.[13] These distributions of students across levels of schooling are consistent with the more widespread implementation of compulsory education in Shandong than in Guizhou.

In public health, provinces differ in the number of hospital beds and the ratio of doctors to the population (Table 7.6). While the figures for Guizhou are lower than those for Shandong and the national average, these indicators do not fully reflect the differences in the level and quality of health-care services provided. The fieldwork revealed obvious disparities in medical equipment and technology between Shandong and Guizhou, although there are no comparable statistics on this aspect of service provision.

In 1993, Shandong had per capita budgetary expenditures of Y218, similar to Guizhou's Y198, yet Shandong provides a much higher level of public services (Table 7.7). Guizhou's inefficient service delivery could explain the discrepancy. The province is less densely populated— there are less than 200 persons per square kilometer—than Shandong, with a population density of 550 persons. The more widely dispersed

Table 7.7: Selected Economic Indicators for Shandong and Guizhou, 1993

Indicator	Shandong	Guizhou	PRC
Total budgetary revenue (Y billion)	19.4	5.7	508.8
Total budgetary expenditure (Y billion)	18.8	6.7	528.7
Population (million)	86.4	34.1	1,185.2
Per capita GDP (Y)	3,222	1,034	2,648
Per capita budgetary revenue (Y)	225	166	429
Per capita budgetary expenditure (Y)	218	198	446

Sources: SSB (1995, pp. 34-35; 1994, p.32); Guizhou Statistical Bureau (1994), p. 91; Shandong Statistical Bureau (1994), pp. 115-116.

---

[13] Although total fertility has declined slightly faster in Shandong than in Guizhou, the difference in distribution is too great to be explained by differences in age structure between the two provinces.

population could well make the service delivery cost per unit higher in Guizhou than in Shandong. Furthermore, relatively more people in Guizhou belong to minority nationalities and their special needs for some public services, such as education, may contribute as well to the higher unit cost of public services in Guizhou. Nonetheless, differences in efficiency cannot possibly explain all of the large gaps noted in Chapter 6. Differences in extrabudgetary revenue and self-raised funds are a more plausible explanation.

BETWEEN URBAN AREAS

Cities in the PRC also vary in the provision of public services. At one extreme are Beijing, Shanghai, and Tianjin, three municipalities with provincial-level status. Literacy rates and the number of hospital beds and doctors per capita in these premier centers of commerce, higher education, and research in the PRC are among the country's highest. In a second group of cities are provincial capitals and major coastal cities, whose health indicators tend to be favorable. Their revenue resources are higher on the average because of their industry clusters or their advantageous location for trade and commerce. The remaining cities in the PRC compose a third group. Our study included two cities in the second group: Guiyang (provincial capital of Guizhou) and Qingdao (a major coastal city). Anshun and Taian, on the other hand, are not provincial capitals, and are not very favorably located.

Public health services in Qingdao and Guiyang are roughly comparable and above the national urban average (Chapter 4). Anshun and Taian provide similar services at a substantially lower level than Qingdao and Guiyang and the national urban average (Table 4.18). The disparity in service provision is also evident in education: compulsory education has progressed further in Guiyang than in Anshun. Greater fiscal capacity (both budgetary and extrabudgetary) allows Qingdao to provide better services and infrastructure than Taian. Extrabudgetary funds were half the size of budgetary funds in Qingdao, but were only a fourth the size of Taian's budgetary funds. While comparable data on extrabudgetary resources are not available for Guiyang and Anshun, Anshun collects only a fraction of Guiyang's budgetary revenue per capita. Since per capita extrabudgetary funds are much lower in Guizhou than in Shandong (Chapter 4), both Guiyang and Anshun are likely to have fewer extrabudgetary resources for local services than counterpart cities in Shandong.

Other studies on the distribution of income across urban areas have found a low level of inequality (Khan et al. 1992; Tsui 1993). Khan et al. (1992) estimated a Gini ratio of 0.23 for urban households in 1988. They found urban subsidies, such as the grain subsidy, to be slightly disequalizing and ineffective in redistributing income among urban residents, particularly in the absence of a means test or income targeting. The egalitarian structure of wages in state and collective enterprises, which employ 90 percent of urban workers, instead serves to equalize urban income to a high degree.

BETWEEN RURAL AREAS

Social services vary between counties in different provinces, within the same province, and to a lesser extent even between townships in the same county. One-third of Guizhou counties still have not attained universal primary education; all counties in Shandong, on the other hand, expect to offer nine years of compulsory education by 1997. The two Shandong counties stand in sharp contrast to the two Guizhou counties in the provision of education and public health services. Every education and health indicator points to more and better-quality social services in Penglai and Qufu as compared with Zunyi and Puding (Chapter 6).

Within Shandong and Guizhou, the counties also provide varying levels of social services. In Shandong, a provincial education official said that education was most advanced in counties along the coast (including Penglai) and slightly less advanced toward the center of the province (including counties like Qufu). A few remaining areas in the mountainous western part of the province had difficulty implementing compulsory education. In 5 percent of counties in Guizhou, government pensions are only Y40 per month versus the provincial average of Y180. Health stations are found in more than half of all villages in Zunyi but are nonexistent in the villages in Puding.

The services offered vary partly because of differences in budgetary expenditures but mostly because of differences in extrabudgetary and self-raised funds. Aside from the cities, the TVEs, which tend to cluster in coastal provinces and in rural areas near cities, constitute the major tax base. In 1993, TVEs generated per capita profits of Y10 in Guizhou and Y206 in Shandong. The uneven distribution of the TVE tax base sharpens rural differences in budgetary and extrabudgetary expenditures. Rural local governments with developed TVEs may have benefited from fiscal decentralization, but many in poor regions with weak industrial bases are forced to cut back on basic services or to levy ad hoc fees and taxes on farm households.

The existence of profitable TVEs explains to a large extent the disparity in social services in the rural areas, as can be seen by comparing the central junior high schools in two townships in Zunyi. The junior high school in Shiban Township is an old, dilapidated two-story structure consisting solely of classrooms. There is no library or laboratory. The teachers live in two rooms on the second floor. In Longkeng Township, the junior high school is in better physical shape. A library and a school office occupy separate rooms, and the teachers are lodged in more spacious quarters. Shiban has no TVEs, while the 762 TVEs in Longkeng contributed a per capita output value of Y2,200 in 1993. Its stronger tax base and extrabudgetary resources have enabled Longkeng to provide better services than Shiban within the same county.

Chapter 6 noted the importance of self-raised funds in sup-porting education and other social services. Local funds help pay the salaries of teachers and public health workers, meet other re-current expenditures, and match higher-level grants for capital out-lays. The capacity to raise local funds for budgetary expenditures depends on the vitality of the local economy, including agriculture and TVEs, and therefore varies widely among rural communities in the PRC.

Not enough grants, earmarked and otherwise, are targeted to ru-ral areas to enable them to offer the same level of service. According to the State Education Commission, to achieve compulsory education goals for the year 2000, central-government grants for the purpose will have to increase many times over to Y1 billion per year during the ninth five-year plan. A number of earmarked central grants are targeted to poorer areas, but the targets are not well defined. In Guizhou, for ex-ample, some prefectures allocated education funds from the province and the center to their counties according to county population and irrespective of the county's school-age population, income, and revenue capacity.

Inadequate funding and increased labor mobility are making it very difficult for all but the wealthiest rural areas to hire and retain well-qualified teachers and medical personnel. Officials in Guizhou reported an exodus of the best-trained and most experienced doctors out of the rural areas starting in the mid-1980s. Some rural doctors and teachers have succeeded in obtaining permanent household registration in the cities while others have simply migrated to more developed rural areas, particularly the coastal provinces. All of them are drawn by the prospect of a higher salary and standard of living and better facilities.

BETWEEN URBAN AND RURAL AREAS

On both the revenue and the expenditure side, the gap between cities and counties is sizeable. The revenue gap is very large owing to the industry-centered tax base. The urban-rural revenue gap exists within better off and poor provinces alike. Prefectural cities in Shandong, for example, collected an average of Y397 per capita in 1992 while nonurban counties in the same province collected only Y66 per capita on the average in 1991 (Table 7.1). In 1993, Guizhou's two prefectural-level cities collected an average of Y497 per capita in budgetary revenue and the nonurban counties, only Y67.

Redistribution through the various channels discussed in "Redistribution Mechanisms in the Fiscal System" and "Net Effect of Intergovernmental Transfers," reduces city expenditures somewhat, relative to revenue, and enhances the fiscal resources of counties slightly. In Shandong, cities had average per capita expenditures of Y326 and revenues of Y397 in 1992, and nonurban counties were able to achieve average per capita expenditures of Y84 and average per capita revenues of Y66 in 1991 (Tables 7.1 and 7.3). The urban-rural gap in expenditures nonetheless remained very large.

Differing needs make it difficult to compare urban and rural fiscal expenditures directly. The greater need of cities for infrastructure investment, especially in the transition period, is commonly cited, in fact, to justify a sizeable urban-rural disparity. To put these needs in the proper context, we break down fiscal expenditures into two parts, as follows:

- Basic (human development) needs - education, public health, social welfare
- Infrastructure needs - water, sewage, electricity, roads, public transport

Basic expenditure needs are the same for both rural and urban governments. However, the infrastructure needs of cities tend to increase and eventually to surpass the infrastructure needs of rural governments as cities regain their economic role in the transition to a market economy. As discussed in Chapters 3 and 4, the financing of infrastructure is critical to the growth of cities. In transition economies, however, cities often do not have enough fiscal autonomy to finance the needed infrastructure, especially during a period of fiscal decline. This is where an important difference between urban and rural governments comes into play. As centers of industry and hence the tax base, cities have some built-in flexibility in responding to the expenditure demand for infrastructure. As the economy flourishes and the demand for urban infrastructure rises, the growth in city revenues will help finance the expenditure. During times of revenue shortfalls, city governments have the option to cut back on infrastructure rather than basic human development services. Rural governments are not so fortunate. Faced with shortfalls in revenue, they must cut back on their basic human development services.

In this light, the degree of urban bias in the fiscal system can be partially inferred from the far superior services provided by cities. In our survey, the four cities had 3.0-8.1 hospital beds per 1,000 population (Table 4.19) while the four counties had 0.8-2.0 (Table 6.17), and the cities also had more and better-trained medical personnel than the counties. All research and teaching hospitals, which are the best equipped, are located in cities. Urban residents can go to these facilities for routine care as well as for complicated cases. Only referral through multiple bureaucratic layers can obtain the same treatment for rural residents.

The cities are also further advanced than the counties when it comes to compulsory education (Chapters 4 and 6). The percentage of students who go on to junior high school and regular senior high school is higher in the urban areas. This is true nationwide and at the provincial level (Table 7.8). Similarly, the illiteracy rate among urban residents all over the country was 12 percent in 1990; for rural residents it was 26 percent. Urban areas in Shandong have an illiteracy rate of only 16 percent, while for the rural areas it is 26 percent. In Guizhou, the rural illiteracy rate of 41 percent is almost double the urban rate of 21 percent.

More importantly, many poor rural areas spend too little per capita to provide the level of basic services called for in government programs and targets, as discussed in Chapter 6. If these government targets are taken to be the defined service needs of the community, shortfalls in provision indicate fiscal gaps in the rural sector.

Differences in the provision of basic human services are only one aspect of the urban bias in the fiscal system. Another is the assortment of subsidies that largely benefit urban residents, and are only partially captured in fiscal expenditure data. These subsidies include price subsidies for urban grain consumption (only half to two-thirds of which are counted in fiscal expenditures—see Wong, Heady, and Woo 1995) and subsidies for housing, medical insurance, and other

**Table 7.8: Distribution of Students, by Level of School
in Cities and Counties, 1993**

	Regular Senior High Schools (%)	Regular Junior High Schools (%)	Primary Schools (%)
Cities			
Nationwide	8.8	28.5	62.7
Shandong	10.8	30.0	59.2
Guizhou	9.9	26.8	63.3
Counties			
Nationwide	3.0	23.0	74.0
Shandong	3.0	27.2	69.8
Guizhou	1.8	15.6	82.6

Source: SSB (1994a), pp. 580-587.

miscellaneous items. A survey of urban and rural households by Khan et al. (1992) revealed that urban residents derived an estimated 39 percent of their per capita disposable income in 1988 from subsidies net of taxes, while rural residents ended up paying 2 percent of their per capita income as a net tax that year. The government in recent years has moved to abolish the urban coupon ration system for grain and other food products but has replaced these with cash subsidies for food paid directly to urban workers.[14] Furthermore, local governments still interfere periodically in local urban food markets in the attempt to hold prices down.

Another government subsidy that disproportionately benefits urban residents is housing. As was pointed out in Chapter 4, housing is a private good, and the government should charge and recover the full cost of providing this good. Yet in the midst of housing reform, most urban residents continue to live in subsidized housing. In 1994, urban residents spent an average of Y79 per capita, or 2 percent of their income, on housing, while rural residents spent nearly twice as much, Y143 per capita, or 12 percent of their income. Living space may be larger in rural homes, but the quality of housing is also lower. Only 10 percent of rural housing is made of reinforced concrete, a common feature of urban residences. Running water and electricity, though fairly standard in urban houses, are still quite rare in rural houses.

Finally, government workers and employees of state-owned enterprises and large urban collectives which are concentrated in urban centers are the primary beneficiaries of subsidized medical insurance. Medical insurance allows most urban residents to consume more health-care services than rural residents who have no coverage. The absence of medical insurance for the vast majority of rural residents makes the provision of public health in rural areas all the more critical.

This imbalance in government transfers contributed to an urban-rural income ratio of 2.42 and a Gini ratio of 0.38 for household income in 1988 (Khan et al. 1992). Inequality between urban and rural areas, as measured by the Gini ratio of household income, is greater than the inequality within rural areas (0.34) and within urban areas

---

[14] Government price subsidies peaked in 1990 at Y38 billion, of which Y31 billion was for grain, cotton, edible oils, and meat. In 1993, the government spent Y30 billion on price subsidies, 85 percent of which were granted in support of those same agricultural products.

(0.23). Data from the State Statistical Bureau indicate that the income gap between rural and urban households has been widening since the mid-1980s. From 1985 to 1994, per capita rural income increased at an average annual rate of 2.4 percent in real terms while per capita urban income grew at an average of 5.9 percent annually. According to the State Statistical Bureau's measures of income, the urban-rural income ratio increased from 1.88 in 1985 to 2.86 in 1994. These findings are consistent with the disparity in the provision of education services, as measured by the distribution of students across levels of school (Table 7.8). The regional gap between Shandong and Guizhou in the share of students attending regular senior high school in cities (10.8 versus 9.9) is smaller than the gap for rural areas (3.0 versus 1.8). The gap is largest between counties and cities—1.8 versus 9.9 for Guizhou and 3.0 versus 10.8 for Shandong.

ISSUES

The examination of equalization issues in this chapter showed that revenue capacity varies greatly between regions, with very substantial differences between provinces; between the urban and rural sectors; and between horizontal units within each sector. These differences are extremely large by international standards.

Mechanisms for redistribution in this system are very active at the subprovincial levels, where large proportions of funds are transferred vertically through revenue-sharing contracts and through "below the line" transfers of earmarked and other subsidies. However, these transfers lack transparency. Remittance rates are largely negotiated, and the distribution of earmarked and other subsidies is ad hoc, with no clearly defined rules.

In spite of the high proportions of revenues redistributed, the net result is often disequalizing, mainly because of the declining share of needs-based transfers and the rising share of earmarked subsidies, which are largely disequalizing. The end of subsidies for urban grain sales should reorient the transfers more toward equalization.

Fiscal decentralization has exacerbated regional disparities and the urban-rural gap, by favoring revenue-producing regions and weakening the overall redistributive capacity of the fiscal system. Specifically, cities and provinces in surplus have benefited by being permitted to retain a growing proportion of their collected revenues, while transfers to regions and sectors in deficit (i.e., rural sectors) have been dwindling. It is not surprising that Shandong's real expenditures per capita have grown faster than Guizhou's, even though Guizhou managed to increase revenue collection more than ninefold from 1980 to 1993, compared with a fourfold increase for Shandong.

The growing reliance on off-budget funds to finance local-government services reflects the government's recognition of the fiscal gaps at lower levels, and efforts to find supplementary sources of finance are tolerated and even encouraged as evidence of "local self-reliance" in solving fiscal problems. Unfortunately, since access to off-budget funds and access to budgetary revenues are highly correlated, the increasing reliance on off-budget resources has amplified regional disparities in the whole system of government finance.

The differential access to funds has led to great differences between provinces, between the urban and rural sectors, and between horizontal units within each sector, in the quantity and quality of services, particularly for such basic needs as education and health. To the extent that many poor localities, especially in the rural areas, provide basic services that fall far short of announced government targets, the fiscal gaps should be recognized, and national remedies undertaken to fill those gaps.

Chapter 8

POLICY RECOMMENDATIONS

by Christine P. W. Wong
and Christopher Heady

T his book shows that local public finance in the PRC is an area requiring urgent policy action. Local governments at the subprovincial levels have unusually heavy spending responsibilities. In 1993, nearly one-half of all the budgetary expenditures of the government were at the local level. Cities and prefectures spent 19 percent of total expenditures, while counties and townships spent 26 percent. (The central government spent about 40 percent, and the provincial governments, 14 percent.) The very large share of local expenditures makes the PRC far more decentralized than the countries visited by teams from the Ministry of Finance (US, Canada, France, Norway, New Zealand, and Australia). The contrast is sharpest with Australia, where local governments spend less than 10 percent of the total. Local governments in the PRC, like local governments elsewhere in the world, are responsible for day-to-day administration and for social services such as basic education, public health, water supply, and sanitation. But unlike other local governments, those in the PRC rely much more on self-financing to provide these services.

Local public finance in the PRC is in a dysfunctional state. Reforms and the emerging forces of the market have brought many changes in the locus and composition of revenues and expenditures, with varying effect across sectors and regions. To date, efforts at fiscal reform have focused primarily on central-provincial relations, leaving local budgets to the discretion of the provinces. Moreover, attention has focused mostly on revenue divisions, leaving expenditures to adjust to the availability of funds. Under fiscal pressure, higher-level governments often devolved expenditures downward while reducing transfers, as they struggled to balance their own budgets. Through the transition, local governments have been saddled with additional major expenditures including social security, urban food subsidies, and social responsibilities devolved from state-owned enterprises (such as child care and kindergartens). A mismatch between revenue and expenditure assignments has emerged and worsened as a result.

While they represented a giant step forward in rationalizing the fiscal system, reforms implemented in 1994 are very much incomplete because changes were specified only in the central-provincial division of taxes and revenues. As long as provinces remain the sole arbiter for revenue assignments for the subprovincial levels, the 1994 reform may be imperfectly transmitted downward. To complete the fiscal reforms needed for a decentralized, market-oriented economy, appropriate revenue and expenditure assignments must be extended to the lower levels of government. This is of particular concern since many localities were already severely underfunded under the previous revenue-sharing regime. By shifting from a negotiated revenue sharing to a fixed share of locally collected VAT and consumption tax, the tax-sharing system may worsen the distribution of fiscal expenditures across regions unless a program of equalization transfers is quickly put in place.

A fundamental reform of local public finance is long overdue. Some scholars have characterized the evolution of local finance as the outcome of reform thinking that has treated local governments much like enterprises in the process of decentralization, with the same expectation that autonomy is bestowed in exchange for savings in state subsidies (Zhou, X., and Yang 1992, p. 52). This seems an apt description of the process whereby local governments are exhorted to reduce their dependence on budgetary transfers by expanding their tax bases, much as SOEs are urged to "turn losses into profits." Unfortunately, this principle of self-financing by each administrative unit runs against the rationale spelled out in Chapter 2 for the efficient intergovernmental division of revenues and expenditures. As noted in earlier chapters, it has also led to growing regional disparities through the past one-and-a-half decades, and these disparities are extremely large by international standards.

Other undesirable outcomes of such fiscal incentives, including increased tax competition and a growing reliance on off-budget financing, were analyzed in *Fiscal Management and Economic Reform in the People's Republic of China* (Wong et al. 1995). These fiscal incentives have been widely noted as being the primary cause of the mercantilist tendencies among local governments in the PRC, besides perpetuating local-government intervention and participation in production, thwarting market-oriented reform (for examples, see Wong 1987, 1988, 1991a, 1992; Zhou, X., and Yang Z. 1992; Gu and Shen 1992).

Many local governments have used off-budget funds to supplement their budgets for local services. But the growing dependence on such funds, particularly among rural governments, has also had problematic outcomes. The size of these funds has been difficult to measure—our best estimate is at least 6-7 percent of GDP, or half as large as the formal budget itself. The importance of off-budget funds in financing local government was illustrated by the comparison of service provision in Shandong and Guizhou in Chapter 6. Shandong was seen to provide far more and higher-quality services per capita despite the virtually identical per capita budgetary revenues of the two provinces, because it had greater access to off-budget funds for primary education and health. Off-budget funds, it was argued in Chapters 5-7, have made the regions even more unequal in the transition. Earlier chapters discussed the adverse effects of multiple budgets on the transparency and efficiency of tax administration and resource allocation. Moreover, significant off-budget spending by government weakens the impact of fiscal policy as a tool of macroeconomic stabilization, and confers substantial de facto control over total spending on lower levels of government.

Finally, budgetary pressures have forced local governments to accumulate payment arrears that pervade the entire fiscal system. Even though local governments are legally not allowed to incur budget deficits, these are common. All four counties in our fieldwork ran slight deficits in 1993. Statistics from Shandong Province show the consolidated budget in deficit nearly every year since 1980. Besides these "open" deficits, payment arrears to enterprises, organizations, and civil servants and between levels of government constitute huge "hidden" deficits for local governments.

The pervasive deficits and payment arrears weaken resource allocation by the government. The system at the local level is said to be so clogged by back debts that new injections into the system are frequently rerouted (often illegally) away from the intended sectors. Examples are poverty alleviation funds for capital investment projects that go instead to meeting backpay for teachers (Park, Rozelle, Wong, and Ren, forthcoming).

LESSONS FROM THE EXPERIENCE OF OTHER COUNTRIES

The study-tour reports on Australia, New Zealand, France, Norway, Canada, and the US provide useful information about how local government finance works in a range of developed market economies. The countries have different systems. The Australian system of intergovernmental transfers, for example, has much greater resource equalization than the US system. Historical diversity and varying opinions of citizens about the importance of equalization and local-government autonomy underlie such differences. Therefore, rather than choosing a single international model of local-government finance, the PRC should adopt the features of the various systems that suit its own circumstances. The most important features are those that are common to the six countries studied.

First, in all the six countries, the tax powers and the expenditure responsibilities of each level of government have a clear legal or constitutional basis. These powers and responsibilities are generally assigned in accordance with the principles discussed in Chapter 2. In the PRC, the new tax-sharing system between the center and the provinces has not produced corresponding changes at the subprovincial level, and doubts as to whether the old revenue-sharing contracts will still apply have spawned uncertainty about financing levels and inevitable reductions in service efficiency. Expenditure responsibilities are also not defined clearly enough and devolution of control to lower levels is not so extensive. Chapters 4 and 6 noted the propensity of lower-level governments in the PRC to make a larger financial contribution to services with more local impact. (This conforms broadly to the principles discussed in Chapter 2.) However, devolution should go further and cities should be given complete control over a larger part of the capital construction budget, which is really local in nature.

Second, in five of the six countries, at least one local tax rate is controlled by local government. Local communities can therefore decide whether or not more service is worth paying higher taxes. Local governments in the PRC cannot make such a choice, but they do impose local fees and levies to make up for a perceived insufficiency in tax revenues. There is no clear legal basis for these fees and levies, which are often deemed onerous and inequitable. A clearly defined local tax that is subject to local control would be both more transparent (because its base would be known) and more equitable.

Finally, local-government expenditure in all the six countries is largely financed with grants from higher levels of government. As discussed in Chapter 2, these grants are meant to equalize financial resources between local governments to a certain extent. The countries studied differ in the degree of equalization intended and achieved, but all want to ensure an acceptable minimum standard of service for all their citizens, wherever they live. The grants to local governments are therefore calculated using transparent formulas, based on objective measures of need. In contrast, individually negotiated contracts governed revenue sharing between the central and local governments in the PRC before the advent of tax sharing. The resultant system of intergovernmental transfers was complex and multistranded. Rather than being based on need, the transfers were politically sensitive and nontransparent, and were typically not reflected as a source of revenue in budget reports. This problem will have been reduced at the provincial level by the tax-sharing system, but its reduction at the subprovincial level requires consistent application of the system throughout the government.

The very active transfer mechanisms at the subprovincial levels were a surprising finding of the study, proving that the PRC could indeed develop an intergovernmental transfer system. The three provinces in the fieldwork redirect downward through revenue sharing and other transfers one-third to one-half of allocable budgetary resources. The same is true at the county level. These findings indicate that the transfers can be better targeted to achieve equalization and resource allocation objectives under a transparent, formula-driven system.

SPECIAL ISSUES IN THE PRC AS A TRANSITION ECONOMY

Many of the current inadequacies of local-government finance in the PRC, such as the insufficient devolution of expenditure responsibilities, arise from the transitional state of the economy. In the move away from the strict control of central planning to a market economy, the government is expected to do less direct management and more indirect management, including creating effective indirect levers of macroeconomic stabilization and a proper regulatory framework.

A fundamental issue is the specification of what exactly the responsibilities of government should be in the PRC. In comparison with market economies, the government has much more involvement with enterprises producing normally marketed goods and services. At the same time, enterprises in the PRC have taken on some responsibilities that are normally the responsibility of government: the provision of education and health care to their workers.

The demarcation between government and enterprises must be clarified to achieve proper functioning of the market and sound local public finance. Market competition falters when enterprises in different places receive different degrees of financial assistance from local government and have different social service requirements. Local governments, for their part, cannot budget properly for their major social functions if they have to fund local industry and if part of their revenue depends on the profitability of the enterprises that they own. The aim should be to relieve enterprises of their role in providing education and health care, and at the same time to eliminate local-government provision of financial assistance to enterprises. Of course, there is an argument for allowing some nongovernmental provision of education and health care, as occurs in many countries, but this should be provided by organizations that are specialized in such provision rather than by enterprises that are simply providing these services as a remnant of the responsibilities they had under central planning.

This separation of enterprises from local government will not be easy. The transfer of social responsibilities to local government is reasonably straightforward, so long as the intergovernmental transfer system guarantees the local government enough funds to take over the financial responsibility. But disengaging the local governments from financial involvement in enterprises is difficult, for two reasons. First, their often substantial investments in their enterprises demand some return. (Provided that the local government makes no management decisions and provides no subsidies, it could, in fact, continue receiving profits from its enterprises, as local governments in some other countries do.) Second, and more importantly, local governments are often called upon to provide capital to small enterprises which find it impossible to borrow from the inflexible banking system. This undesirable practice draws governments into what should be purely commercial decisions, and invites the encroachment of politics on the market mechanism. But to stop the practice, banks must become more able to meet the financial needs of small enterprises.

One social service that local governments have taken over from the enterprises is pensions. The removal of this responsibility from the enterprises is fundamental to the move toward a market economy, as discussed in Chapter 4. But the pension funds will move into deficit soon and will thus require subsidies from local governments unless the pension schemes are managed more efficiently, the levels of contributions and benefits changed, and the pooling systems expanded into a national pension scheme.

A further problem arising from the transition is the large expenditure on subsidies, which are a major drain on local-government finance. To eliminate these subsidies, there must be a clear distinction between public and private goods now provided by the government. Local governments should then gradually do away with subsidies for private goods, such as housing, and consider transferring this provision to nonstate bodies. With public funds in short supply, social objectives, such as different aspects of health and education, must also be prioritized. Funds should then be devoted to ensuring that the highest priorities are carried out all over the country before lower priorities are met. This calls for the sort of intergovernmental transfers discussed in the previous section.

The government's limited resources and its inability to offer and fund a full range of social services to the rural population must likewise be acknowledged. Fortunately, rural areas can still rely on the communitarian ethic and families to provide much of the social safety net, although this ethic is expected to weaken gradually as modernization proceeds. The government needs to recognize that it cannot always treat the rural and urban populations separately. Separate (inferior) programs or no programs at all for the rural population will not be acceptable in the future. But in light of the government's limited resources, gradually reducing urban subsidies is more realistic than trying to extend these subsidies to the rural populace.

A particularly important priority in the transition is infrastructure. Each level of government should budget some funds each year for infrastructure maintenance and operations. Given the lumpiness of infrastructure investment, governments should not be restricted to financing infrastructure out of current revenues but should have the right to issue bonds or otherwise borrow funds provided they prove to an oversight board that they can repay the loans. The user fees to be collected as a result of the investment can be used to show augmented fiscal capacity. Such limited borrowing for investment presents a better option than selling state assets at prices below their true value. It must be ensured that the infrastructure investments lead to no further increase in overall investment rates in the PRC, which are already at very high levels. But there is no reason why their good financial returns should not recommend them over some of the investments in state-owned enterprises, where rates of return are often lower. Infrastructure borrowing should therefore be allowed to compete for a fixed total of bank borrowing, set at a level to prevent unacceptable rates of inflation.

ISSUES OF URBAN PUBLIC FINANCE

The transition process has sharply accelerated urbanization. At the annual growth rate of 5 percent over the past 15 years,[1] urban population has more than doubled since the start of market liberalization. With the trend expected to continue, urban population should more than double again before the year 2010.[2] This rapid growth in urban population creates three issues for municipal finance: how to finance the increased demand for urban services and infrastructure; how to rationalize and streamline the administrative hierarchy to define the expenditure responsibilities of provinces and cities and to give cities enough autonomy to carry out their expanded economic role; and how to cope with the swelling population of rural migrants, who are currently not incorporated into urban development plans and have little access to urban services.

---

[1] This estimate includes the "floating population."

[2] For the population to double in 15 years, annual growth must average 4.7 percent. At an average annual growth of 5 percent, the population will double in about 14 years.

Urban governments do not have the degree of autonomy needed to raise revenues and allocate expenditures. Especially critical is the financing of infrastructure, which is essential for economic growth and a better quality of life. Without new investment, many of the shortfalls in urban infrastructure services, especially in transportation, piped water supply, power supply, and communications, will increase, particularly as demand is driven up by rising per capita income. It is estimated that to meet the increased demand for transportation and communications infrastructure alone, the PRC would need to invest more than $500 billion over the next ten years (SCMP 1995). Most of these upgrades and investments will take place in cities.

The present system of urban finance must be revamped to meet the increased need for urban infrastructure and services. Funds for urban construction in the PRC, and in most of the cities visited, now come mainly from enterprise taxes and from asset (land) sales. Urban households, the beneficiaries of many municipal services, have generally not paid the full costs of the services. The principle of making the users pay points to a need to raise more revenue from user fees, especially from the household sector. The recent consumer boom in major cities indicates that the average urban household is much better able to pay for housing and municipal services than in the past. Since raising user charges to cost recovery levels will be unpopular among urban residents, this should be done gradually to minimize adverse consumer reaction.

Municipal governments should also have greater autonomy to issue bonds or borrow for infrastructure investments according to the guidelines set out in the previous section. Borrowing for long-lived infrastructure is both efficient and equitable—after all, the present taxpayers cannot in fairness be made to pay the full cost of investment while subsequent generations are allowed to reap free benefits. Relieving the current budget of the burden of investment finance will reduce incentives for the hasty sale of state assets and the overuse of user fees such as road tolls and multiple fees on new urban construction. Since cities "own" very substantial state assets such as land, housing, and production enterprises, the orderly and rational management of these assets, as well as their marketability, depends on reforming municipal finance to create the right incentives and regulatory framework.

Improved management of urban facilities to achieve their most efficient use is equally critical but has not been given sufficient attention by the government. Proper mechanisms to ensure better management and maintenance will be important. Personnel must be better trained to evaluate the performance of municipal projects. As the government becomes less preoccupied with industrial production and turns to providing and managing infrastructure, there must be a corresponding change in the departmental structure of urban government. Past rigidity in urban land-use and infrastructure planning should give way to greater flexibility to match changing business and consumer demand. Urban planning and management must also be strengthened to make urban services more efficient and responsive to local needs.

To confer greater autonomy on cities, jurisdictional ambiguities and conflicts in the administrative structure should be reduced. More economic management powers have been devolved to large cities in the last decade to enable these urban centers to respond more flexibly to local conditions and forge horizontal market networks outside of the vertical administrative system. However, as noted in Chapter 3, continued ambiguity in the administrative and economic powers of provinces and line-item cities has muddled responsibilities among the different levels of government and sowed dispute. Reforms have not eliminated the administrative restraints on economic interaction between cities. In general, the present system of local governments consists of too many layers. It is compounded by the many piecemeal and ad hoc features introduced in the reform era, some of which do not conform to the current provisions in the Constitution.

The PRC has implemented for more than three decades an urban development strategy of "promoting the growth of small and medium-sized cities and controlling that of large cities." Officials take this to mean that they should restrict the number of large urban centers and their (nonagricultural) population sizes. This view is based on a simplistic notion of optimal city size which is difficult to define. The present stage of development in the PRC and its scarce capital resources still call for selective development, but limiting the growth of large urban centers, with their many scale economies, would be premature. Many of the so-called "big city" problems in the PRC today are often due to reasons other than size.

Finally, regarding the issue of rural migrants, the current division of city populations into those with urban entitlements and those without is bound to create social conflict. The latter group, including permanent residents who carry agricultural household registrations and temporary residents (the "floating population"), is about half the size of those with urban entitlements. The "without" group is either denied access to many basic urban services, such as education and medical care, which are subsidized for other residents, or forced to pay high fees for them. In fact, many cities totally ignore the needs of the "without" group in planning for services and infrastructure.

Urban governments cannot be expected to end the discrimination overnight as most of them cannot afford the increased costs of providing even the basic services to the "without" group. Moreover, a better deal for the "without" group would induce even more people to move to the cities from the countryside, further overburdening the system in the short run. However, for reasons of equity and efficiency as well as good politics, discrimination against this segment of the population cannot be maintained indefinitely. Failure to provide basic services to this group may result in other problems that can be more costly to society at large. At bottom, the answer lies in doing away with urban-biased policies that create and widen rural-urban gaps. The government should continue to reduce urban subsidies (e.g., by charging the full costs of urban services) and use the resources thus freed up for equalization transfers. At the same time, cities should include their entire urban populations, regardless of residency status, in their development plans and budgets.

RETHINKING RURAL PUBLIC FINANCE

The fiscal gap is most critical at the county level. Lacking the flexibility of cities to adjust expenditures to revenue growth, rural governments nonetheless provide basic services to some 800 million people, as noted in Chapters 5-7. The murky division of expenditure responsibilities among counties, townships, and villages often leaves key services to be provided by the lower levels. Many villages have expenditure responsibility for basic services including supplementary finance for primary education, basic health care, and welfare for the aged and indigent under the "five guarantees" (*wubaohu*) program, along with their other functions like militia training and cadres' salaries. To prevent this situation from imposing an excessive financial burden on farm households, the county or the township budget should be strengthened to take on more of the financing responsibility for these services.

Indeed, rural public finance in the PRC as a whole urgently needs to be strengthened and rationalized. The conduct of rural public finance in the PRC has not fundamentally changed since the 1960s and 1970s, and self-reliance remains very much the guiding principle today, with two salient features. First, despite the large and growing gap in income and revenue capacity between the rural and urban sectors, rural government can call on no formal program of transfers, other than the poverty alleviation programs, and continues to be treated as a residual claimant of state resources. Indeed, it was noted in Chapter 5 that when the township was set up as a formal level of fiscal authority, explicit recognition was given to "self-raised funds" as a part of the "broad-based budget." SRF is but a new name for what was collected as "public accumulation" under the collective structure, comprising the remitted profits of collective enterprises and various fees collected from rural households. The second feature is that expenditure assignments remain murky, with a high degree of overlap in the service responsibilities at the county and township levels. For example, in about half of the counties in the PRC, basic education is a county-level responsibility, and in the other half it is a township responsibility.

This concept of a self-reliant rural public sector is no longer workable now when rural conditions are so fundamentally different. Decollectivization has rendered taxation much more difficult. It is harder to monitor and tax not only rural household incomes but also the profits of those descendants of the commune and brigade enterprises, the township and village enterprises (TVEs). TVEs are mostly privately owned, but even those that are still owned by collectives no longer yield their profits directly to collective coffers. Rural public finance must change to suit the rural economic transformation brought by decollectivization.

To provide adequate financing for their assigned expenditure responsibilities, the rural sector should be more fully integrated into the national system of government finance, both as taxpayers and as recipients of equalization transfers. So far this incorporation has been partial and confined mostly to the revenue side where, under protests mounted by urban industries, TVEs have been brought under increasingly stringent tax collection (Wong 1988). At the same time, however, expenditure responsibilities of the township level remain largely outside budgetary considerations. In 1993, the township-level budgets remitted Y18.7 billion in fiscal surplus upward to higher levels, mainly because in many localities in-budget expenditures are highly restricted at the township level. A wide range of fiscal expenditures are forced outside the budget, where items such as salaries for community teachers are financed by off-budget resources.

Expenditure responsibilities must also be divided more clearly among counties, townships, and villages to improve efficiency and equity. A single level of government should take charge of the main services such as education, health, and social welfare to make fiscal gaps easier to identify and the services more uniform. To cut down on bureaucratic duplication, rural finance should be unified at one level, the county level, since townships are generally too small to be effective redistributive units. But townships in rich coastal regions like Guangdong Province have significant revenue capacity and can form the basic level of rural government instead of counties which, in such cases, may be phased out. Villages, on the other hand, have no formal financing capability and so should not be asked to support programs like the "five guarantees" (*wubaohu*) which are mandated by national policy. Budgetary planning at the higher levels must also take rural expenditure needs fully into account, and provide for transfers and grants to finance expenditures that the government deems necessary and worthwhile. The central and provincial governments can finance these grants jointly. The widening gap between urban and rural incomes seems to justify an expanded program of fiscal transfers to the rural sector for the sake of greater equity.

The division of responsibility among the state, the community, and households also requires rethinking. On the one hand, the collective economy left behind a communitarian ethic that enables a level of service provision that exceeds the expected level based on income considerations, and the development of off-budget funding has established a pattern of local financing for these services. Nevertheless, the new rural public finance must recognize explicitly the limited revenue capacity of the sector and the disincentive effect of high tax rates. At the same time, rural infrastructure such as roads and large-scale irrigation schemes have public goods characteristics that make their provision by government efficient.

RETHINKING POVERTY ASSISTANCE

The mid-1980s saw poverty programs in the PRC shifting in focus from income maintenance ("consumption relief") to income-generating development assistance (see Chapter 6). A concomitant shift in funding also occurred. From being confined almost exclusively to grants, the programs have increasingly extended repayable loans. Loans made up more than half of the nearly Y10 billion in poverty alleviation funds provided by the central government in 1994. Only a portion of the funds was included in the budget. Roughly Y2 billion was issued as "fiscal credits" through the Ministry of Finance and local finance departments, and another Y2.5 billion was issued through the Agricultural Bank of China at subsidized interest rates.

A major part of these fiscal credits and subsidized loans for poor areas goes to TVEs, a vital component of income-generating development assistance programs. Township enterprises in central and western PRC, where poverty is concentrated, also gained access in 1992 to Y5 billion in credit from banks, and in 1994 to another Y5 billion. The emphasis on TVE development for poverty alleviation is defended on the grounds that these enterprises employ rural surplus labor, raise rural incomes, and are a major tax revenue source for local governments.

Many poverty alleviation programs lay stress upon the revenue-generating feature of TVEs and, in fact, use per capita fiscal revenues along with per capita income and food consumption as an indicator of poverty (Lyons 1992). This uncommon use of per capita revenue figures makes higher fiscal revenues an important target of poverty programs. The "3/5/8" antipoverty program adopted by the Fujian Province Party Congress in 1986, for example, hoped to meet the basic needs of the great majority of households in "poor" counties within three years, eliminate the budget deficits of the counties within five years, and turn the deficits into revenue surplus within eight years (Lyons 1992). Similar programs in other provinces include cases where quota subsidies for three to five years are given as a lump-sum advance to counties in deficit. The counties are encouraged to invest the funds in productive enterprises to expand their tax base and achieve fiscal self-sufficiency and eventual fiscal surplus (Wong, Heady, and Woo 1995). In these programs, local governments tend to favor enterprises at the county and township levels, which are easier to tax, over smaller-scale enterprises run by villages and individuals. However, it is in small-scale enterprises at and below the village level where employment in poor areas has grown fastest (World Bank 1992).

Unfortunately, stressing fiscal revenue generation ignores inherent regional disparities in revenue capacity. Many poor regions are poor because of their unfavorable resource endowments—bad location, low access to markets, dearth and inferior quality of land, and shortage of skilled labor. In such regions, investment returns are likely to be lower on the average than elsewhere in the country. Studies have, in fact, shown that TVEs in poor areas have had less success than those in more developed, coastal areas in absorbing surplus rural labor and increasing rural incomes (see, for example, Byrd and Lin 1989). A poverty alleviation strategy that gives undue emphasis to revenue expansion tends to produce, besides TVEs, "tourism spots," hotels, restaurants, amusement parks, and sports complexes—all entities that are easy to tax under the current fiscal system. In the early 1990s, local governments built thousands of "development zones" in their eagerness to attract wholesale markets for leather goods, garments, animal skins, and other products and thus expand their tax base. In a number of cases, these zones were built with funds intended for poverty alleviation and for other uses, such as education. When these investments fail—as many inevitably do—nonrepayable debts and misspent future subsidies drive the localities into even more desperate financial straits. In some cases, the local governments continue to support the loss-making enterprises, including state-owned enterprises managed by counties.

This book has pointed out that it is inefficient and inequitable for local governments at the county and township levels to strive for fiscal self-sufficiency. Two other flaws in the fiscal system—the limited rural tax base and the links between local government administration and rural enterprise management—skew policy in favor of rural enterprise development in poor regions. Measures should be taken to broaden the rural tax base and to separate government administration from enterprise management.

Instead of focusing on revenue generation, poverty alleviation strategies should focus on removing the resource disadvantages that most commonly cause poverty. Improving infrastructure by investing in both physical and human capital is essential. Such investments are more likely to increase fiscal capacity in poor areas in the long run than government-directed investment in rural enterprises. Poverty alleviation strategies must also acknowledge the need in some areas for entire populations to relocate. Therefore, policies that encourage labor mobility should be considered supportive of poverty alleviation. It should also be recognized that grants, and not loans, are needed in cases of extreme poverty. One very effective poverty assistance program, the Food for Work Program, is financed with grants and matching local funds. This program directly benefits the poor by developing infrastructure and introducing other improvements in poor regions. The government should proceed with plans to allow the better-developed coastal provinces to graduate from poverty alleviation programs, possibly at a faster pace, so limited resources can be redirected to where they are most needed. The fiscal needs of poor regions for providing basic services, such as education, public health, and social security, should be met through transfers.

POLICY RECOMMENDATIONS

To ensure adequate funding for the expenditure responsibilities of local governments, intergovernmental fiscal reform should revamp revenue and expenditure divisions, centralizing some functions while decentralizing others. Ten main policy recommendations are presented in the following paragraphs. The order of presentation was chosen for ease of exposition and does not reflect relative importance or the order in which the policies should be introduced. The recommended sequence is shown in Table S.1 in the Summary.

First, the PRC should set up a formal program of intergovernmental transfers, to achieve a few well-defined policy goals, such as poverty alleviation and minimum standards for basic services (education, health, social security). The transfers should be determined according to a transparent formula, which uses objective measures of financial resources and expenditure needs. From a modest level, the transfers can be increased gradually as the minimum standards for the basic services increase. Although this book cannot recommend a specific formula for lack of data with which to simulate the effects of alternative transfer formulas, the following principles should apply:

- Past expenditure levels or expenditure components, such as the number of government employees, should not determine expenditure needs; otherwise, past inequities would be perpetuated and local governments would pursue policies simply to gain additional transfers. The measurement of needs should be based on objective variables such as the number of school-age children (for schooling needs) and the population density (for ease of service delivery).
- Instead of variables that can be manipulated, such as revenue collected, taxes collected from the area by the central government (VAT and consumption tax) or local GDP or both should be used to measure financial resources.
- Needs and resources will both be difficult to measure accurately at first. Therefore, the cost of education per child, for example, should first be measured with the help of a simple formula, such as one that merely guarantees a particular amount of finance per child. Even just allocating education funds by number of school-age children would be an improvement over current population-based formulas. While regional cost variations may preclude uniform service, the unfilled need is too large for the implementation of this scheme to be postponed by the search for the "perfect formula."

The system of intergovernmental transfers could be achieved through modifications in the current system of vertical transfers or through the introduction of a (horizontal) system of direct transfers between local governments, under the supervision of the central government. In a horizontal system, local governments could take part in drawing up the formula and can ensure the acceptability of the system to the richer areas that will be giving up resources. A horizontal element would also make it easier to combine interprovincial and intraprovincial transfers. The combination is essential for two reasons. Poorer provinces cannot guarantee acceptable levels of service on the strength of their own resources. At the same time, the richer provinces will be more inclined to make the supplemental transfers if they know that the resources will go to the neediest areas of the poorer provinces. The latter consideration also suggests that there should be some earmarking of transfers to keep the provinces from diverting funds away from the communities for which they are intended.

Second, the PRC should reform off-budget finance. The fee and levy structure should be examined, and legitimate fees and levies should be included in the formal system of budgetary accounting. Those that are really taxes in that they are not imposed for a specific service should be treated like other taxes, included in the tax-sharing system, and counted as a financial resource in the proposed system of intergovernmental transfers. Genuine user fees, on the other hand, should be retained by the local government to finance the services for which they are charged. Finally, local governments should be allowed to keep the remitted profits from enterprises that they own, provided that the enterprises have paid all the taxes to which they are legally subject.

Third, the PRC should make the system of earmarked funds more efficient. There are hundreds of categories of earmarked funds at the provincial, prefectural, and county levels. Most of these grant categories are carry-overs from the period of more centralized budget management, especially in the allocation of investment funds. Most earmarking is either ineffective or hampers the ability of local governments to respond most effectively to local needs. Earmarking should be confined to those few cases where investment projects have regional or national impact, or where it will ensure that aid for poor communities does reach its intended beneficiaries.

Fourth, local governments (especially municipal governments) should be given greater autonomy to set local taxes and users' charges and should be allowed to borrow for infrastructure investments. Local governments should set those taxes that will not distort the allocation of resources in the economy, chiefly the property tax, the land-use tax, and the personal income tax. The yield from property and land-use taxes can be increased through such means as reducing exemptions, while the yield from the personal income tax has recently been increasing rapidly. The revenue from these taxes can therefore give local governments a substantial degree of choice regarding how much service to provide. User charges are also important revenue sources for local governments, and concern about their effect on the price level and the cost of living should not be exaggerated. The doubling of water charges, for example, would increase the overall price level by less than one-half of one percent. User charges that already take up a large share of household budgets or that have to be raised more substantially can be raised gradually so that the rate of increase in workers' standards of living simply slows down.

Fifth, the PRC should consolidate county and township finance. Rural counties and their townships overlap the most in their service responsibilities. In poor areas, where townships and villages are too small to adequately fund basic services such as primary education, public health, and social welfare (*wubaohu*), financial responsibility should be recentralized at the county level. Townships in some richer areas have enough financial resources of their own and should be given full financial responsibility. These moves will clarify service responsibility and simplify the system of intergovernmental transfers. In the long run, townships in poorer areas and counties in the richer areas could become superfluous and could be dissolved to produce a less stratified local government, more like the local governments in other countries.

Sixth, the PRC should clarify the expenditure responsibilities of different levels of government to improve the efficiency of public services and to establish revenue needs under the intergovernmental transfer system. Ideally, the law should specify the service responsibilities of each level of government. But beyond merely codifying current practice, some changes should be made. As discussed in the previous paragraph, education, health, and social welfare services should be made the responsibility of only one level of government in rural areas: counties in poorer areas and townships in better-off areas. In urban areas, municipal governments are already responsible for these key services. But the responsibility for urban infrastructure could be allocated more properly: cities should generally hold this responsibility, and the provinces should confine themselves to projects affecting large parts of the provinces.

Seventh, the PRC should clearly define the revenue division and tax assignments of the different levels of government. There are really two parts to this recommendation: the consistent extension of the 1994 tax-sharing system below the provincial level; and the allocation of the 15 local taxes among the levels of government.

Regarding the extension of the tax-sharing system, the only issue is whether the same formula used in center-province sharing should apply to subprovincial tax sharing. Clearly, subprovincial levels must pass upward at least as high a proportion of the VAT and consumption tax as the provinces must submit to the center; if not, the provinces may not be able to provide the necessary funds to the center. Passing upward a higher proportion of the taxes (or receiving a smaller share of increased revenues) would be tantamount to transferring more resources to the provincial level. However, this book argues that the most important service responsibilities should be allocated to the lowest levels of government. As these levels are also underfunded, there is no real reason to transfer additional resources to the province level. It is therefore recommended that the formula used for center-provincial sharing be used for subprovincial sharing.

As for the 15 taxes, it is sensible to allocate them all to the same level of government to avoid the expense of setting up local tax bureaus at more than one level. It is also sensible to allocate them to the level of government that is mainly responsible for providing health, education, and social services, for it is at that level that the funds are needed, and decisions to increase locally controlled tax rates can be made to improve services.

Eighth, the PRC should refocus its poverty alleviation programs. The transfer system should meet the fiscal needs of poor areas for minimum levels of service. The current strategy of supporting enterprises that will increase the local tax base undermines the move toward a market economy. Investment in education and infrastructure can have a greater long-term effect on improving fiscal capacity.

Ninth, the PRC should set up procedures for arbitrating taxpayer complaints. The immediate aim of this policy recommendation is to lessen the widespread abuse of local levies. The procedures would also accord with international practice. It is generally recognized that a proper tax system requires mechanisms for protecting citizens from the unreasonable actions of officials.

Tenth, the PRC should combine the local pension schemes into a national scheme. Since the success of the transition depends on the maintenance of a social safety net, the latter cannot be left to the local level, where the quality of management is highly variable. The financial viability of the pension system requires reductions in the level of benefits, at least for new scheme members, and the reductions can be achieved in an orderly manner only if they are coordinated from the center. Also, national pooling is required to ensure that the pension scheme can deal properly with workers who move between areas during their working lives.

ANNEX: THE FIELDWORK SITES

This book is based on fieldwork undertaken in two provinces in the PRC, Shandong and Guizhou. In these two provinces, four cities (Qingdao, Taian, Guiyang, and Anshun) and four counties (Qufu, Penglai, Zunyi, and Puding) were visited. These sites were selected to cover a wide range of income levels and socioeconomic conditions.

SHANDONG PROVINCE

Shandong Province, located in the eastern portion of the PRC, is one of the coastal provinces in the lower reaches of the Yellow River. Its coastal length makes up one-sixth of the country's total.

Shandong has three levels of subprovincial administration. At year-end 1992, Shandong had 5 prefectures, 12 prefecture-level cities, 28 county-level cities, 70 counties, 37 city districts, 929 towns (*zhen*), and 1,474 townships (*xiang*). In 1993, more counties achieved the status of cities, changing the number of county-level cities to 31 and of counties to 67.

Among the more developed provinces in the country, Shandong in 1994 ranked third in terms of provincial gross domestic product (GDP), behind Guangdong and Jiangsu. Per capita GDP was Y4,466, slightly higher than the national average (Table A.1).

The industrial sector accounted for about half of Shandong's total GDP in 1993. Its output of Y136 billion was the third highest among all provinces. In 1994 about 25 percent of the gross material product of industry came from state-owned enterprises, and 55 percent, from collectively owned enterprises. The comparable national averages were 34 percent and 41 percent, respectively.

Shandong is an important agricultural province. Agricultural output was Y60 billion in 1993, the highest in the country. The share of the sector in total output has, however, been declining, from 32 percent in 1978 to 22 percent in 1993. Township and village enterprises (TVEs) have played an important role in the rural sector. In 1992, TVEs employed 11.2 million, or 31.9 percent of Shandong's rural labor force.

Table A.1: Selected Economic Indicators
for Shandong and Guizhou

	Shandong	Guizhou	PRC
Gross domestic product			
Sectoral share (%)	100.0	100.0	100.0
Agriculture (1993)	21.5	32.1	19.9
Industry (1993)	48.9	37.4	47.6
Services (1993)	29.6	30.6	32.5
Population (million, 1994)	86.71	34.58	1,198.50
Per capita GDP (Y, 1994)	4,466	1,507	3,755
Per capita revenue (Y, 1994)	155.6	92.4	435.4
Per capita expenditure (Y, 1994)	252.8	219.6	483.3

Source: SSB (1995).

GUIZHOU PROVINCE

Guizhou is an inland province in the southwestern region of the PRC. As of 1993, Guizhou had two cities (Guiyang and Liupanshui), four prefectures (Zunyi, Anshun, Bijie, and Tongren), and three ethnic autonomous prefectures (Qiandongnan, Qiannan, and Qianxinan) under the jurisdiction of the provincial government. At the next lower tier, there were 9 cities and 77 counties, districts, and special districts under the jurisdiction of the prefectures.

Between 1979 and 1993, Guizhou's GDP grew at an average rate of 9.3 percent per annum, slightly faster than the national average. Despite this rapid growth, however, the province remained at the bottom 20 percent of the country in terms of GDP and had the lowest per capita GDP among all provinces in 1994, when GDP stood at Y52 billion, or Y1,507 per capita. The industrial sector accounted for 37 percent of total output, while both agriculture and services accounted for about 32 percent each in 1993. As of 1993, over 85 percent of the entire population of the province resided in the rural areas. Limited off-farm employment opportunities kept about 90 percent of the rural labor force employed in agriculture, forestry, animal husbandry, and fishery. The agricultural sector produced 70 percent of the total rural output, while the rural industrial sector produced 18 percent.

Guizhou is one of the least industrialized provinces in the country. Since 1979, industrial output has grown at a slightly slower pace than the national average growth rate of 10.2 percent. In 1993 output of the industrial sector was Y16 billion, equivalent to less than 1 percent of total national industrial output. State-owned enterprises produced 70 percent and collectively owned enterprises 16 percent of the total gross material output of industry in 1994.

THE FOUR CITIES

Qingdao

Qingdao, on the southwestern part of the Shandong Peninsula, is one of the PRC's designated coastal open cities and also a line-item city. Greater Qingdao includes five county-level cities under its administration. Qingdao City proper is the largest city in Shandong Province, and is the PRC's fourth largest port and a major industrial city. It has developed a full range of light industries and machinery industry. In 1993 its GDP totaled Y37 billion, having grown at an average annual rate of 26 percent in nominal terms since 1990. Qingdao has been successful in attracting foreign investment in recent years.

Taian

Nestled in the southern foothills of Taishan in central Shandong, Taian derived its name from the mountain which is a national tourist site. It was upgraded to a prefectural-level city in 1985. At present it administers two districts, three counties, and two county-level cities. Taian's GDP totaled Y10 billion in 1991. Of this total, 35 percent came from agriculture, 45 percent from industry, and the rest from services. The city is a major agricultural base in Shandong. Food grains, cotton, meats, and poultry are the major farm products. The major industries are coal, machinery building, metallurgy, and power.

Guiyang

Guiyang sits on the eastern slope of the Yunnan-Guizhou Plateau. It is the capital city of Guizhou Province and a major transportation hub in southwestern PRC. This prefectural-level city administers five districts and one town. Guiyang's GDP in 1993 was Y6.13 billion. Sixty-two percent came from industry, and only 4 percent came from agriculture. Guiyang's industries are more of the heavy-industry type and include metallurgy, machinery, and chemicals. In 1993 the city was named an "inland open city" and was allowed to offer concessionary tax rates to foreign investors. At the same time, a high-tech development zone and an economic and technology development zone were also set up.

Anshun

Anshun is a major center in western and southwestern Guizhou and is linked with Guiyang by a first-grade expressway. The city administers 10 towns and 7 villages, 2 suburban offices, and 4 street offices. In 1993 Anshun had a GDP pf Y994 million. Industry contributed 38 percent of the total and agriculture, 22 percent. Anshun has a strong industrial base as a result of the massive state investment in the "Third Front industri- alization" era. Its major industries are related to machinery building. About 80 percent of the management personnel and workers are in state- owned enterprises.

THE FOUR COUNTIES

Qufu

Qufu is located in southwestern Shandong, 120 kilometers due south of the provincial capital city of Jinan. It was elevated to a county-level city in 1986. Qufu's GDP has grown by 19 percent per annum since 1980; by the end of 1993 it totaled Y1.7 billion. Per capita GDP was 15 percent below the provincial average of Y3,222 and rural per capita income was slightly below the provincial average of Y953. Qufu had 244 industrial enterprises above the township level and 3,773 TVEs in 1993.

Penglai

Penglai is a county-level city in the prosperous eastern peninsula of Shandong Province. It has 3,056 industrial enterprises, with 72 at the county level, 124 at the township level, and 2,860 at the village lvel. In 1993 Penglai's GDP was Y3.6 billion (Y7,248 per capita), more than double the provincial aver- age. Rural incomes, at Y1,436 per capita in 1993, were also well above the provincial average.

Zunyi

Zunyi, one of the most prosperous counties in Guizhou Province, is located in the heart of a fertile agricultural area. It accounts for one-seventh of the province's grain output and one-ninth of its total production of oilseed. Zunyi also grows tobacco, and tobacco and liquor taxes constituted the main source of its revenue growth in the 1980s. Half of the county's GDP of nearly Y2 billion came from agriculture and 31 percent came from industry. Per capita GDP is 50 percent above the provincial average of Y1,034 and per capita rural income of Y721 exceeds the provincial average of Y580. Among the county's 1,600 TVEs, more than 500 are loss-making.

Puding

Puding is among the nationally designated "poor counties" in Guizhou. While its population is relatively small, its population density is the highest of all counties in the province. There is a severe shortage of farmland. Karst hills cover 84 percent of the county and there is only 0.05 hectare per capita of relatively poor-quality farmland. In 1993 the county's GDP was Y300 million, or Y8,333 per capita. Rural per capita income was only Y348, well below the provincial average. About 33 percent of output came from agriculture and 37 percent from industry. Puding has long been a county in deficit, dependent on a variety of subsidies from above. In recent years, however, the county's TVEs have grown rapidly. In 1993 Puding was named one of the four advanced counties in economic growth and promotion of TVEs in Guizhou Province.

REFERENCES

Association for Statistical Information Exchange. 1993. "A Collection of Statistical Materials About Coastal Open Cities, Special Economic Zones, Line-Item Cities (1992)."

Bahl, Roy, and Johannes Linn, 1991. *Urban Public Finance in Developing Countries*. New York: Oxford University Press.

_____. 1992. *Urban Public Finance in Developing Countries*. New York: Oxford University Press.

Banister, Judith. 1987. *China's Changing Population*. Stanford: Stanford University Press.

Bao, Zhonghua. 1995. *Zhongguo chengshihua daolu yu chengshe jianshe (The Path of Urbanization and Urban Construction in China)*. Beijing: Zhongguo chengshi chubanshe.

Bater, James H. 1980. *The Soviet City*. London: Edward Arnold.

Bird, Richard M. 1986. *Federal Finance in Comparative Perspective*. Toronto: Canadian Tax Foundation.

_____. 1992. *Tax Policy and Economic Development*. Baltimore: Johns Hopkins University Press.

Bird, Richard M., and Christine I. Wallich. 1992. "Local Government Finance and Intergovernmental Relations in Transition Economies: Broadening the Framework for Analysis." CECPE, October 1992. Washington, D.C.: The World Bank.

Bird, Richard M., Robert D. Ebel, and Christine I. Wallich. 1995. "Fiscal Decentralization in Transition Economies: A Long Way to Go." *Transition* 6(3).

Brennan, G. and J. M. Buchanan. 1980. *The Power to Tax: Analytic Foundations of a Fiscal Constitution*. Cambridge: Cambridge University Press.

Byrd, William, and Lin Qingsong. 1989. *Rural Industry in China*. New York: Oxford University Press.

Chan, Kam Wing. 1985. "Urbanization Issues in China's Development." In *China Insight*, ed. Min-sun Chen and Lawrence N. Shyu. Ottawa: Canadian Asian Studies Association.

_____. 1994. "Urbanization and Rural-Urban Migration in China Since 1982: A New Baseline." *Modern China*, 20(2): 243-281.

_____. 1994. *Cities with Invisible Walls: Reinterpreting Urbanization in Post-1949 China*. Hong Kong: Oxford University Press.

_____. 1995. "Migration Controls and Urban Society in Post-Mao China." Working Paper No. 95-2. Washington: Seattle Population Research Center.

Chen, Minzhang, ed. 1994. *China Yearbook of Public Health 1993*. Beijing: People's Medical Publishing House.

Chen, Pi-chao. 1976. *Population and Health Policy in the People's Republic of China*. Occasional Monograph Series No. 9. Interdisciplinary Communications Program. Washington, D.C.: Smithsonian Institution.

China Daily. 1993. 3 May.

_____. 1994. 24 September.

Chinese Urban Economic and Social Development Research Association and China Administration Management Society. 1993. *Zhongguo chengshi nianjian* (The Almanac of Chinese Cities). Zhongguo chengshi nianjian she.

Deng, Xinsheng. 1993. "Hainan Peasants Bear Excessive Financial Burden." *Zhongguo wujia* (Prices in China) 11:30-34.

Dowall, David. 1993. "Establishing Urban Land Markets in the People's Republic of China." *APA Journal* 59(2): 182-192.

Economic Information Daily. 1994. 2 September.

Editorial Committee of Dangdai Zhongguo Series. 1990. *Dangdai Zhongguo de chengshi jianshe* (China Today: City Construction). Beijing: Zhongguo shehui keshe chubanshe.

Exhibition on Social Development in China. 1994. September. Beijing.

FBIS. 1993. FBIS-CHI-93-154. 12 August.

_____. 1993. FBIS-CHI-93-215. 9 November.

Fung, Ka-iu. 1980. "Suburban Agricultural Land Use Since 1949." In *China: Urbanization and National Development,* ed. C. K. Leung and Norton Ginsburg. Chicago: University of Chicago.

Furusawa, K. 1990. "Rural Enterprises Under Reconsideration." JETRO, *China Newsletter*, no. 88, Sept.-Oct.

GHK (Hong Kong) Ltd. 1995. "PRC: Urban Sector Review." Report prepared for the Asian Development Bank.

Gu, Songnian, and Shen Liren, eds. 1992. *Hongguan jingji feneng tiaokong yangjiu* (Exploration of the Vertical Division of Macroeconomic Management). Nangjing: Jiangsu People's Press.

Guangmin ribao. 1989. 3 March.

Guizhou Statistical Bureau. 1994. *Guizhou Tongji Nianjian 1994* (Statistical Yearbook of Guizhou 1994). Beijing: China Statistical Publishing House.

Hare, Denise Marie. 1992. Rural Non-Agricultural Employment, Earnings, and Income: Evidence from Farm Households in Southern China. Ph.D. dissertation, Stanford University.

He, Chengming. 1992. *Difang caizheng xuw* (A Study of Local Finance). Shenyang: Dongbei caijing daxue chubanshe.

Hebei Statistical Bureau. 1992. *Hebei jingji tongji nianjian 1992* (Hebei Economic and Statistical Yearbook 1992). Beijing: China Statistical Publishing House.

Hong Kong Government. 1995. *Hong Kong 1995.* Hong Kong: Government Printing Department.

Hou Ruili. 1994. "For the Future of a New Generation." *China Today* (September): 28-31.

Hu, J. 1995. "The Imperative of Shanghai Hospitals Serving the Whole Country." *Shanghai Statistics* (4):27-8.

Hu, Tiyun. 1992. "Establishing County-Level Cities for Promoting the Development of Local Economy." In *Zhongguo xianzhen nianjian* (Yearbook of Counties and Towns in China). Beijing: Zhongguo xianzhen nianjian chubanshe.

Hua, Kuiyuan. 1993. "Urban Infrastructural Construction, Development Problems and Prospects in China." in *Zhongguo chengshi yu quyue fazhan: zhanwen ershishiji* (Urban and Regional Development in China: Looking into the 21st Century), ed. Yue-man Yeung. Hong Kong: Hong Kong Institute of Asia-Pacific Studies, Chinese University.

Huang Kehua, 1993. *Gaige Kaifang Zhongde Shandong Caizheng* (Shandong's Finance in the Process of Opening and Reform). Jinan: Shandong People's Press.

Jingji ribao. 1994. 18 September.

Khan, A. R., K. Griffin, C. Riskin, and R. Zhao. 1992, "Household Income and its Distribution in China." *The China Quarterly*, 132(12): 1029-61.

Kirkby, Richard J. 1985. *Urbanization in China: Town and Country in a Developing Economy 1949-2000 A.D.* New York: Columbia University Press.

Knight-Ridder. 1994. 17 February.

Koshizawa, Akira. 1988. *Chengshihua jingcheng he chengshi jianshe de zhanwan* (Urbanization Process and the Prospects of Urban Development). In *Medium- and Long-Term Outlook for the Chinese Economy,* Japan-China Association on Economy and Trade. Beijing: Jingji chubanshe.

Lai, David C., Xian-yao Zhao, and Xi-xin Liang. 1992. "Dalian: Its Industrial Development and Urban Growth." In *China's Coastal Cities: Catalysts for Modernization,* ed. Yeung and Hu. Honolulu: University of Hawaii Press.

Lardy, Nicholas R. 1978. *Economic Growth and Distribution in China*. New York: Cambridge University Press.

Lee, Yok-shiu. 1989. "Small Towns and China's Urbanization Level." *The China Quarterly*, 120.

Li, Mengbai, and Yin Hu. 1991. *Liudong renkou du dachengshi fazhan de yingxiang ji duice* (Impact of Floating Population on the Development of Large Cities and Recommended Policy). Beijing: Jingji ribao chubanshe.

Li, Yang. 1992. "Financing Urban Infrastructural Investments." *Jingji yanjiu* (Economic Research) (10): 45-51.

Lin, Justin Yifu. 1991. "Education and Innovation Adoption in Agriculture: Evidence from Hybrid Rice in China." Mimeo.

Liu, Guangren, ed. 1992. *Hukou guanlixue* (Study of Household Registration Management). Beijing: Zhongguo Jiancha chubanshe.

Liu, Ta. 1993. "On the Establishment and Development of Land Market in China." *Jingji kexue*, no. 2.

Lu, Lei, Hao Hongsheng, and Gao Ling. 1994. "1990 nian zhongguo fen sheng jianlue shengming biao" (Abridged Life Tables by Provinces in China in 1990). *Renkou Yanjiu* (Population Research) (3):52-59.

Lyons, Thomas P. 1992. "China's War on Poverty: A Case Study of Fujian Province, 1987-1990." Hong Kong Institute of Asia-Pacific Studies, The Chinese University of Hong Kong.

McGee, T. G. 1991. "The Emergence of Desakota Regions in Asia: Expanding a Hypothesis." In *The Extended Metropolis: Settlement Transition in Asia*, ed. Norton Ginsburg et al. Honolulu. University of Hawaii Press.

McLure, Charles, Jr. 1993. "Vertical Fiscal Imbalance and the Assignment of Taxing Powers in Australia." Essays in Public Policy. Hoover Institution on War, Revolution, and Peace, Stanford University.

Ming Pao. 1994. 3 October.

_____. 1995. 30 September.

Ministry of Construction. 1988. *Chengshi jianshei tongji nianbao 1988* (Annual Statistical Report of Urban Construction 1988).

_____. 1992. *Chengshi jianshei tongji nianbao 1992* (Urban Construction Annual Report 1992).

_____. 1993. *Chengshi jianshei tongji nianbao 1993* (Urban Construction Annual Report 1993).

_____. 1993. "Special Report on Urbanization in China." Unpublished report.

_____. 1994. *Chengshi jianshei tongji nianbao 1994* (Urban Construction Annual Report 1994).

Ministry of Finance (MOF). 1992. *China Finance Statistics 1950-1991.* Beijing: Kexue chubanshe.

_____. 1992. *Zhongguo Caizheng Nianjian* (Chinese Fiscal Yearbook). Beijing: Science Press.

_____. 1993. *Finance Yearbook of China 1993.* Beijing: Zhongguo caizheng chubanshe.

Ministry of Internal Affairs. 1985. *Zhonghua renmin gongheguo xingzheng qu jiance 1985* (A Handbook of Administrative Regions in the PRC 1985). Beijing: Zhongguo ditu chubanshe.

_____. 1987. *Zhonghua renmin gongheguo xingzheng qu jiance 1987* (A Handbook of Administrative Regions in the PRC 1987). Beijing: Zhongguo ditu chubanshe.

_____. 1994. *Zhonghua renmin gongheguo xingzheng qu jiance 1994* (A Handbook of Administrative Regions in the PRC 1994). Beijing: Zhongguo ditu chubanshe.

Ministry of Public Health. 1994. *Chinese Health Statistical Digest 1993.*

Naughton, Barry. 1992. "Implications of the State Monopoly over Industry and Its Relaxation." *Modern China* (January): 14-41.

_____. 1995. "Cities in the Chinese Economic System: Changed Roles and Conditions for Autonomy." In *Urban Spaces in Contemporary China,* ed. Deborah Davis et al. Wilson Center Press and Cambridge University Press.

Nongye Jingji Wenti (Issues of Agricultural Economics). 1990.

Oates, W. E. 1972. *Fiscal Federalism*. New York: Harcourt Brace Jovanovich.

Ody, Anthony. 1992. *Rural Enterprise Development in China, 1986-90.* World Bank Discussion Papers, China and Mongolia Department Series, no. 162.

Ofer, Gur. 1976. "Industrial Structure, Urbanization, and the Growth Strategy of Socialist Countries." *Quarterly Journal of Economics* 90(2): 219-244.

Oi, Jean. 1992. "Fiscal Reform and the Economic Foundations of Local State Corporatism in China." *World Politics* 45(1), October.

Paine, Lynn. 1992. "The Educational Policy Process: A Case Study of Bureaucratic Action in China." In *Bureaucracy, Politics, and Decision Making in Post-Mao China,* ed. Kenneth G. Lieberthal and David M. Lampton. Berkeley: University of California Press.

Park, Albert, Scott Rozelle, Christine Wong, and Ren Changqing. Forthcoming. "Distributional Consequences of Reforming Local Public Finance in China: Evidence from Shaanxi." Mimeo, Stanford University.

Pepper, Suzanne. 1995. "Regarding the Initiative for Education Reform and Development." *China Review 1995.*

Population Census Office, ed. 1993. *Zhongguo 1990 nian renkou pucha ziliao* (Tabulation of the 1990 Population Census of the People's Republic of China). Beijing: China Statistical Publishing House.

Prud'homme, Remy, 1987. "Financing Urban Public Services." In vol. 2 of *Handbook of Regional and Urban Economics,* ed. Edwin Mills. Netherlands: Elsevier Science.

Qingdao People's Press. 1994. *Qingdao Statistical Yearbook 1993.*

Renmin ribao. 1985. 8 September.

Schiffer, Jonathan. 1991. "State Policy and Economic Growth: A Note on the Hong Kong Model." *International Journal of Urban and Regional Research*, 15(2): 180-196.

Sha, Jicai, and Jingchun Cai, eds. 1994. *Gaige kaifang de renkou wenti yanjiu* (A Study of Population Problems under Reform and Opening). Beijing: Beijing Daxue chubanshe.

Shandong Academy of Social Sciences. 1992. "Problems in Changing Counties to Cities and Policy Measures." In *Zhongguo xianzhen nianjian* (Yearbook of Counties and Towns in China). Beijing: Zhongguo xianzhen nianjian chubanshe.

Shandong Statistical Bureau. 1992. *Shandong Tongji Nianjin 1992 (Shandong Statistical Yearbook 1992)*. Beijing: China Statistical Publishing House.

_____. 1993. *Shandong Tongji Nianjian 1993* (Shandong Statistical Yearbook 1993). Beijing: China Statistical Publishing House.

_____. 1994. *Shandong Tongji Nianjian 1994* (Shandong Statistical Yearbook 1994). Beijing: China Statistical Publishing House.

Shi, Xiaoyi. 1994. "On Upgrading China's Township Enterprises." *Guanli shijie (Management world)* (5): 142-149. Translated in Foreign Broadcast Information System (FBIS) CHI-95-016, 24 September.

Sing Tao Daily. 1988. 14 June.

_____. 1994. 8 February.

_____. 1995. 31 March (English edition).

_____. 1995. 1 October.

Solinger, Dorothy. 1985. "'Temporary Residence Certificate' Regulations in Wuhan, May 1983." *The China Quarterly* (101): 98-103.

_____. 1989. "Urban Reform and Relational Contracting in Post-Mao China: An Interpretation of the Transition from Plan to Market." *Studies in Comparative Communism*, 22(2/3): 171-185.

_____. 1993. *China's Transition from Socialism*. M. E. Sharpe.

South China Morning Post International (SCMP) Weekly. 1995. 6 May, p. B-5.

Spiegel, Mark. 1994. "Gradualism and Chinese Financial Reforms." *Federal Reserve Bank of San Francisco Weekly Letter*, no. 94-44.

State Council. 1983. "Supplement to State Council Regulation Regarding Urban Nonagricultural Individual Economy." In *Siying he geti jingji shiyong fagui daquan* (A Practical Encyclopedia of Regulations Regarding Private and Individual Enterprises, 1988). *Beijing: Renmin chubanshe.*

_____. 1984. "Several Stipulations Concerning Rural Individual Industrial and Commercial Enterprises." In *Laodong fagui xuanbian* (A Compilation of Selected Labor Regulations, ed. Ministry of Labor and Personnel. Beijing: Laodong renshi chubanshe.

_____. 1984. "Temporary Regulations Regarding Reduction and Exemption of Enterprise Income Tax and Industrial and Commercial Tax in Special Economic Zones and 14 Coastal Open Cities." In *Coastal Open Cities and Special Economic Zones Handbook,* ed. Wenxiang Wang. Chinese edition. Beijing: Zhongguo guoji guangbo chubanshe.

_____. 1984. "Answer to the Questions Raised by the Xinhua News Agency Reporter: Policies About Further Opening 14 Coastal Cities." In *Jingji tizhi gaige shouce* (Handbook of Economic System Reforms), ed. Jiye Wang and Yuanchun Zhu, 1987. Beijing: Jingji ribao chubanshe.

_____. 1990. "Temporary Regulations on Sales and Transfers of Urban Land-Use Rights."

State Council and State Statistical Bureau. 1993. *Tabulation of the 1990 Population Census of the People's Republic of China*, vol. 2. Beijing: China Statistical Publishing House.

State Economic System Reforms Commission (SESRC). 1984. "Summary of Work Meetings on City Economic System Reforms Test Points." In *Jingji tizhi gaige shouce* (Handbook of Economic System Reforms), ed. Jiye Wang and Yuanchun Zhu, 1987. Beijing: Jingji ribao chubanshe.

State Education Commission. 1993. *Zhongguo jiaoyu jingfei fazhan baogao* (Report on the Development of Education Funds in China). Beijing: Tertiary Education Publishing House.

State Statistical Bureau (SSB). 1983. *Zhongguo tongji nianjian 1983* (Statistical Yearbook of China 1983). Beijing: Zhongguo tongji chubanshe.

350

_____. 1989. *Zhongguo tongji nianjian 1989* (Statistical Yearbook of China 1989). Beijing: Zhongguo tongji chubanshe.

_____. 1990. *The Forty Years of Urban Development.* Beijing: China and Statistical Information and Consultancy Service Center.

_____. 1992. *Zhongguo tongji nianjian 1992* (Statistical Yearbook of China 1992). Beijing: Zhongguo tongji chubanshe.

_____. 1993. *1992 National Sample Survey on the Situation of Children National Final Report.* Beijing: China Statistical Publishing House.

_____. 1994. *Zhongguo tongji nianjian 1994* (Statistical Yearbook of China 1994). Beijing: Zhongguo tongji chubanshe.

_____. 1994. *Zhongguo tongji zhaiyao 1994 (A Statistical Survey of China 1994).* Beijing: Zhongguo tongji chubanshe.

_____.Various years. *Zhonguo chenshi tongji nianjian (Urban Statistical Yearbook of China).* Beijing: Zhongguo tongji chubanshe.

_____. 1995. *China Statistical Yearbook 1995* (English edition). Beijing: China Statistical Publishing House.

Sun Tanzhen. 1994. "Jiaoyu jingfei de chuocuo yu zhengfu gonggong zhineng: Yicheng xian anli (The Raising of Education Funds and the Public Function of Government: A Case Example of Yicheng County)."

Ta Kung Pao. 1994. 21 September.

Tan Jee-Peng and Alain Mingat. 1992. *Education in Asia: A Comparative Study of Cost and Financing.* Washington, D.C.: The World Bank.

Tang, Wing-Shing, and Alan Jenkins. 1990. "Urbanization: Processes, Politics, and Patterns." In *The Geography of Contemporary China,* ed. Terry Cannon and Alan Jenkins. London and New York: Routledge.

Tsui, K. Y. 1993. "Decomposition of China's Regional Inequalities." *Journal of Comparative Economics,* 17(3): 600-627.

United Nations. 1980. "Pattern of Urban and Rural Population Growth." *Population Studies,* no. 68. Department of International Economic and Social Affairs.

_____. 1987. "The Prospect of World Urban Population." *Population Studies*, no. 101.

Wang Bingqian. 1990. "Report on the Implementation of the 1989 State Budget and the 1990 Draft Budget, at the Third Plenary Session of the Seventh National People's Congress," 21 March. In *Renmin ribao*, 8 April 1990.

Wang Siping. 1994. "Summary Report of the Sample Survey on School Attendance in Project Counties of Guizhou." *China Population Today*, 14-17 April.

Wang, Xinhui, Deyuan Cui, and Qin Zhang. 1987. "A Consideration and Assessment of the Line-Item Reform in Central Cities. "*Jianghan luntan* 10:3-36.

Wen Wei Po. 1987. 21 July.

_____. 1994. 1 September.

West, Loraine A. 1994. *Regional Variation and Its Consequences for Rural Basic Education in China*. World Bank McNamara Fellowship report.

West, Loraine A., and Christine P. W. Wong. 1995. "Fiscal Decentralization and Growing Regional Disparities in Rural China: Some Evidence in the Provision of Social Services." *Oxford Review of Economic Policy*, 2(4), December 1995.

Whiting, Susan. 1993. *The Micro Foundations of State Capacity in Reform China: Implementation of Tax and Credit Policy in the Rural Industrial Sector*. Chapter 2 of Ph.D. dissertation, University of Michigan.

_____. 1995. "The Micro-foundations of Institutional Change in Reform China: Property Rights and Revenue Extraction in the Rural Industrial Sector." Ph.D. dissertation, University of Michigan.

Wong, Christine P. W. 1982. "Rural Industrialization in the People's Republic of China: Lessons from the Cultural Revolution Decade." In *China Under the Four Modernizations,* ed. Joint Economic Committee, U.S. Congress. Washington, D.C.: United States Government Printing Office.

_____. 1987. "Between Plan and Market: The Role of the Local Sector in Post-Mao China." *Journal of Comparative Economics,* no. 11, September.

_____. 1988. "Interpreting Rural Industrial Growth in the Post-Mao Period." *Modern China*, January.

_____. 1990. "The Coastal Development Strategy." Unpublished paper.

_____. 1991. "Central-Local Relations in an Era of Fiscal Decline: The Paradox of Fiscal Decentralization in Post-Mao China." *The China Quarterly*, no. 128, December.

_____. 1991. "The Maoist 'Model' Reconsidered: Local Self-Reliance and the Financing of Rural Industrialization." In *New Perspectives on the Cultural Revolution,* ed. William Joseph, Christine Wong, and David Zweig. Cambridge: Harvard University Press.

_____. 1992. "Fiscal Reform and Local Industrialization: The Problematic Sequencing of Reform in Post-Mao China." *Modern China*, 18(2), April.

_____. 1994. "Subprovincial Finance in the People's Republic of China: A Pilot Study in Hebei Province." Report for the Ministry of Finance and Asian Development Bank, February.

Wong, Christine P. W., Christopher Heady, and Wing Thye Woo. 1995. *Fiscal Management and Economic Reform in the People's Republic of China.* Hong Kong: Oxford University Press.

World Bank. 1980. *World Development Report 1980*. New York: Oxford University Press.

_____. 1990. *China: Revenue Mobilization and Tax Policy*. Washington, DC: World Bank.

_____. 1990. *China: Long-Term Issues and Options in the Health Transition.* Washington, D.C.: The World Bank.

_____. 1992. *China Strategies for Reducing Poverty in the 1990s*. Washington, D.C.: The World Bank.

_____. 1994. *World Development Report 1994: Infrastructure for Development.* Washington, DC: World Bank.

_____. 1994. *Averting the Old Age Crisis.* Oxford: Oxford University Press.

World Resources Institute and International Institute for Environment and Development. 1994. *World Resources 1994*. New York: Basic Books.

Xiang Huaicheng, ed. 1994. *Zhongguo caizheng tizhi gaige* (The Reform of China's Fiscal System). Beijing: Chinese Financial Press.

Xiao, Bin. 1991. "Shuangxi bingli, shengshi geyi" (Develop a Dual System that Suits Both Provinces and Cities). *Tianjin shehui kexue* 1:56-60.

_____. 1993. *Zhongguo chengshi de lishi fazhan yu zhengfu tizhi* (Historical Development of Cities and Government Systems in China). Beijing: Zhongguo zhengfa daxuchubanshe.

Xinhua. 1993. 25 February. Translated in FBIS-CHI-93-040 (3 March 1993): 17-31.

Xu, Huadong, et al. 1985. "Tan xiao chengzhen de jianzhen wenti" (On the Question of Designations of Small Towns). *Chengxiang jianshe* (Urban and Rural Construction) 2:34-35.

Yang, Shuzhang. 1994. "An Analysis of School Age Children Not Attending School." *Renkou yu jihua shengyu* (Population and Family Planning) 3:58-63.

Yao, Xinwu, and Yin Hua. 1994. *Basic Data on China's Population.* Beijing: Zhongguo renkouchubanshe.

Ye, Xingqing. 1991. "Analysis of Government Revenues and Expenditure in Remote Regions." *Jingji Kaifa Luntan* (Tribune of Economic Development), March.

Yeh, Anthony Gar-On, and Fulong Wu. 1994. "Changes and Challenges of the Main Shaping Force of Internal Structure of Chinese Cities." Paper presented at the Fourth Asian Urbanization Conference, Taipei,China, 1-5 January 1994.

Yeh, Anthony Gar-On, and Xueqiang Xu. 1989. "City System Development in China, 1953-86." Working Paper No. 41. Centre of Urban Planning and Environmental Management, University of Hong Kong.

Yeung, Yue-man. 1991. *The Urban Poor and Urban Basic Infrastructure Services in Asia: Past Approaches and Emerging Challenges.* Occasional Paper No.7. Hong Kong Institute of Asia-Pacific Studies, The Chinese University of Hong Kong.

_____ and Xu-wei Hu. 1992. "China's Coastal Cities as Development and Modernization Agents: An Overview." In *China's Coastal Cities: Catalysts for Modernization,* ed. Yeung and Hu. Honolulu: University of Hawaii Press.

Zhang, Yimin. 1993. "Investigation of County Level Primary and Secondary School Fee Collection." *Zhongguo wujia* (Prices in China) 3:7-9.

Zhao, Ziyang. 1982. "Report on the Sixth Five-Year Plan." In *Fifth Session of the Fifth National People's Congress, 1983*. Beijing: Foreign Language Press.

Zheng, Yan Shao, ed. 1994. *Zhongguo yanhai kaifang chengshi liyong waizi falu wenti (Legal Questions about Using Foreign Funds in Coastal Open Cities in China)*. Shanghai: Shanghai shehui kexue chubanshe.

Zhongguo fangyu (Chinese Territories). 1994. No. 3.

Zhou, Junli. 1994. "Spatial and Functional Structure of System of Cities in China: A Cross-Sectional Analysis." Unpublished Ph.D dissertation, Brown University.

Zhou, Xiaochuan, and Yang Zhigang. 1992. *Zhongguo caishui tizhide wenti yu chulu* (Issues and Solutions for China's Fiscal and Tax Systems). Tianjin: Tianjin People's Press.

_____. "Achievements and Problems in the 1994 Tax Reform." Paper presented at the Conference entitled The Next Steps for Economic Reform in China, September 1994.

Zhou, Yixing. 1988. "The Relationship Between Urban Industrial Output and Urban Size in China." *Jingji yanjiu* (Economic Research), 5:74-79.

Zhuang, Mu. et al. 1993. *Fangdican zhidu* (The System of Real Estate). Beijing: Beijing Jingjixueyuan chubanshe.

CONTRIBUTORS

KAM WING CHAN, associate professor with the Department of Geography of the University of Washington, has done research mainly on urban development and internal migration in the PRC. Dr. Chan is the author of *Cities with Invisible Walls: Reinterpreting Urbanization in Post–1949 China* and was guest editor of a recent special issue of *Chinese Environment and Development* dealing with Chinese internal migration.

CHRISTOPHER HEADY is professor of applied economics at the University of Bath (UK). Dr. Heady has published papers on a wide range of topics in public finance and development economics, and has worked on public finance in the PRC since 1988. His interest in transition economies has extended to countries in central Europe, particularly the Czech Republic.

LORAINE A. WEST works with the US Department of Commerce as a statistician economist with the Eurasia Branch of the International Programs Center, Bureau of the Census. She does research on economic and demographic issues concerning the PRC and other Asian countries. Among Dr. West's areas of study are social security reform and subnational demographic changes in the PRC, local-government provision of education and health-care services in rural PRC, and subnational variation in the socioeconomic characteristics of Viet Nam.

INDEX

In this index, administrative units below the provincial level are listed together with their respective provinces in parentheses.